HARVARD EAST ASIAN MONOGRAPHS

80

LANDLORD AND LABOR IN LATE IMPERIAL CHINA
CASE STUDIES FROM SHANDONG

Li Heng-qing, Gong Zi-zhen, and Gong Chuan-jie of Dongfanliu village. (See note 1 to Chapter 4, p. 276.)

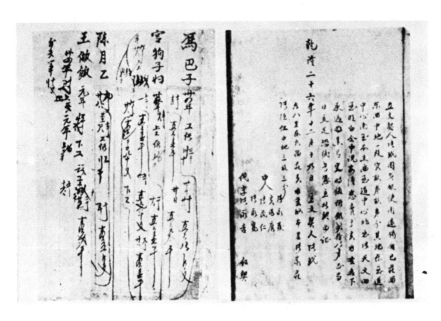

Pages from Taihe Tang Wage Labor Account Book

LANDLORD AND LABOR IN LATE IMPERIAL CHINA
CASE STUDIES FROM SHANDONG

by
Jing Su and Luo Lun

Translated from the Chinese
with an Introduction
by
Endymion Wilkinson

Published by
Council on East Asian Studies
Harvard University

Distributed by
Harvard University Press
Cambridge, Massachusetts
and
London, England
1978

This book is produced by the John K. Fairbank Center for East
Asian Research at Harvard University, which administers research
projects designed to further scholarly understanding of China,
Japan, Korea, Vietnam, Inner Asia, and adjacent areas. These
studies have been assisted by grants from the Ford Foundation.

Library of Congress Cataloging in Publication Data

Ching, Su.
    Landlord and labor in late imperial China.

    (Harvard East Asian monographs ; 80)
    Translation of Ch'ing tai Shan-tung ching ying ti chu
ti she hui hsing chih.
    Bibliography: p.
    Includes index.
    1. Farm tenancy—Economic aspects—China—Shantung—
History. 2. Peasantry—China—Shantung—History.
3. Shantung, China—Rural conditions. I. Lo, Lun,
joint author. II. Title. III. Series.
HD151.C52S513   333.5'3'095114   78-7606
ISBN 0-674-50866-1

FOREWORD

Scholars outside the People's Republic of China have long been interested in studies of local agricultural and marketing systems in China in historic times. Through the use of sources available in American and other libraries external to China some progress has been made in understanding these local systems. But foreign scholars have had only limited access to China itself and almost no access for meaningful research in China's rich collections of original source materials. Chinese scholars, on the other hand, have been preoccupied over the past decade by the Cultural Revolution and the various upheavals in the education system that followed in the path of the Cultural Revolution. If time has been available for substantial historical scholarship during this past decade, the results of that scholarship have not yet found their way into print.

Such a paucity of major historical scholarship on China has not always characterized the post-1949 period in China. The study of Jing Su and Luo Lun of Shandong University published in China in 1959 was one of many works on Chinese economic and social history published in that period and before. Jing and Luo's study stands out in part because it is one of the few studies we have of north China developments at the local level in the Qing period. Of greater significance are the kinds of sources the authors were able to draw upon in their study. Interviews, questionnaires, account books, and land deeds were used extensively to supplement the more "conventional" gazetteers, collected writings, and the like. This study of the local Shandong economy and society, therefore, illustrates the enormous potential for new kinds of data and more sophisticated analysis for those with access to these rich sources.

Endymion Wilkinson has done much more than provide us with a translation of the study of Jing Su and Luo Lun. He has written an introductory essay that is itself an important piece of scholarship and one that puts Jing and Luo's analysis in the context of both Western and Chinese Marxist scholarly traditions.

After graduating in history and Oriental studies from Cambridge University in 1964, Endymion Wilkinson taught in the People's Republic of China for two years. He received his PhD from Princeton in 1970 and for the next four years was Lecturer in the History of the Far East at the University of London. During these years his publications included *The History of Imperial China: A Research Guide* and *The People's Comic Book.* Since 1974 Dr. Wilkinson has been serving in the Directorate-General for External Relations of the Commission of the European Communities and is currently posted in Tokyo in the Commission's Delegation to Japan.

Dwight H. Perkins
John K. Fairbank Center for
East Asian Research

ACKNOWLEDGMENTS

I should like to express my thanks to Dr. Charles Curwen, my former colleague at the School of Oriental and African Studies, University of London, who read through an early draft of the translation with scrupulous care and saved me from many a slip and error. I am indebted to Professor Dwight Perkins for encouraging the book's publication in this series and also for writing the Foreword. Sheila Marian and Florence Trefethen of the John K. Fairbank Center for East Asian Research, Harvard University, edited the manuscript. I alone am responsible for the finished product, which I trust has fairly caught the meaning of the original.

Endymion Wilkinson
Tokyo, 1978

CONTENTS

TABLES

MAPS

INTRODUCTION

The total land area of the north China province of Shandong (Shantung) is about the same as a medium-sized European country like Austria or Portugal. In 1400, the population of Shandong was of the order of 5 million. By 1900, this had risen to approximately 35 million. No changes in technology or organization remotely resembling an industrial revolution had taken place in Shandong or in any other part of China during these centuries. How, then, did this growth in population come about? What effects did it have on the economy and society of the province? In what directions was the Chinese economy developing before the impact of the Western industrial system in the nineteenth century? How was the nature of that impact conditioned by the traditional economy?

Although the authors of this unusual and provocative study, Mr. Jing Su and Professor Luo Lun of Shandong University, are not primarily concerned with the causes and effects of population growth, they are very much concerned with economic and social change in Shandong between 1650 and 1900 and, by implication, with the broader questions outlined above.[1] Their argument goes as follows. By the sixteenth and seventeenth centuries, sizable commercial and handicraft towns linked to local and national markets became apparent in Shandong as well as in many other provinces. This urban growth was made possible by increases in agricultural production which, in turn, stimulated specialization and increased commercialization in the agricultural sector with important repercussions for rural society. Large numbers of peasants fell into debt and were forced either into the towns to find what work they could, or to make a living as rural wage laborers. At the same time, a new wealthy stratum of landlords who managed their estates with wage labor began to emerge in the villages. It is this stratum, a kind of rural bourgeoisie, that forms the main focus of Jing and Luo's study. Jing and Luo conclude that the emergence of managerial landlords farming for profit was a protocapitalist phenomenon, confirming the statement made by Mao Ze-dong:

1

"As China's feudal society developed its commodity economy and so carried within itself the embryo of capitalism, China would of herself have slowly developed into a capitalist society, even if there had been no influence of foreign imperialism."[2] The scholastic background and political implications of this conclusion need not detain us here.[3] The value of Jing and Luo's study derives not so much from the originality of their argument and its conclusion as from the region to which they have applied the argument and from the kinds of data they have used in its articulation.

Regional and local studies of Chinese history in the Ming and Qing periods (1368–1644, 1644–1911) are still extremely rare. The few such studies that have been made have concentrated on south China, which is far better documented than the north.[4] It is therefore highly unusual to find a local historical study of a dry-farming northern province such as Shandong. It is even more unusual to find in such a study a wealth of conventional written historical sources (local gazetteers, collected writings, and the like) used in conjunction with such "unconventional" materials as interviews, questionnaires, account books, and land deeds. Whatever reservations we may have about the authors' main thesis, at the very least it has led them to study the interaction of historical changes at the provincial level (largely using conventional written sources) with changes in the economic behavior of individual households (using unconventional sources). The result is a uniquely documented study that throws a great deal of light on the economy and society of north China between 1650 and 1900. In what follows, I have tried to supplement the authors' argument where this seemed necessary and to check the reliability of their sources where this proved possible. For the reader's convenience, I have also aggregated a considerable amount of the raw data in the authors' Appendixes.

The Development of Commercial and Handicraft Towns

Jing and Luo begin their study by successfully demonstrating that the two main towns on the Grand Canal in Shandong, Linqing, and Jining, as well as Zhoucun and Yanshen in central Shandong, grew considerably in size from at least the sixteenth century onward.

They do this most convincingly by using such indicators as the extension of city walls or the increase in the number of streets and by quoting qualitative evidence on the trade and handicraft industries of the towns.

Occasionally they have been able to find statistics that indicate the size of the handicraft industries. In Linqing, for example, the fine silk scarf or *hada* firms were famous throughout China; they numbered more than 700 "loom shops" which employed a total of 5,000 weavers in the town. In Jining, the tobacco-curing industry had an annual turnover of 2 million taels and was run by 6 families who employed some 4,000 laborers. The authors also give some interesting details on the size of one of the condiment works in Jining; it employed about 400 workers and annually used 1,375 metric tons of grain, 200 tons of vegetables, 150 tons of salt, and 100 tons of coal in the manufacture of its products. (See Chapter 5, Section 2.)[5] Each of the four towns manufactured products which were marketed not only throughout the province but also throughout the whole of China. Linqing produced felt, silk goods, and bricks; Jining's manufactures included tobacco and pickled vegetables; Zhoucun was a collection point for wild silk and cotton; and Yanshen exported glass and coal. (See Chapter 1, Sections 1–4.)

Absolute statistics on the population of Chinese towns are almost totally lacking in the traditional sources because the government collected taxes (and counted households and other tax units) by district, making no distinction between the district town and its surrounding rural areas. The authors sum up the traditional evidence on Linqing's and Jining's populations and reckon that both towns probably numbered about 100,000 inhabitants by 1600. They make no estimates for the populations of Zhoucun and Yanshen. On the basis of twentieth-century statistics for the four towns, with allowances made for changed conditions, the authors' figures of about 100,000 for Linqing and Jining, and an estimate of between 25,000 and 50,000 for Zhoucun and Yanshen in the eighteenth and nineteenth centuries, would appear reasonable.[6]

The authors argue that the growth of commercial and industrial towns was a new phenomenon which created new forms of demand and acted as a catalyst to the rural economy. The key question, therefore, is not the absolute size of these towns but their growth relative to total population growth and the degree of change in urban-rural population ratios, leading to the consideration of changes in the ratio of urban to rural industries and the estimation of changes in local, regional, and national trade flows. As Lenin put it: "One cannot conceive of capitalism without an increase in the commercial and industrial population at the expense of the agricultural population." And he noted that in the case of Russia, "The percentage of urban population is constantly growing, that is, the population is being diverted from agriculture into commercial and industrial occupations. The towns are growing twice as fast as the rest of the population ... The population of the towns which are important industrial and commercial centres is growing much more rapidly than the urban population generally."[7]

This is a point and these are questions that the authors can scarcely have been expected to document, given the absence of relevant statistics in the traditional sources. But these questions deserve a much fuller discussion than Jing and Luo give them.

The growth of urban centers, for example, takes on a different aspect when seen in the context of general population growth in north China at this time. Between 1600 and 1900, the population of the whole of China grew from about 200 million to 410 million, and this growth took place mainly in north China, where the population rose from 60 million in 1600 to 200 million in 1900. During the same period, the population of the south rose from about 140 million to 210 million. In 1290, only 10 percent of the Chinese people lived in the north. By 1900, this had risen to 45 percent.[8] The growth of urban centers in the north, then, took place within the context of an overall growth of Chinese population. It should not be seen in terms of a sudden imbalance of urban-rural population ratios of the type Lenin had in mind.

The very few statistics in the traditional sources on urban-rural ratios suggest that, even in the most urbanized areas of the south, close to cheap river and coastal transport, at the very most no more than 25 to 30 percent of the population of a given district

lived in the district town.[9] There is no evidence to indicate that
urban-rural ratios were rapidly upset in Shandong in the late traditional period; they probably fluctuated between 10 and 15 percent,
depending on local conditions. In 1942, Jining had been served by
a railway line for over thirty years but, even so, only 22 percent of
the population of the prefecture lived in the town.[10]

The development of Linqing and the other three Shandong
towns examined by the authors should also be seen in the context
of the growth of intermediate market centers. Although Jing and
Luo quote interesting qualitative evidence on the growth of a small
market town in central Shandong (Mingshui, see Chapter 3), there
is plentiful quantitative evidence they do not quote to show that
the growth of such intermediate centers was a general phenomenon
throughout Shandong and the rest of north China.[11] It was a
phenomenon, moreover, that coincided with the overall growth of
population in north China at that time. In Zhangqiu, for example,
the district in which Mingshui is situated, there were only 10
market towns with periodic markets in 1550; by 1600 there were
17, and by 1700 there were 27. Thereafter the pace slowed down.
In 1850 there were 30; and in 1907, 31.[12]

Towns in Shandong along the Grand Canal and in the center
of the province (such as Linqing, Jining, Zhoucun, and Yanshen)
undoubtedly grew from the sixteenth century onward. But so did
the rural population, and so did the population of the smaller
market towns. There is a great deal of difference between the
effects of such overall growth in the various levels of the marketing
system and the sudden growth of one level of the system leading
to imbalance and adjustments at the other levels. Overall growth
can be accompanied by increasing specialization of agricultural
production, the increased marketing of agricultural surplus, and
the breakdown of customary village relations and their replacement
by monetary/contractual relations. Sudden growth in one level of
the system, however, such as towns, can trigger these same changes
but at a pace that, given a favorable social and political environment,
may eventually induce structural change.

Jing and Luo quote many sources to show that social values as reflected in the life styles of the merchants in these towns were changing. As one disapproving Confucian official complained, "Even the men servants wear silk, and the attendant maids are decked out in great finery. Many who are not necessarily gentry put on banquets and theatricals in Linqing. Marriage and burial ceremonies far surpass the accepted rites. Here pride and extravagance are equally in evidence and artfulness and deceit are the norm."[13] The merchants ignored the old sumptuary regulations, and contemporary literature is full of the archaically aristocratic pretensions of *nouveaux riches* young bloods with lots of money but no real (Confucian) culture. It is no accident that the first full-length novel whose hero is one of these northern *nouveaux riches* is set in Linqing.[14]

Although the merchants often lived ostentatious and, in Confucian terms, disreputable lives, they did not present a serious ideological or political threat to Confucianism or to the imperial state structure. Late imperial China was very different from feudal Europe, not the least with respect to the role played by the towns. In China there were no competing centers of power, no kings, feudal lords, or bishops, for the townsfolk to play off against each other. On the contrary, the Chinese town was typically an integral part of the unitary structure of the Confucian state. It never became an independent corporate entity, sharply differentiated from the surrounding countryside, fighting for political and economic rights. Chinese merchants learned to work within the existing state structure and ideology. Their luxurious living habits and ostentatious display of wealth were signs of a flourishing sub-culture rather than of a rising middle class.

Jing and Luo provide plentiful evidence to show that a number of towns in Shandong grew considerably. They also show that merchants in these towns lived luxurious and colorful lives. But they have not shown that these towns grew so rapidly relative to the rest of the population as to introduce the possibility of fundamental change throughout the economy and society. Nor have they shown that the political and social environment was favorable to such changes.

The Commercialization of Agriculture

In Chapter 2, the authors quote from a large number of historical sources to show that there was an increase in the specialization of agriculture. Large quantities of food grains were shipped to the towns on the Grand Canal and along the rivers of the province.[15] New industrial and commercial crops, such as cotton, tobacco, and peanuts, were introduced into the province, and the cultivation of older industrial crops, such as the leaves for wild silkworm cultivation, was extended.[16] Throughout the province, there was a great increase in the number of periodic village markets and small market towns, although this is a point the authors do not discuss.[17]

Scholars have long recognized the importance of cheap transport in the economic development of certain regions of China. In the late traditional period, the three relatively advanced areas were the Yangzi delta region or Jiangnan (Suzhou, Hangzhou, Songjiang, Jiaxing, Huzhou, and Nanjing were the main towns), the southeast coastal region (Quanzhou, Zhangzhou, Fuzhou, and Canton were the main towns), and the Grand Canal region (Yangzhou, Xuzhou, Jining, Linqing, Jinan, and Tongzhou).[18] Jing and Luo do point out the importance of the Grand Canal in the development of Linqing and Jining, but they do not discuss the effects of the canal's gradual desuetude in the nineteenth century on these towns or their hinterlands. Nor do they discuss the secondary transport systems in Shandong provided by the rivers and by the imperial roads.[19] Commercialization of agriculture within the province was uneven, and one of the main reasons was the absence of readily available cheap transport covering the whole province.

Jing and Luo have some interesting things to say about the commercialization of agriculture, derived from their case studies in Part II and from questionnaire data in the Appendixes. In Chapter 2, they simply quote as much evidence as they have been able to find in traditional historical sources.

The Differentiation of the Peasantry

The conclusion of Chapter 3 is that the growth of new towns

and the consequent stimulus to commercialized agriculture led to the creation of two hostile classes in the villages. On the one hand, there was the small number of landlords who had been able to take advantage of the new economic opportunities and, on the other hand, there was the large number of peasants who had been forced to sell their land and either to work as wage laborers for the land-lords or to shift to the towns. I have already suggested that the probable impact of the towns was far less than the authors argue. In Appendix A they themselves supply plentiful evidence to show that Shandong villages in 1900 can hardly be said to have been characterized by two hostile classes. In Table A, I have aggregated all the authors' data on village landholding.

Table A shows that the single largest category in the villages at this time were the owner-peasants. Jing and Luo argue in Chapter 3 that the tenantry system was gradually being replaced throughout the Qing dynasty by the landlord/wage-labor system, yet their data show that an average of 16.9 percent of the households in the villages were tenants as apposed to 17.1 percent who were wage laborers. This can hardly be said to be a replacement.[20] Further-more, 40 percent of the wage-laborer households in Jing and Luo's sample derived the major portion of their income from small plots of land. Strictly speaking, then, only 10.3 percent of the house-holds in the village relied wholly on wages. A total of 70.2 percent of the households in all owned their own land (3.8 percent + 4.6 percent + 55 percent + 6.8 percent).

If Jing and Luo are correct in supposing that the villages were characterized by two hostile classes, then it would be reasonable to expect this hostility to be reflected in the numerous outbreaks of rural violence that occurred in Shandong in the nineteenth century. In fact, nobody, including Jing and Luo, has yet produced any evidence to show that there is any connection between the inci-dence of landlord/wage-labor relations and the incidence of such outbreaks. On the contrary, one scholar attempted to find such a correlation in an analysis of the numerous outbreaks of rural vio-lence in the decade 1853–1864 and came up with a complete blank. Village hostility was predominantly antiofficial and antitax.[21]

Table A

Class Structure of 200 Villages in Shandong, c. 1900

Region of Shandong	Percentage landlords	Percentage rich peasants	Percentage owner-peasants	Percentage tenants	Percentage wage laborers	Percentage others
Central Shandong (Jinan/Zhoucun)	2.5	3.5	64.7	9.8	13.2	6.3
Grand Canal	2.8	5.1	62.3	10.9	15.8	3.1
North Shandong	0.9	3.7	52.0	11.0	31.9	0.5
Shandong promontory	2.8	4.2	55.7	23.7	13.2	0.4
South and West Shandong	9.8	6.6	42.3	29.3	11.7	0.0
AVERAGE	3.8	4.6	55.0	16.9	17.1	2.0

Source: Calculated from data in Chapter 4 and Appendix A.

The percentages of total land owned by the different categories of landholder are not given by Jing and Luo, except for three villages in central Shandong. (See tables 5, 10, and 19.) In these villages, the distribution of land was clearly very uneven, as suggested by other surveys of north Chinese landholding. Up to 25 percent of village households farmed less than 10 mu, which they either owned, part-owned, or rented. These households increased their income by working as wage laborers, peddlers, porters, and so forth. Most households in the villages were owner-peasants typically farming between 10 and 30 mu. (See Chapter 7, Section 3.) Between them these two categories of landowner farmed approximately 80 percent of all village land. The remaining 20 percent was owned by land-lords, many of whom did not live in the villages but in market towns, district towns, and larger cities. Absentee landlordism was not a new feature of the Chinese landholding system in the nine-teenth century.[22] Only a very few of the landlords owned over 10,000 mu. Most owned a few hundred mu. The evidence of land-holding conditions in Shandong is summarized by Ramon Myers, who concludes that, as population continued to increase in the twentieth century in Shandong, farms became even smaller in size while the number of comparatively large farms declined.[23] Jing and Luo's data suggest that, by the 1890s, Shandong society, in com-mon with that of the rest of China, was characterized by "a social continuum with a restricted overall range."[24] This is, of course, not to say that there were no inequalities. On the contrary, they charac-terized each tightly packed rung of the rural social structure.

One of the features of this farming system was that, at each level of landholding, farming was combined with other activities. Part-owners and small tenants, as noted above, increased their in-come by working as laborers, peddlers, porters, and so forth, as did small owner-peasants. Medium landowners typically ran businesses in the market towns, while large landowners resident in district towns and larger cities rented out most of their land and invested in urban business. This feature is another indication of the degree to which the agrarian economy had become commercialized.

Micro-Studies of the Managerial Landlord Economy

In late traditional China, writers recognized distinctions of wealth in using categories such as rich, middle, and poor families. Great importance was also attached to status divisions, which were conventionally linked to the classical fourfold functional divisions of scholar, farmer, craftsman, and merchant, and therefore not necessarily directly linked to wealth. The so-called "gentry" (*jinshen*) were an important status group in the scholar-official category. They were made up of those who had qualified for office in the imperial bureaucracy by passing the imperial examinations as well as those who were retired officials. The gentry of late imperial China formed the core of the local elite in each district. There were an average of 20 to 40 gentry households in each district, and as a rule they lived in the district towns in which the offices of the district magistrate were located. Although the gentry were often absentee landlords owning country estates and having extensive business interests, not all gentry were necessarily large landowners and by no means were all landowners gentry; high status was gained by proximity to office, and officeholding was approached through education in Confucian ideology and examination.[25]

One of the extremely valuable points about Jing and Luo's study is that most of the landlords in their sample were situated one or two steps down on the social ladder from the local and central elite, the gentry and officials, upon whose activities both traditional Chinese historical sources and modern secondary sources are focused. Their study, therefore, throws light on a stratum— village or market town rural entrepreneurs—that has hitherto been neglected in the literature.[26]

The core of their study is the presentation and analysis of interview and questionnaire data on 134 "managerial" landlords and two "rentier" landlords, on wage-labor conditions in 144 villages, and on the class structure of 200 villages. The data relate to conditions in Shandong in about 1900.

The authors begin by presenting detailed materials on the family histories and economic activities of three "typical" managerial landlords and their laborers (Chapter 4) and on two rentier landlords (Chapter 5). These materials were gathered mainly in interviews by the authors themselves. The data on village class structure, the remaining 131 landlords, and the laborers in 141 villages are presented in summary form in Chapter 6 and in statistical form in the Appendixes. These data were gathered for the authors by local cadres and primary school teachers using questionnaires.

The distribution of the data among the five regions of Shandong into which the authors divide the province is shown in Table B.

Table B

Distribution of Data

Regions of Shandong	Villages		Landlords		Laborers	
	Number	Percent	Number	Percent	Number	Percent
Central Shandong	83	41.5	55	41.0	55	38.1
Grand Canal	25	12.5	11	8.2	16	11.1
North Shandong	38	19.0	22	16.4	23	15.9
Shandong promontory	30	15.0	19	14.1	19	13.1
South and West Shandong	24	12.0	27	20.1	31	21.5
TOTALS	200	100.0	134	100.0	144	100.0

Source: Calculated from data in Chapter 4 and Appendixes.

The authors' definition of "managerial landlord," (a term of their own coining) is a landlord who employed 3 or more long-term laborers and who directly managed part of his estate and sold part of his surplus product for profit. They engaged in a wide variety of rural business enterprises, and most of them lent money at high interest rates. "Rich peasants" employed wage laborers and to a certain extent engaged in commerce, handicrafts, and usury, but they employed fewer laborers and farmed smaller amounts of land than the managerial landlords. The scale of their nonfarming activities was also smaller. Managerial landlords are distinguished from the more common type of Chinese landlord, the "rentier landlord," here defined as a landlord who managed none of his estate directly and who rented out at least 50 mu to tenants. According to these definitions, managerial landlords could also rent out parts of their estate, and indeed many of them did so.

The authors argue that managerial landlords were a new phenomenon in Chinese society of the Qing period (1644–1911) and that they had begun to farm for profit using wage labor in response to the opportunities provided by the new commerical and handicraft towns whose rise Jing and Luo outline in Part I.

Sixty-six of the landlords in Jing and Luo's sample had originally made their money in business and then invested part of it in land. Sixty had worked their way up through the ranks of the peasants, and only eight owed their fortune to having served as an official in the imperial bureaucracy as is shown in Table C.

The large number of landlords in the sample who had worked their way up through the ranks of the peasantry owed their success to the fact that they were good farmers. The relative unimportance of privilege in acquiring land at this level of the landholding hierarchy (as shown by the small percentage of landlords who had originally been officials) and the corresponding importance of economic means suggest the extent to which agriculture had become commercialized. The close connections between town and country are also shown by the high percentage of landlords who had originally made their money in business in the towns. It was both socially acceptable and profitable to invest urban wealth in the countryside. It was even more profitable, if less socially acceptable, to invest rural wealth in the towns. As Table D shows, most of the landlords, whatever their origins, ran businesses in the towns (in the smaller market towns if they were small landlords and in the larger towns if they were large landlords) in addition to lending money, renting out land, and farming with wage labor.

Table C

Origin of Wealth of 134 Managerial Landlords

	Farming		Business		Official		Totals	
	Number	Percentage	Number	Percentage	Number	Percentage	Number	Percentage
Central Shandong	21	38.1	30	54.5	4	7.2	55	41.0
Grand Canal	8	72.7	2	18.1	1	9.0	11	8.2
North Shandong	12	54.5	9	40.9	1	4.5	22	16.4
Shandong promontory	6	31.5	11	57.8	2	10.5	19	14.1
South and West Shandong	13	48.1	14	51.8	0	0.0	27	20.1
TOTALS	60	44.7	66	49.2	8	5.9	134	100.0

Source: Calculated from data in Chapter 4 and Table 29.

Table D

Number of Landlords Conducting Nonfarming Activities

	Total number of landlords	Number and percentage conducting non-farming activities		Number and percentage conducting no non-farming activities	
Central Shandong	55	47	85.4%	8	14.5%
Grand Canal	11	9	81.8%	2	18.1%
North Shandong	22	18	81.8%	4	18.1%
Shandong promontory	19	18	94.7%	1	5.2%
South and West Shandong	27	24	88.8%	3	11.1%
TOTALS	134	116	86.5%	18	13.4%

Source: Calculated from data in Chapter 4 and Table 30.

Most of the landlords, too, took several generations to build up their fortunes, and early in this process they diversified their operations to include farming, business, and moneylending. This is well illustrated in the family histories of the three managerial and two rentier landlords presented in Chapters 4 and 5.

It took four generations and two centuries for the Shujing tang Bi family to amass 900 mu of land.[27] The increase in the family's land went hand in hand with the growth of its silk-weaving works.

Shujing tang Bis

	Amount of land (mu)	Number of looms
Early 18th century	30	1
Late 18th century	100	1+
Early 19th century	300	20
Late 19th century	900	72

The growth of the Shujing tang Bi family coincided exactly with the development of Zhoucun as a silk marketing center 10 miles from the family's home village. (On Zhoucun, see Chapter 1, Section 3, and on the Shujing tang Bis, see Chapter 4, Section 2.)

The Taihe tang Li family (see Chapter 4, Section 1) took 155 years to get 515.5 mu. Their most rapid period of expansion came at a time when they began to run a miscellaneous goods store and a wine shop, and to make loans in neighboring villages and market towns. The other family histories given by the authors tell the same story. Increased landholding went hand in hand with increased business and moneylending activities, and these, in turn, coincided with the growth of both urban and rural population and the increase in numbers of market towns and larger urban centers.

In some cases, families dramatically increased their lands as the result of sudden opportunities presented by natural calamities during which people were forced to sell land in order to survive. Others were able to use government office as a road to riches. The Sun family of Jining, for example, took eight generations and a period of 325 years to rise from rich peasant to president of a central ministry. The most dramatic rise in the family's fortunes came in the fifth generation when Sun Yu-ting became a Grand Secretary and Provincial Governor. He bought 30,000 mu and a half interest in a soy-sauce factory. His grandson was also a high official (president of the Zongli Yamen and the Board of War at the end of the nineteenth century) and used his power to buy more land and to expand the condiment works. (See Chapter 5, Section 2.)

Such dramatic changes of fortune were the exception. In general the process of land accumulation was a slow and hazardous one. Chinese families divided their properties equally among all sons, so estates were constantly broken up, and the status of families could fall very rapidly. The Taihe tang Li family bought 515.5 mu over a 155-year period in no less than 104 separate purchases. In the fifth generation, a rapid succession of family divisions coupled with poor management practically returned the Lis to the status of small owner-peasants.

Traditional Chinese society was much more fluid than the feudal societies of Europe or Japan, to say nothing of a caste society such as India's. This fluidity was brought about in large part by the absence of customary or legal barriers to the disposal of family wealth.

The amount of land owned by the landlords varied greatly but, in general, by the end of the nineteenth century only a few landlords in the whole province owned more than 10,000 mu (about 1,700 acres). In each district, there were probably a few dozen owning between 1,000 and 10,000 mu. Most of the landlords owned less than 1,000 mu. These proportions are reflected in Jing and Luo's sample. I have calculated the number of landlords with holdings of different sizes in each region in Table E.

Altogether the landlords in Jing and Luo's sample (excluding the two rentier landlords in Chapter 5) owned 234,678 mu, of which 186,003 mu (80 percent) were rented out to tenants. Only 48,675 mu (20 percent) were directly farmed with wage labor. It makes better sense then, as I argue below, to regard direct farming

Table E

Amounts of Land Owned by 134 Landlords in Shandong, c. 1900

| | to 499 mu | | to 999 mu | | to 4,999 mu | | over 5,000 mu | |
	Number	Percent	Number	Percent	Number	Percent	Number	Percent
Central Shandong	40	71.4	9	16.0	6	10.9	0	0.0
Grand Canal	7	58.3	1	8.3	1	8.3	2	25.0
North Shandong	13	59.1	6	27.3	3	13.6	0	0.0
Shandong promontory	4	21.1	7	36.8	7	36.8	1	5.3
South and West Shandong	7	28.9	4	15.3	11	37.3	5	18.5
TOTALS	71	52.9	27	20.1	28	20.8	8	6.7

Source: Calculated from data in Chapter 4 and Appendix B.

Table F

Average Amounts Owned by Landlords and Methods of Management Used

Regions of Shandong	Total amount owned (mu)	Number of landlords	Average amount owned (mu)	Average amount farmed with wage labor (mu)	Average amount rented out (mu)	Percent of total amount in each region farmed with wage labor
Central Shandong	25,538	55	464	297	167	64.0
Grand Canal	29,180	11	2,652	312	2,340	11.7
North Shandong	13,900	22	631	480	151	76.0
Shandong promontory	41,260	19	2,171	254	1,917	11.7
South and West Shandong	124,800	27	4,622	501	4,121	10.8
TOTALS	234,678	134	1,751	363	1,388	20.7

Source: Calculated from data in Chapter 4 and Appendix B.

Table G

Amounts of Land Farmed With Wage Labor
by 134 Landlords—Summary

Amount of land managed with wage labor (mu)	Number of landlords	Percentage of total landlords in survey
Less than 100	10	7.4
100–199	37	27.6
200–299	20	14.9
300–399	27	20.1
400–499	13	9.7
Sub-total	107	79.8
500–599	4	2.9
600–699	7	5.2
700–799	4	2.9
800–899	0	0.0
900–999	3	2.2
Sub-total	18	13.4
Over 1,000	9	6.7
TOTAL	134	100.0

Source: Calculated from Chapter 4 and Table 28.

as one aspect of landlord activities, rather than as the defining feature of a special type of landlord, the "managerial landlord."

The average amounts of land farmed with wage labor and rented out differed considerably from region to region, as is shown in Table F.

Jing and Luo are not so much concerned with the land rented out by these landlords or with landlord/tenant relations as with the land directly managed by the landlords using wage labor. They demonstrate that there were definite limits to the size of farms managed directly. (See Chapter 6, Section 1, Tables 21–28.) I have recalculated their findings in Table G to include the data on the three landlords introduced in Chapter 4.

From Table G it is clear that 500 mu was the point at which marginal costs rose so rapidly as to make direct farming unprofitable. Land acquired after that was rented out to tenants in small plots. The average size of a directly managed farm was 363 mu.

An important finding of Jing and Luo's study is that yields on landlords' directly managed land were higher than on peasant and tenant land. Altogether they provide yield statistics for various crops on about one-third of the managerial landlord lands and on poor peasant and tenant land in the same places. (See Tables 12, 34, and 35.) Yields varied greatly throughout Shandong, depending on the quality of the land, on the level of the inputs, and on such random factors as weather. In Table H I have averaged all of Jing and Luo's data on yields.

Landlords' yields were about 30 percent higher than poor peasant yields. Partial corroboration of these figures comes from the American agronomist F. H. King, who visited Shandong in the early years of this century and recorded that "one of the large farmers, owning 10 acres (60 mu), stated that his usual yield of wheat in good season was 160 catty (jin) per mu."[28] King's farmer owned just enough land to come into the category of small managerial landlord, the average of whose wheat yields in Jing and Luo's sample came to 165 jin per mu.

The yields given for two of the "typical" managerial landlords in Chapter 4 (Taihe tang and Jinxiu tang) are, however, much higher than the landlords' average yields in the rest of the sample. Also the yields the authors quote for poor peasants and tenants in the same villages as these two "typical" landlords are much lower than the poor peasant yields in the rest of the sample. The result is that Taihe tang and Jinxiu tang yields are shown to be almost twic as high as poor peasant and tenant yields in the same villages. (See Table I.) In the light of the rest of the sample these are clearly not very typical yield figures.

On the whole the landlords were able to produce higher yields

Table H

Average Yields on Landlords' Directly-Managed Land and on Poor Peasant Land

| Crop | Size of sample | | Average land-lord yield (jin per mu) | Average poor peasant yield (jin per mu) | Average landlord yields as a per-centage of poor peasant yields |
	Landlords	Peasants			
Wheat	43	44	165	123	134
Kaoliang	43	44	232	178	130
Millet	42	43	323	255	127
Maize	22	23	212	165	128
Cotton	14	17	113	89	127

Source: Tables 12, 34, 35.

Table I

Comparison of Taihe and Jinxiu Yields
with Poor Peasant and Tenant Yields

Crop	Average Taihe tang and Jinxiu tang yield (jin per mu)	Average poor peasant and tenant yield in the same villages (jin per mu)	Average Taihe tang and Jinxiu tang yield as % of poor peasant and tenant yield in the same villages
Wheat	180	93	193
Kaoliang	310	163	190
Millet	358	200	179
Maize	242	156	155

Source: Calculated from Tables 12 and 34.

than the peasants as a result of owning better land and of providing superior inputs (labor, animals, fertilizer, and implements). Superior inputs enabled them to produce more labor-intensive crops and also to use more intensive cropping patterns.

Long-term laborers employed by the landlords worked for periods of between one month and a year. They frequently owned small plots of land, but in some cases they owned none at all.[29] The authors show that, in 60 percent of the villages surveyed, the long-term laborer's only source of income was his wage. (See Table 32.) In general, half the wage was paid in money, the other half in the form of meals. In Chapter 4, Sections 1 and 2, they attempt to show how low the laborers' money wages were by calculating their purchasing power in terms of 1950s currency and prices. Such a conversion means practically nothing because of the numerous currency changes in the interim. The authors also use 1900s grain prices in their calculations that are three times higher than all other 1900s grain prices in their study. The result is to severely deflate the purchasing power of laborers' cash wages in the 1900s. Nobody would suggest that Chinese rural wage laborers were well paid at the turn of this century, but it would be interesting to have some comparative data and to know whether their wages were rising, falling, or stationary at the end of the nineteenth century. The authors provide no data on this.[30]

Short-term laborers were employed during the busy seasons by the day or by the month at special rural labor markets, usually in the local market town. (See Chapter 6, Section 4.) They owned small plots of land, and their family income was derived from their land, their wages, and secondary occupations such as peddler, stone-cutter, porter, and mat-weaver.

The landlords employed large numbers of both long- and short-term wage laborers, and Jing and Luo are undoubtedly right in stressing the importance of adequate labor in raising yields. (See Chapter 7, Section 2.) They give the numbers of laborers employed by thirteen of the landlords. In Table J, I have drawn these data together from the various chapters in which they are given to show the number of mu per long- and short-term laborer.

There appears to be no correlation between the size of the farm and the number of long-term laborers employed, which is not surprising since each landlord ran a different mix of business activities in addition to farming; therefore, funds available to pay for labor varied from farm to farm. The average number of mu per long-term laborer given by Stenz in his study of Shandong farming at this time was 50, which accords fairly well with the average of 37 in the above sample.[31] Of the three "typical" landlords presented in Chapter 4, only the Taihe tang Li family appears to be typical in the number of laborers they employed. The Shujing tang Bi family and the Jinxiu tang Meng family both had far more laborers than the average.

The authors explain that one or two of the long-term laborers on each farm acted as foremen or overseers (*da huoji*) whose duties included helping the landlord plan the farming operation and hiring the short-term laborers, whose work in the fields was supervised by the subforemen. The foremen often acted as guarantors for the

Table J

Mu per Long- and Short-Term Laborer on 13 Managerial Landlords' Farms

Finding number (see Appendix B) and landlord's name	Amount of land farmed with wage labor (mu)	Number of long-term laborers	Number of short-term laborers	Mu per long-term laborer	Mu per short-term laborer
74 Zhou Shu-sheng	777	6	60	129	12
112 Chen Mao-de	600	6	14	100	42
Ch. 4 Shujing tang Bi	600	30	50	20	12
95 Yue Zhao-xing	500	14	20	35	25
Ch. 4 Taihe tang Li	472	13	30 av.	36	15
Ch. 4 Jinxiu tang Meng	450	37	50	12	9
42 Wang Jin-han	400	9	25 av.	44	16
100 Ma Zeng-shou	400	29	30	13	13
127 Yang Zhong-qin	340	21	40	16	8
72 Han Zhao-li	260	10	18	26	14
57 Li Meng-yue	200	11	14	18	14
41 Lu Guo	200	10	24	20	18
52 Li Xiao-jie	120	6	15	20	8
AVERAGES	409	15	30	37	15

Source: Calculated from data in Chapters 4 and 7.2 and Appendix B.

hired labor. Jing and Luo do not discuss what part the landlords themselves actually played in the running of the farm; it presumably varied according to the number and extent of their other businesses, but, in general, they appear to have acted through their foremen rather than directly supervising or dealing with the other laborers. Thus, in a farm manual written for his sons by a managerial landlord from Shenxi province in the first part of the nineteenth century, the farmer is urged to check this or that activity of the foremen. Certain matters required personal supervision, for example, guarding the crops just before harvest: "The owner himself should not take it easy at home but he should pace up and down two or three times in the fields each evening and check that the laborers are not asleep. You live a prosperous and easy life at home all year round," the author continues, "so that the only hardship you have to put up with is the week or two's rush and the extra special care and attention involved at harvest time." Another task the owner himself was urged to supervise personally was the mixing and preparation of compost.[32]

Jing and Luo provide adequate evidence that the managerial landlords had more draft animals, sheep, and pigs than the peasants. This enabled them to plough larger areas deeper and more quickly. It also enabled them to collect much larger amounts of fertilizer. As Table K indicates, the actual figures they give for fertilizer used by the three "typical" landlords in Chapter 4 are astonishingly high.[33]

Table K

Average Amounts of Fertilizer per Mu of Three Typical Landlords

Taihe tang Li	4,237 jin per mu (31.7 tons per hectare)
Shujing tang Bi	4,666 jin per mu (34.9 tons per hectare)
Jinxiu tang Meng	4,444 jin per mu (33.3 tons per hectare)

Source: Calculated from data in Chapter 4.

On the average, peasants in the same villages as these three landlords used about half as much fertilizer per mu. F. H. King in *Farmers of Forty Centuries* mentions that a farmer with a 60-mu farm, whose wheat yields were as good as the average managerial landlord's wheat yields in Jing and Luo's sample, applied 5,333 pounds of compost per acre (978 jin per mu). In other words Jing and Luo's three typical landlords applied over four times as much fertilizer as King's farmer (who applied half as much as Jing and Luo's peasants).[34] In Chapter 7, Section 3, the authors give the estimate of 1,200 jin per mu of fertilizer for wheat cultivation, which would be a more typical figure. In fertilizer use as in other respects, the three "typical" landlords were not so typical.

Other advantages enjoyed by the managerial landlords were superior implements and relatively compact estates. While the peasants were often still using hoes or human traction ploughs, the landlords had iron ploughs drawn by oxen; while the peasants sowed the seed by hand, the landlords used seeding drills; and while the peasants winnowed the grain by hand, the landlords used winnowing fans. Curiously enough, the authors leave out of their account one of the most important inputs of all—irrigation. They do suggest, however, that, here too, adequate supplies of labor gave the landlords the edge over poorer farmers.

Better quality land and relatively compact estates, as well as superior inputs of labor, animals, fertilizer, and implements, enabled the managerial landlords to run a far more efficient farming operation than the peasants. Their efficiency was reflected in higher yields per mu.

What crops did the landlords grow and what percentage of those crops did they market? Jing and Luo give details only of the crops grown by two of the three landlords presented in Chapter 4. The other landlords grew the same crops (wheat, kaoliang, millet, maize, cotton, and legumes), but we are not told how much land was sown to each crop. This is clearly a key question in estimating to what extent the landlords were producing for household consumption and to what extent they were producing for the market.

No details of the landlords' household or farm budgets have survived, so the authors are forced to attempt to answer these questions by estimating the total annual production of all crops of one landlord (the Taihe tang Li family, see Table 6) and by subtracting the amount presumed to have been consumed by the household and the laborers. The remainder was available for sale on the market. The Li family produced a minimum of 74 tons (all crops) annually. The 100 household members, farmhands, shopkeepers, and other dependents annually consumed about 24 tons. By this reckoning, a minimum of 50 tons, or 67.5 percent of the total farm output, would have been available for sale. How much this grain would have fetched and how the proceeds would have been used can be estimated by using scattered information supplied by the authors. If two-thirds of the grain for sale was coarse grain and one-third wheat, the 50 tons would have fetched roughly 1,835 strings of cash (based on the average price of wheat given in Table 31 of 25 cash per jin and the price of coarse grain at 15 cash per jin). The laborers' annual wages came to 742 strings (14 long-term laborers at an average wage of 21.2 strings plus 3,600 short-term laborers' working days at an average day-wage of 124 cash). The land tax would have come to about 120 strings (at an estimated 250 cash per mu). After meeting these expenses, Taihe tang would have been left with about 975 strings. Miscellaneous expenses, such as cattle feed, hog feed, seed grain, tools, repairs, and so forth, may have come to about 350 strings, leaving Taihe tang with an estimated profit of 625 strings. This figure could well have been much higher, as the landlords had adequate storage facilities and were therefore able to store their grain and sell it in the spring and summer when prices were twice as high as in the autumn and winter. If Taihe tang's grain sold at 35 cash per jin for wheat and 22.5 cash per jin for the coarse grains (half as much again as in the above estimates), then they would have been left with a final profit of about 1,500 strings. The total cost of all Taihe tang's lands was exactly 9,979 strings of cash plus 573 taels. (See Tables 2, 3, and 4.) With allowance for depreciation of the cash during the course of the nineteenth century and conversion of the taels to cash at the rate of 1,500, the total cost of the land comes to between 15,000 and 20,000 strings of cash. If the annual profit from the farm came to between 625 and 1,500 strings, then the annual return on the original investment came to between 3 and 10 percent. These are only approximate calculations, but they can be checked against the budget of a Shandong farm near Jining of about the same size as Taihe tang's and at the same period. The return on the original investment of this farm reckoned in the same way was 25 percent but its land was one quarter as expensive as Taihe tang's. Had the land been as expensive, the return on the original investment of this farm would have been about 6 percent, which is the same order of magnitude as the return on Taihe tang's farm.[35]

At the end of the nineteenth century, Taihe tang was making an annual profit of 4,500 strings from its businesses plus an undisclosed amount from its extensive money-lending activities. (See Chapter 4, Section 1.) If it made 1,500 strings from these activities, total profits from the business side would have been 6,000 strings or between four and ten times the profit made from the farm. But the farm, it should be remembered, also provided all the food for the workers in the businesses, plus the household's consumption needs.

Unfortunately, the authors do not provide enough data to make similar calculations possible for any of the other landlords in their sample. Nor have they been able to find enough statistics to enable checking for possible correlations between farm size and household size. They do point out, however, that the managerial landlords frequently had very large households (50 to 100 members, if servants, laborers, and dependents are included). For this reason, they stress that production for household consumption was an important aim of the managerial landlords. But it was clearly not the only aim. A considerable portion of total farm output was marketed, and the farm was run at a small profit.

The landlords maintained a lavish style of life; they lived in immense walled-in compounds, surrounded by large numbers of servants and often by their own private guards. At festivals and at family celebrations they spent huge sums of money feasting and entertaining large numbers of guests, often hiring a private opera company for the occasion. The big landlords of the Meng clan owned the ultimate sign of luxury in a land-scarce society, a private pleasure park. It was stocked with "peacocks, cranes, mongolian larks, monkeys, and so forth, and in it were cultivated many rare and precious plants and flowers." (See Chapter 4, Section 3.)

Most of the landlord families included neither scholars nor officials and, for this reason, their names do not appear in the traditional historical sources. One of them summed up his attitude toward education by saying, "There's no point in us studying; the poor kids have already done it for us." (See Chapter 5, Section 1.) He was presumably referring to the children of the poorer families in his clan, for, even if the landlords were scornful of education, they still recognized its utility, and many provided the funds for clan or family schools.

If these landlords did not, on the whole, attempt to climb into the ranks of the Confucian gentry through the regular channels of the imperial examination system, they certainly attempted to raise their status by purchasing official titles. Many of them, too, were active in district and village affairs, sometimes joining the local informal sub-bureaucracy and always using their influence in the local networks of entrenched wealth and power through which the gentry and the officials of the central government acted.

The preceding outline of the managerial landlord economy poses a number of questions the reader himself may well have begun to ask.

First, how accurate are the details of Jing and Luo's survey? It was, after all, based on questions put to people in the 1950s about conditions in the 1890s and 1900s. Second, if the details are reasonably accurate, how widespread were the managerial landlords? In other words, how representative of overall landlord behavior is Jing and Luo's sample? Third, the authors' thesis on urban development, commercialization of agriculture, and the differentiation of the peasantry presented in Part I was based on standard historical sources dating mainly from the seventeenth to nineteenth centuries.

Their survey data based on interviews and questionnaires relate mainly to the decade 1890–1900. If the details of the survey are accurate and if it is representative, how well does it fit with the thesis on the earlier economic and social changes in Shandong outlined in Part I?

How accurate are the details of the authors' sample? They themselves warn: "We had to rely on the memories of old men. Memories can be mistaken and facts distorted, and furthermore we were not able to administer the questionnaire directly." (See note to Appendixes.)

Sources with a direct quantitative bearing on the same landlords or on the same villages of Shandong at this time are extremely difficult to find. Nevertheless several examples of direct corroboration have already been given. Alexander Armstrong in 1891 remarked on a condiment works in Jining that employed 500 workers. Jing and Luo's informant (who had been the firm's last accountant) told them it had employed 400 workers in about 1900. The Royal Asiatic Society's landholding survey of 1888 covered some of the same districts as those in Jing and Luo's survey and confirms their breakdown of village class structure. Many of the details on farming practice recorded by F. H. King and P. G. M. Stenz also corroborate Jing and Luo's findings. Only one of the villages covered in J. L. Buck's survey of Chinese agriculture also appears in Jing and Luo's sample (Xiawei in Yishui district). Buck gives the total population in 1930 as 170 households, while Jing and Luo's questionnaire gives the population of the same village c. 1900 as 160 households.[36]

There is no reason to suppose that Jing and Luo's informants should not have remembered exactly details such as the number of households in their villages or the amount of land owned by different families. Indeed the small amount of evidence summarized above suggests that they had remarkably accurate memories. Granted that the details of the sample are reasonably accurate, how representative is it?

The authors state that they began their study by gathering data on the three landlords from central Shandong presented in Chapter 4. They then sent out questionnaires to 197 villages all over Shandong to find out how widespread landlords similar to the original three were. Managerial landlord/wage labor relations of production were found in 74 percent of the villages, while an average of 25 percent of the villages in each region had only managerial landlord/wage labor relations of production. From this the authors conclude that "the economic forms of managerial landlords such as Taihe tang, Shujing tang, and Jinxiu tang were not isolated phenomena." (See Chapter 6.)

Unfortunately, the authors do not say how the 197 villages of their control sample were selected, so there is no means of knowing how typical these villages were of the total of about 100,000 Shandong villages. The 197 villages contained a total of 28,034 households. Of these, 390 (1.3 percent) were managerial landlords and 507 (1.8 percent) were rentier landlords. The village sample shows therefore that, even if the managerial landlords were widespread, they were still outnumbered by rentier landlords. (See Appendix A.)

From the 390 managerial landlords in the sample, 131 were selected (here again, we are not told how they were selected) and data were gathered on their farming practices. (See Appendix B.) I have already pointed out that these data show that, in several important respects, the original three "typical" managerial landlords of Chapter 4 were not so typical. They had higher yields and more laborers and applied more fertilizer than the average, and their business operations were probably larger than those of the 131 landlords in the control sample. Moreover, their farms were on the highly commercialized plain which lay to the east of the provincial capital. Despite these differences, there is no doubt that, by the end of the nineteenth century, there was a wealthy stratum of rural entrepreneurs in Shandong, engaged in farming part of their land as well as in business and in moneylending. The question remains, precisely how extensive was this stratum? The authors' answer is to give the percentage of villages in their control sample in which managerial landlord/wage labor relations of production were found. They provide data in their village sample that show that 1.3 percent of the landlords were managerial and 1.8 percent were rentier. The control sample of 131 landlords in Appendix B also shows that 263 of the managerial landlords (60 percent) rented out more than 50 mu. In all they rented out a total of 186,003 mu, which was no less than 80 percent of the total land they owned. Only 48,675 mu or 20 percent of their land was directly managed. Direct farming was in no sense the most common method of management used by landlords, even by the "managerial landlords."

In general, Jing and Luo's data on 131 landlords in Appendix B reveal that, the more land owned, the less farmed directly; the less land owned, the more farmed directly. Thirty-six of the landlords out of the 134 in the entire survey (27 percent) owned 1,000 mu or more. Of these, only 7 directly cultivated more than half their land and 25 cultivated less than a quarter. At the other end of the scale, 31 landlords (23 percent) owned between 120 and 280 mu. Of these, only 4 directly managed less than half their land and none less than a quarter. Nineteen of them directly managed all their land. The cut-off point at which marginal costs rose so rapidly as to make direct farming unprofitable was 500 mu. In some regions the authors' data cluster at one point on this scale of landholding. For example, the 22 landlords in north Shandong directly managed 76 percent of their land (they owned an average of 631 mu), while the 27 landlords in south and west Shandong only directly managed 10.8 percent of their land (they owned on the average 4,622 mu). It seems likely that this reflects how the sample was selected rather than objective conditions in these regions. In other words, there is every reason to suppose that there were plenty of large landholders directly managing only a small percentage of their land in north Shandong, just as there were small landholders in south and west Shandong managing a large percentage of their land.

The picture suggested by Jing and Luo's data on landholding accords well with what is known of Chinese landholding from other sources. Typically, Chinese landlords rented out their land in small plots to tenant cultivators rather than farming it directly themselves. Within this system, and particularly in north China, landlords hired wage labor and directly managed a portion of their land.

The following description of farming in Qufu (central-south Shandong) in the 1920s, for example, underlines this characteristic of north Chinese landholding and incidentally accords very exactly in every other respect with the picture suggested by Jing and Luo's data:

> There are a large number of freeholders owning more land than they can cultivate themselves. In the farming season there is always a shortage of labor and farmers have to engage assistance from neighboring districts. If a freeholder owns more land than he can cultivate himself, he may let a part to poor friends or relatives at a nominal rent. Usually, however, he cultivates his property with hired labor. In the latter case, a number of hands are employed under a foreman and a large proprietor sometimes has five or six foremen each controlling a number of laborers ... The foreman is responsible for recruiting labor, and most of the hands are his friends or fellow-townsmen, for whose behavior he is responsible ... A hand employed by the season is discharged in October...[37]

Jing and Luo chose one characteristic aspect of the north Chinese landlord system—direct management—as the focus of their argument and they have a great many interesting things to say about it. The focus of their argument, however, should not be allowed to obscure the overall features of the landholding system suggested by their data. Direct landlord farming with wage labor was indeed fairly widespread in Shandong c. 1900, as Jing and Luo point out. But most landlord-owned land (including that owned by "managerial landlords") was rented out to tenant cultivators, and between 65 percent and 80 percent of all land was farmed by small peasant owners.

How well do the survey data presented in Parts II and III fit with the argument of Part I based on historical sources?

"In arranging and setting forth the survey material on the class structure of the villages," the authors write at the beginning of Chapter 6, "we have made the assumption that it was not something that had developed overnight but, on the contrary, that it had gradually developed over a long period of time and that it had largely inherited certain special features of the class structure of these villages from the past. For this reason, we believe it is perfectly possible, on the basis of the class structure of the villages in the late Qing, to discern the broad outlines and main developmental directions of the class structure of Shandong villages throughout the Qing dynasty (1644–1911)."

This is the only passage in which the authors explain their use of survey materials on the decade 1890 to 1900 to corroborate changes supposedly taking place in Shandong over the previous three centuries. It is hard to see how survey materials relating to a single point in time can be used to suggest "developmental directions."

Here, as elsewhere, the authors would appear to be less interested in the process of economic and social change in Shandong over time than in fitting their survey and historical data into an ideal model of how feudal societies develop into capitalist societies. If one part of the 1890s survey data appears to fit the model and one part of the historical data (say urban growth in the seventeenth century) also appears to fit the model, then the later survey data "corroborate" the earlier data. Little attempt is made to follow secular trends, such as changes in population, prices, or wages. Even categories such as "managerial landlord" appear to be required by the model rather than suggested by the data in the Appendixes (which show that the landlords directly managed only 20 percent of the land they owned, a point not made by the authors in the text). This one feature of landlord management is apparently sufficient to permit labeling these landlords "managerial landlords," a category that snugly fits into the Leninist model put forward in Part I. Clearly these landlords farmed for profit, and clearly they did so by exploiting destitute peasants in new capitalist relations of production. They were able (so the argument continues) to sell their surplus produce because of the new urban demand created by the rise of commercial and industrial centers such as Linqing and Jining. As long as all or some regions of Shandong can be assumed to have had all or some of the features of this model at some point in the last three centuries they can then be assumed to have been part of a common process. In this way data from one period are thrown in with data from another period, and such matters as place and time are virtually ignored. For example, if it is true that Linqing and Jining (Grand Canal region) grew rapidly from the sixteenth century on, how did their growth make itself felt on other regions of the province? Why did the other two towns selected by the authors develop two centuries later than Linqing and Jining? How was landlord farming actually connected with urban demand? Certainly the landlords employed wage labor (a sufficient definition of "rural bourgeoisie"?), but the authors make little or no attempt to show that the landlords grew cash or industrial crops for the towns whose growth they examined in Part I.[38]

If I felt Jing and Luo's simplistic Leninist model a fruitful one in the Chinese context, it would be worth pursuing these points in greater detail. Enough has been said already, however, to suggest that this particular model does not even begin to fit the traditional Chinese case: there was, for example, no rapid and massive increase of urban population at the expense of the agricultural population in north China before the opening of the treaty ports, and the identification of certain Shandong landlords as "managerial" rather than "rentier" is not even supported by the authors' data. One is tempted to dismiss the authors' argument with Lenin's own tart comment: "Of course, infinitely diverse combinations of elements of this or that type of capitalist evolution are possible, and only hopeless pedants could set about solving the peculiar and complex problems arising merely by quoting this or that opinion of Marx about a different historical epoch."[39]

To dismiss the authors' argument in this way would, however, do less than justice to the cautious qualifications with which they have hedged it in Part III, especially in their Preliminary Conclusions. It would also obscure the paradox that, in attempting to apply a practically unworkable thesis, the authors have been led to collect and publish unique data of a type too often overlooked by students of Chinese history.

Late traditional China was characterized by a considerable

growth in population, particularly in the north. Shandong was no
exception. Indeed, thanks to the relatively cheap transport provided by the state-run Grand Canal, this region was one of the
commercially advanced areas of the country. Sizable towns grew
up along or near the canal, often with specialized handicrafts or
commercial functions. These towns, however, were not centers of
change or disruption either in the economy or in the body politic.
Their populations grew at about the same pace as the rural population, and the townsfolk produced no alternate set of values to
challenge the Confucian gentry state. Here was no clash of a nascent
bourgeoisie with a hostile feudal ruling elite. On the contrary, the
functions of merchant, landowner, and official in late traditional
China were often performed by the same individuals (or family
members) who shared a common ethic of mutual adjustment and
accommodation.

Population growth stimulated and was, in turn, sustained by
intensification, specialization, and commercialization of the agricultural economy (of which the towns were an integral part). There
was also expansion into marginal areas (made possible by the introduction and spread of crops such as the potato) and into hitherto
unsettled areas. Where a shift to crops such as the sweet potato took
place, a rapid increase of small and very small farms became possible, since such crops can support many times more people per unit
of land than can cereals. The power elite in most villages were
successful entrepreneurs who had taken advantage of new moneylending and business opportunities to increase their landholdings.
About 20 percent of the land in the villages was owned by about
5 percent of the households. The remainder was held in small plots
by peasant freeholders. Not only did the successful rural entrepreneurs invest profits from market towns and cities in country estates,
but they also fairly often ran comparatively efficient "home-farms"
using hired labor. Profits from the sale of surplus produce from
these farms were not high, their primary purpose presumably being
to feed the landlord's household and its dependents. Most of the
landlords' land was rented out in small plots to tenants.

The traditional Chinese economy might simply have continued

to intensify with periodic Malthusian crises. It might also have found new areas of expansion. New institutions and new technologies might also have been invented, although there are no indications in the available historical evidence that any of the preconditions or characteristics of an industrial revolution were present. As it happened, the nineteenth and twentieth centuries saw both Malthusian crises and overseas migration. But by then the terms of the traditional equation had begun to alter dramatically due to the arrival of the Western powers and elements of the industrial system. And that is the point at which Jing and Luo chose to end their study.[40]

NOTES ON THE TRANSLATION

Romanization. In the romanization of Chinese names and terms, the Pinyin system has been used throughout, except for "Peking" and "Canton."

Maps. The original text included only one map, which is reproduced here as "Map 2: Regions of Shandong." "Map 1: Central Shandong" has been added by the translator to make the geography of the region somewhat clearer.

Illustrations. The original text was illustrated with twenty-eight pictures, of which only two have been reproduced here in the frontispiece.

Annotations. All annotations or additions by the translator are enclosed in square brackets.

Terminology. "Peasant" is usually used in the sense of "owner-peasant" as distinct from "tenant." Occasionally it is also used more broadly to cover both "owner-peasants" and "tenants."

PREFACE (1957)

In writing on the economic and social significance of managerial landlords in Shandong during the Qing period, we have sought to use a comparatively compact body of data from one province to answer the following questions: How extensive was the use of hired labor in rural Shandong during the Qing? What was the average amount of land cultivated by managerial landlords using hired labor? How diversified were the economic activities of managerial landlords? What were the practices relating to the hiring of long- and short-term farm laborers at that time? What was the level of their wages? What was their social status, and so forth? To put it in one sentence, we have attempted to show the basic tendencies of differentiation of the peasants and the economic and social significance of the managerial landlords.

Marx pointed out in *Capital* that "the economic structure of capitalist society has grown out of the economic structure of feudal society. The dissolution of the latter set free the elements of the former."[1]

In feudal society, agricultural production is the most important form of production. In China, the feudal relations of production of landlords and tenants were the basic relations. The appearance of managerial landlords and agricultural wage laborers was, therefore, a new phenomenon. To research and ascertain the nature of this phenomenon, especially as it had developed from the late Ming into the Qing period, will help the understanding of the development of the beginnings of capitalism in Chinese agriculture.

AUTHORS' NOTE (1959)

The draft of this small volume was completed in June 1957 and put in the publisher's hands in December. In the intervening two years, we have not been able to find the time to make any alterations. Now, as the volume goes to the printers, we have made a few minor corrections to the final draft, which remains substantially the same as upon its completion two years ago.

Our original intention had been to use field data and written sources to corroborate each other and, using typical sources from each locality, to relate them to the overall picture of the economy of Shandong in the Qing period at the same time as pursuing our main theme. On rereading the book, it strikes us that we fell far short of achieving this aim.

We hope that our readers will point out the gaps and weaknesses in our argument caused by our own lack of knowledge and by the limitations of our sources.

In gathering our questionnaire materials, we received the help and encouragement of many people, and we should like to take this opportunity to thank them all.

The authors
28 June, 1959
Shandong University

WEIGHTS AND MEASURES*

Area

mu (shimu)	1/15 hectare; 1/6 acre
qing	100 mu; 6 1/2 hectares; 17 acres

*Capacity***

sheng	1/10 dou; 1 liter; 0.22 gallons
dou	10 sheng; 10 liters; 2.2 gallons
hu	nominally 10 dou but in practice 5 dou
dan	10 dou; 100 liters; 22 gallons

Weight

jin (shijin: catty)	1/2 kilo; 1.1 lbs.
picul (shidan)	100 jin; 50 kilos; 110 lbs.
20 piculs	1 metric ton

*Length****

cun	1/10 chi; 3 centimeters; 1 1/3 inches
chi	10 cun; 1/3 meter; 13 inches
zhang	10 chi; 3.3 meters; 11 ft.
li	150 zhang; 1/2 kilometer; 1/3 mile

Currency

1 string of cash	nominally made up of 1,000 copper cash
tael	one ounce of silver, nominally exchanged for 1,000 cash
RMB (*Renmin bi*)	the currency of contemporary China, reckoned in yuan, dollars

sui	"year" (in the Chinese system a person is regarded as being one year old at birth and two years old at the beginning of the next calendar year)

41

[* In Parts II and III, the authors have converted traditional, regional forms of the Chinese units of measurement given here to their post-1929 market system (*shizhi*) forms whose metric and British Imperial equivalents are listed. Units of measurement in Part I have not been so converted, and therefore their equivalents should not be regarded as completely accurate.

** The authors state that 1 dan (capacity measure) of kaoliang in the early part of this century in central Shandong (Zhangqiu district) weighed 550 jin and that 1 dan of wheat weighed 700 jin. A province-wide Japanese survey of weights and measures in Shandong at this time shows variations of between 380 and 800 jin per dan of kaoliang (*Shina shōbetsu zenshi, Santōshō*, Tokyo, 1917, p. 1173).

*** The cun, chi, and zhang listed here are the market system ones. In traditional China, these measures (as indeed all others) varied greatly, but, in general (especially when used for textiles), they were considerably longer than their post-1929 market system (*shizhi*) forms.]

Part I

THE DEVELOPMENT OF THE REGIONAL ECONOMY
OF SHANDONG DURING THE QING PERIOD

Our central theme concerns the analysis of the economic and social significance of the managerial landlords in Shandong during the Qing period [1644–1911]. Already long before the Qing, the basis of the feudal system, the feudal landlord economy, had begun to break up, so that what we are discussion is, in fact, the early appearance of capitalism in the rural sector. This phenomenon cannot be understood in isolation. Other aspects of the economy that are closely linked to the rural sector have to be taken into consideration also. As is well known, the key to the genesis and development of capitalism is the formation of the market. In the final period of feudalism, the development of regional economies took place within the context of the development of the national market. It is for this reason that, before discussing the managerial landlord economy itself, we turn first to the development of the regional economy of Shandong.

We have singled out three main aspects of this topic: the growth of local markets; the development of commercial agricul-

43

ture; and the differentiation of the peasants. Rather than attempt a complete analysis of local markets in Shandong at this time, we have chosen four of the most flourishing commercial and handicraft centers to serve as examples. Commerce and handicrafts developed on the basis of agricultural growth and, in turn, stimulated this growth, leading in some areas to increasing commercialization of agriculture and increased commercial activity in general.

No sooner had commercialization penetrated the agricultural sector than the insatiable feudal landlord class, on the one hand, stepped up their extravagant and wasteful style of life, while, on the other hand, they made every effort to preserve their already diminishing feudal powers. As for the exploited middle and poor tenants, the semi-owner-peasants and the owner-peasants, the commercialization of agriculture meant that it was both easier to lose as well as to obtain land. As a result, the tendency within the peasant class was for the rich to become richer and the poor poorer. In the course of this increasing polarization, far more peasants lost their land and became poorer than became richer. Those who lost their land either stayed in the countryside and became wage laborers or went to the newly flourishing commercial and handicraft centers to become handicraftsmen. In these ways, new class relations were gradually evolving.

The key time period for the changes we are discussing was roughly from the late seventeenth to the mid-nineteenth century. From the Manchu conquest in 1644 to the end of the seventeenth century, the ruling order in Shandong was unstable. Apart from the landlords and scholar-gentry, who had quickly submitted to the Manchu conquerors, a large number of uprisings broke out in these years. The Yulin forces, for example, which operated in Chaocheng, Guancheng, Yuncheng, and Chengwu districts, had a very large number of followers and covered a wide area. In 1655 they were threatening the provincial capital, Jinan, as well as a leading commercial center, Linqing. The towns in these years had not fully recovered from the devastation of the Manchu conquest, let alone begun to flourish. From the latter half of the nineteenth century, the gradual penetration of foreign capitalism into the national economy altered its natural course, giving rise to problems which lie outside the theme of this book. However, in clarifying certain questions, various post-Opium War [1842] conditions are discussed, just as certain pre-Qing tendencies which throw light on our central theme are also brought up.

Chapter 1

THE DEVELOPMENT OF COMMERCIAL
AND HANDICRAFT TOWNS

The increase in number and growth of commercial and handicraft towns attest to the flourishing nature of the commodity economy at this time. A number of cities in Shandong that had been famous since ancient times, such as Jinan, Qingzhou (modern Yidu), and Yanzhou, were political rather than commercial or handicraft centers, and they owed their fame to the fact that they were the seats of the feudal court's provincial governors and prefectural magistrates, their large staff of bureaucrats and clerks, and the scholar-gentry and prominent families of the province. Their size and expansion were intimately connected with the feudal landlord class and its bureaucratic political arm. It is not this type of town that concerns us, but rather the commercial and handicraft centers that had begun to appear from the sixteenth century on and whose rise was closely connected with the development of their agricultural hinterlands and the national market. These towns, as a result of the development of a commodity economy, had grown up by breaking away from the self-supporting natural economy. Four of these new towns have been selected for discussion here. Linqing and Jining were situated on the Grand Canal and had expanded from the sixteenth century on. Zhoucun and Yanshen lay between Jinan and Qingzhou and began to develop in the later eighteenth century. [See Map 1.]

1.1 Linqing
Linqing was an important center on the Grand Canal. It had begun to develop when the canal was opened in the Yuan dynasty [1267–1368] and gradually became the main commercial and handicraft center in the northwestern part of the province.[1] According to the following description, it was already an imposing walled town in the mid-fifteenth century: "Linqing is a place where ships from

46

all over the empire congregate and where high officials and important people pass through. Large numbers of soldiers and commoners as well as merchants and traders gather here; ships' masts are crowded together in rows, and smoke rises in a cloud. It is an important staging point between north and south China."[2] By the early sixteenth century, commerce in Linqing was quite advanced and under the direction of Zhao Ji-jue, an assistant director of the Inspector-General (*Bingbei fushi*), a tamped earth wall of 20 li was erected, and this was soon expanded again. By the end of the sixteenth century, Linqing had already become one of the large towns of the north.

Local sources contain many descriptions of the town which, although probably exaggerated, do give some idea of its flourishing state. "Our sub-prefecture was founded in the Western Han... during the Ming dynasty as a center of Grand Canal as well as riverine communication, it has been the vital supply link for the capital and is famed throughout the empire."[3] "Linqing was raised from being a district to a sub-prefecture. It is of vital strategic importance for the capital as well as the juncture of communications lines of the empire, precious goods are stored here in great quantities and thousands of boats glide along the banks of the Wen and the Wei Rivers. Travelers pass on their way through; merchants bustle around; and peasants are busy weaving."[4] "Built on the intersection of the Wen and the Wei Rivers, Linqing is an important town between the ancient states of Qi and Zhao. Merchants and traders come from every direction by boat and overland; they build up great stores here from which they sell their goods. The town clothes the empire, and its people live by profit."[5] "I came into the sub-prefecture and saw the large number of fine houses, the mass of people bustling to and fro, the many thousands of transport boats stem to stern on their way north up the Grand Canal, and, in the town market, carriages and crowds of people, surpassing both Linzi and Jimo."[6]

In the course of its development, Linqing suffered a number of setbacks of one kind or another. In 1600, as a result of the extremely heavy taxes imposed by the feudal court and its agents, several thousand people rose and chased away the tax commissioner, Ma Tang. In the *Veritable Records of the Ming* (Shenzong, *juan* 376), the President of the Board of Finance, Zhao Shi-qing, in a memorial dated 1602, recorded that receipts from the trade tax since 1599 "had been decreasing year by year" and that, "in previous years, there had been 38 merchants dealing in miscellaneous goods passing through the tax station but now, because of the heavy duties imposed on goods in transit, all but 2 have gone bankrupt." He went on to say that "21 out of 32 satin stores had closed; that 45 out of 73 cotton goods stores had closed; that 41 miscellaneous goods stores had also closed; and that none of the Liaozuo cloth merchants [from northeast China] were left." During this period, extremely heavy taxes clearly acted as a brake on the development of commerce.

Before and after the fall of the Ming, Linqing was sacked several times by the Qing armies, and the developing town suffered severe damage. An inscription of 1686 records that "Linqing was originally a center of commerce but, since the armies sacked it, it has become ever more empty . . . merchants and tradesmen have scattered like stars and only two- or three-tenths of its former glory remains."[7]

Apart from these setbacks, Linqing was taken and used as a base for fierce attacks on the Qing rulers by the armies of Li Zi-cheng at the end of the Ming, by the forces of Wang Lun of Shou Zhang's uprising in 1774, by the Taiping armies in 1855, and by the forces of Song Jing-shi of Tang Yi in 1863. While the fighting was going on, it naturally had a profound influence on economic development.[8]

Population

One source is clearly exaggerating when it puts the population at close to one million.[9] We estimate that between the sixteenth and eighteenth centuries the population of Linqing was in the neighborhood of 100,000. This much lower estimate would still make Linqing a considerable center, for, in a self-sufficient feudal economy, a commercial and handicraft town of 100,000 population was comparatively large.[10] As the *District Gazetteer of Linqing* put it: "At the height of its prosperity, the town stretched without a break for several tens of li, the shops bunched together like the teeth of a comb as far to the north as Tawan and as far to the south as Toucha."

As a result of the peasant wars at the end of the Ming and the depredations of Qing troops, Linqing's population had probably dropped to about 100,000 before the middle of the eighteenth century and declined even further in the course of the uprisings of the late eighteenth and the nineteenth centuries to approximately 50,000, which remained fairly stable down into the 1930s.

Trade and Handicrafts

During the Qing period, Linqing's commerce and handicrafts flourished. According to the President of the Board of Finance Zhao Shi-qing's 1602 memorial already quoted, there were at least "32 satin stores" in the town at the beginning of the seventeenth century as well as "73 cotton goods stores" and a large number of miscellaneous goods stores. A great many local products were collected at Linqing for processing before being sent out to the neighboring district and market towns and indeed, in some cases, to towns all over the empire. These products included cotton, felt, indigo, wax, saffron, honey, wool, dried jujubes and melons, and so on. In addition, large numbers of handicraft products, some of them very famous, were manufactured in Linqing itself as well as in the neighboring villages. According to the entry in the *Imperial Encyclopaedia,* "Political Divisions" section: "Fine Linqing silk is used for kerchiefs and curtains both strong and beautiful, which are sold in other regions . . . the best sheepskin coats and felt mats are made at Linqing . . . the felt produced at Linqing is better than that produced anywhere else." The products listed in the 1784 edition of the *Gazetteer of the Independent Sub-Prefecture of Linqing* (section on "Local Products") include the following four-teen local handicraft products: cotton head towels, silk head scarfs, kerchiefs, felt, fur clothes, glue, sugar, yeast, velvets, red ribbons, gauze silk, raw silk, cotton cloth, and brocade. The same gazetteer (section on "Markets") lists the following streets in Linqing: Fruit Lane, White Calico Lane, Cooper's Lane, Charcoal Works, Grain Market, Idol Prints Lane, Leather Lane, Incense Lane, Black Bowl Market, Cooking-pot Market, Wicker Oil-basket Lane, Woven Mat Works, Saddler's Lane, Yeast Lane, Horse Market Street, Sheep Market, and Ox Market. These street names clearly show that Linqing was a commercial and handicraft center with close connections with the everyday life of people in surrounding villages. Leather Lane, Saddlers Lane, Horse Market Street, Ox Market, and Sheep Market were all connected with the buying and selling of agricultural products, while the cloth, charcoal, grain, and cooking-pot markets dealt in basic necessities. In the section on Dong-a district, Yanzhou prefecture, the *Imperial Encyclopaedia* records that, "Yanzhou (Qufu) is not far from Linqing and Zhangqiu and its people are able to buy all their daily necessities from small traders at these places."

Not only was Linqing a local market center, but it also tied in very closely with other markets in every part of China. "Linqing is a major center in the trade between north and south China; goods from all points of the compass are collected here; other places cannot compare with its volume of sales. Far more tribute goods are bought here than from neighboring prefectures."[11] Both the fine white open silks of the southeast and the furs and woolen stuffs of the northwest can be found stocked at Linqing."[12] "Local supplies of grain are insufficient to provide for the town, which as a result depends upon grain merchants. The grain brought down the Wei River on sailing boats comes mostly from Henan; glutinous millet comes upstream from Tianjin. Most of the grain coming up the Wen River comes from around Jining. The cotton cloth and silk also all come from the same area. Stem to stern, the boats come from hundreds of miles, bringing coarse grains and rough cloths for the town supplies. Fine and beautiful gift items come packed aboard the grain tribute vessels, and they are easily hidden."[13] From the Ming on, there were "Qingzhou cloth merchants" in Linqing who sold their goods in Qingzhou.[14] And there were even "Liaozuo cloth merchants" from Linqing who marketed their goods in north-

east China.[15] We also know traders from Taicang in Jiangsu sold
their cloth in Linqing[16] and, during the Qing, merchants from
Dengzhou prefecture "traveled all the way to sell their goods at
Linqing."[17] In the market at Xuanhua prefecture, Hebei province,
there was a Linqing cloth and silk store,[18] and one source even
records that Linqing's silk was "mostly sold at the capital while a
small part was sold in places as far away as Tibet."[19] The red and
yellow ceremonial presentation silk scarves (*hada*) made in Linqing
were retailed in Mongolia, Chahar, and Suiyuan.[20]

As Linqing's commercial economy expanded, the lifestyles of
the "upper crust" of the townsfolk began to change markedly from
the old ways. As a seventeenth-century writer put it, Linqing is "a
place at which people from all quarters gather and in which large
numbers of merchants congregate. Common sights are gentry and
their women going out on excursions, and the rich flaunting their
jewels and presenting dances and entertainments at their homes to
the accompaniment of banquets and feasts."[21]

An eighteenth-century source records that "in Linqing...
people live by their wits making profits in business; when they are
not busy, they give parties with much drinking and song, going on
for days and nights without resting. Their young men throw their
weight around, killing and robbing and shamelessly committing
other such crimes."[22] The preface to the 1749 edition of the
Gazetteer of the Sub-Prefecture of Linqing states that "even the
menservants wear silk, and the attendant maids are decked out in
great finery. Many who are not necessarily gentry put on banquets
and theatricals in Linqing. Marriage and burial ceremonies far surpass the accepted rites. Here pride and extravagance are equally in
evidence, and artfulness and deceit are the norm."[23]

Although these descriptions were written by officials for inclu-
sion in official publications and, as a result, are probably exaggerated,
they do give an indication of the extravagant lifestyle of the "upper
stratum" of Linqing.[24]

During the Qing period, there were various official establish-
ments in Linqing. Apart from the prefectural and sub-prefectural
yamens there were such specialized organs as the Linqing Granary

under the Board of Revenue, the Linqing Trade Tax Office (also under the Board of Revenue), the Branch Building Bureau (under the Board of Works), and a Sluice Gate Office for the Grand Canal (also under the Board of Works). Since the early fifteenth century, "there were three granaries in Linqing in which were stored the annual tribute of Henan and Shandong."[25]

The Trade Tax Office was established in 1429 under "censors and a bureau secretary from the Board of Finance to oversee the tribute rice and trade tax collection."[26] The Sluice Gate Office was set up in 1526 and it "collected tunnage (*duanzai*) and voucher dues (*zhijia*)."[27]

At the beginning of the fifteenth century, "brickmaking kilns were set up in Shandong and Henan, and they were put under the direction of a branch building bureau of the Board of Works established in Linqing. The annual quota was one million city-wall bricks. Later, kilns were found throughout the province," and Linqing was the center of the industry. "The Board set a fixed price for bricks" and, as a result "of setting up kilns and inviting merchants to manage them, brick production in Linqing doubled over what it had been in the past."[28] At that time, there were 11 brick kilns in 6 different localities of Linqing. These exploitative organs of the Ming dynasty were inherited by the Qing court. By 1748, another 12 places in Linqing had brick kilns. Although these "officially supervised, privately operated" (*guandu minban*) brickworks were set up to meet the needs of the government, they acted as a spur to the development of Linqing's handicraft industries and economic life in general, and this was because the officials fixed the price and bought up the product and invested considerable sums in the kilns and in transportation.

The Linqing Tax Station was an important source of revenue for the feudal state and a lucrative post for greedy and corrupt officials. It was "set up in the early Ming under the joint supervision of the Board of Finance and the Board of Works. In the late seventeenth century, it was placed under the Provincial Governor of Shandong and, in the second half of the eighteenth century, it was under the direct control of the Prefect of Linqing. At that time the annual receipts were between 20,000–30,000 taels and 60,000–70,000 taels. Money taken in excess of this quota went in squeeze (embezzlement). There was a local saying: "Whether the goods are sufficient or not, the quota is 66,000 taels";[29] 66,000 taels is a very large sum, and it shows how important the Linqing Tax Station was and that trade was well developed in the town.

1.2 Jining

Jining is another important town situated on the Grand Canal. It served as the main commercial and handicrafts center for southwest Shandong. As a walled town it is slightly older than Linqing, its brick walls having been built in 1370. At that time, Jining was mainly an administrative and military center. Later, because of the grain tribute and other traffic on the Grand Canal, the town's commerce and handicrafts began to develop rapidly and, by 1622, an "outer" and much larger wall with a perimeter of over five miles was constructed around the old walls.[30]

An eighteenth-century source describes Jining as "a meeting point between north and south, the goods from the Yangzi and Huai valleys are collected here . . . and people from every direction gather bustling in its markets. It is quite different from the cultural centers of Zou and Lu." The same source continues, Jining is situated "on the northern bank of the Grand Canal; to the south it controls the area down to Peixian and Xuzhou (in Jiangsu) and to the north the Wen and Si rivers join within its borders. It thus commands an important position on the Grand Canal. The wealth of the Yangzi and Huai valleys and merchants from every direction gather here. Its people are only interested in trade, and they live on the profits from it; they pay no attention to farming or sericulture."[31] From the mid-sixteenth century on, Jining had already become a large town with abundant supplies of goods.

Just as in Linqing, many of the streets of Jining were named after the occupations of the people who lived and worked in them. Although most streets were not named in this way, the ones that were give us some idea of the range of commercial activities and handicrafts carried on in the town. According to the section on streets in the 1840 edition of the *Gazetteer of the Independent Sub-Prefecture of Jining* (printed in 1859), the following street names related to trade: Cotton Cloth Market Main Street, Cotton Market Street, Porcelain Alley, Paper Store Street, Ginger Shop Street, Date Store Street, Fruit Passage, Big Charcoal Ditch, and Little Charcoal Ditch. Then there were those streets in which people bartered domestic animals such as Ox Market Street, Donkey and Horse Market Street, Mule Market Street, and so forth. Finally there were those named after handicrafts, for example, Shipbuilders Street, Copper Beaters Street, Foundry Street, Bamboo Basket Weavers Passage, Comb Market Street, Wicker Oil-basket Passage, Rope Twisters Street, Distillers Alley, Sugar Store Street, Sugar Store Alley, Paperworks Street, Flourmill Street, Incense Store Alley, Yeast Street, Leatherworks Street, Serge Passage, and so forth. The names suggest the important part played by local products in trade in Jining at this time. The handicrafts, too, appear mainly to have been concerned with processing local products or manufacturing daily necessities.

Jining's shift from being primarily an administrative, military center to a handicraft and trade center can be seen in the rapid growth in the number of streets in the town.

Table 1 shows that the total number of streets within the walls of Jining had more than doubled between the seventeenth and the nineteenth centuries, while the number of streets outside the walls had more than quadrupled in the same period. We can tell from houses that have survived from this period that most of those living within the walls were officials and gentry (*guanliao, jinshen*) and ordinary people with no business connections. Most of those living outside the town walls, on the other hand, were merchants and handicraftsmen. The fact that the number of streets outside the walls showed a much greater increase than those within clearly indicates that Jining was developing in the direction of a commercial and handicraft center closely linked to its rural hinterland.

Population

There are no surviving sources that give the early population

Table 1

Growth in the Number of Streets in Jining Between
c. 1673 and c. 1840

	Number of streets c. 1673	*Number of streets c. 1840*	*Increase*
Within the walls:			
N-W Quarter north/south streets	6	15	9
N-W Quarter east/west streets	6	9	3
N-E Quarter north/south streets	6	18	12
N-E Quarter east/west streets	4	10	6
S-W Quarter north/south streets	6	12	6
S-W Quarter east/west streets	6	16	10
S-E Quarter north/south streets	4	10	6
S-E Quarter east/west streets	7	17	10
TOTAL	45	107	62
Outside the walls:			
streets outside the north wall	5	11	6
streets outside the south wall	24	90	66
streets outside the east wall	8	57	49
streets outside the west wall	6	25	19
TOTAL	43	183	140

Source: *Gazetteer of the Independent Sub-Prefecture of Jining,* 1859 edition,
   juan 4, pp. 15–17.

of Jining. A source dating from 1621 remarks: "Its inhabitants are
crowded together and number several tens of thousands of families;
its merchants and traders, too, must number several tens of thousands."[32]

   In 1622 when the town was resisting the armies of the peasant
leader Xu Hong-ru, the prefectural magistrate Zheng Yu-qiao
recruited "militia from every quarter of the town amounting to
several tens of thousands of men."[33] This suggests that the popula-

tion of Jining in the early seventeenth century may have been over 100,000. During the fighting and confusion at the end of the Ming period, and in particular the massacres attendant upon the invasion of the Manchu armies, its population must have dropped considerably. In 1644 Jining and three neighboring districts had a ding quota of 17,590, whereas at the beginning of the century it had been 49,554. By 1669 the quota for Jining had been increased to 20,890.[34] Even as late as 1767 Jining still had only something over 70,000, which was still below the probable Ming population. For 1840 there is a comparatively reliable total population estimate for the town that gives 20,845 households. If five is taken to be the average household size, this gives a total of over 100,000.[35]

Because Jining was a developed commercial and handicraft center, there were many brokers and agents who set up their own brokerage organizations. They were in no sense the internal organizations of individual merchant groups and handicraft workers, but they were rather a means whereby the officials organized the collection of taxes from their members. In trades or professions that were fairly well-developed the officials farmed out the taxes on a yearly quota basis to guarantors in the brokers' guilds. These guarantors or agents were "tax farming merchants" (baoshui shang). They requested guild licenses from the officials and paid guild taxes. From the merchants and handicraftsmen, they collected the taxes on incoming and outgoing goods and other taxes. Incoming goods had first to go through the brokers' guilds where a percentage was paid. Any goods not going through the brokers were "smuggled goods," and they were not allowed to be traded. Although the guilds were very much a device for controlling their members, the presence of such organizations in Jining reflects, to a certain degree, the extent of trade and handicrafts in the town.

By the end of the Ming period, these exploiting middlemen were sufficiently powerful in the town to heavily influence the relations between the merchants and handicraftsmen on the one hand and the officials on the other. Though orders were issued to abolish the brokers' hold on business, they could not be completely successful. In 1639 a stone stele was erected on behalf of the cloth merchants entitled "Record of a Request to Abolish the Brokers and Disencumber the Merchants," and a similar one entitled "Record of a Request to Do Away With Our Troubles" was erected on behalf of the ginger merchants. The cotton merchants' stele reads in part: "The cloth merchants should be placed under the same regulations as the linen merchants, and, in accordance with the Provincial Treasurer's ruling, should be taxed only at the rate of .003 taels per bolt." The ginger merchants' stele reads in part, "In order to relieve the ginger merchants, the following five points should be taken up: forbid shabby goods; outlaw dishonest merchants; do away with brokers; stop sharp practices in the market; and forbid fraud among the porters. Fix a tax of .008 taels per hundred hu to be levied on all our goods between Tongji bridge and Wenshenfang, and allow no further taxes to be added."[36]

The two stelae suggest the volume of the cotton cloth and ginger merchants' trade in Jining at this time.

When the Manchu armies came into China in the 1640s, Jining's trade and handicrafts suffered a serious setback, and it was not until the early eighteenth century that they gradually began to revive. The Ming system of brokers' guilds continued under the Qing, and the guild tax quotas reflect the gradual revival of the town's trade. According to Wu Sheng, who was prefectural magistrate of Jining from 1693 until his death in 1706, the "trade tax quota" in Jining at that time was set at 1,218 taels and the "miscellaneous brokerage tax" at 65 taels.[37]

These are official figures and, as such, underestimate the actual amounts collected and leave out the sums taken as squeeze by the brokers among others. That the town's trade had begun to recover is seen more clearly in the number of guilds in existence by the beginning of the eighteenth century. According to Wu Sheng, there were over 18 with "plenty of capital and goods."[38] Another source from about ten years later (1719) refers to the "thousands of carters, boatmen, porters, and coolies who daily enter and leave the town," which suggests the extent of its recovery by this date.[39]

Throughout the Qing dynasty, Jining had a flourishing transport industry. An eighteenth-century source records that, because

Yanzhou prefecture (in which Jining was situated) had "no pine, cedar, or other woods of its own to use for materials," its people bought "timber from the Yangzi valley which came up the Grand Canal, and timber from Shanxi which came east down the Xin River and by way of Ji and Bu feeder canals into the Grand Canal."[40] According to the record of establishment of the Yixian coal bureau, "During the eighteenth and early nineteenth centuries the district was a meeting point and merchants came in large numbers; when the coal pits were increased in number, several thousand boats would come to carry several million piculs of coal up the Grand Canal."[41]

The coal used at Yanzhou and Caozhou came up the Grand Canal through Jining on the grain tribute boats. Apart from the through traffic up and down the canal, there were all the goods coming into the prefecture as well as the local products waiting to be shipped out. Right up until the closure of the canal in 1900, Jining served as an extremely busy transshipment center which employed large numbers of boats, carts, wheelbarrows, and so forth. The Jining carters', porters', and boatmen's guilds referred to in the sources were among the most important in the town.

By the mid-eighteenth century, Jining's trade and handicrafts had undergone further development. Not only was the town an entrepôt and distribution point for timber and bamboo from the Yangzi valley and central China plain, sugar from Zhejiang, porcelain from Jiangxi, tung-oil from Hubei, iron tools from Shanxi, and other goods carried on the Grand Canal and sold in Yanzhou, Caozhou, and Hebei, but it was also a collection point for the local products of the lower Yellow River and Yanzhou prefecture region. These included cotton, jujubes, persimmons, pears, the buds of *cedrala odorata* [*xiangchunya*, used as a vegetable], and *materia medica*. These products were shipped south from Jining to the Yangzi provinces. Food crops, cotton cloth, coal, and so forth from around Yanzhou were also shipped in large quantities up to Linqing, Dezhou, and other towns to the north.[42]

During our visit to Jining in February 1957, we were able to question a number of old gentlemen, including Yuan Wen-pu (82 sui), Zhou Lin-gan (76 sui), Wang Qing-xi (a former boatman, 73 sui), and others, on trade in Jining before the closure of the Grand Canal in 1900.[43] Every year in the tenth lunar month, the grain tribute boats set out up the canal carrying the tribute rice from Suzhou and Hangzhou. Since they were exempt from trade taxes, their captains, helmsmen, and crews used the boats to carry goods such as timber, bamboo, porcelain, iron implements, crystallized sugar, silks and satins, tung-oil, Shaoxing wine, paper, and miscellaneous items. They would sell off these goods along the way. Those with plenty of capital would sell luxury items, while those with less cash could sell coarse goods. The tribute boats would reach Jining at the end of the fourth lunar month each year and stop there to spend the festival of the fifth day of the fifth month. Over half of the private cargo would be sold in Jining, the remainder being disposed of later in Dongchang and Linqing. The boats would start loading up with local products as soon as they set out on the return journey down the canal from Tongzhou lock [just outside Peking at the head of the canal]. They would pass Jining on the return journey in the eighth lunar month and would buy there jujubes, pears, persimmons, hill haws, walnuts, *cedrala odorata* buds, peanuts, capsicum, bricks, leather and fur goods, and so forth. On the return journey, the tribute rice boats were classified as private traders and their cargoes were taxed. Although these interview materials relate to conditions at the end of the nineteenth century, they accord well with written sources from earlier periods on Jining's trade and, for this reason, we have included them here.[44]

Handicrafts

Jining's tobacco-processing industry began to flourish because large areas of its and Ziyang district's hinterland came to be planted to tobacco. In his *Grand Canal Diary* of 1829, Bao Shi-chen notes Jining's "biggest export is tobacco leaf. Six families operate the business which has an annual turnover of two million taels. Some 4,000 workers are employed altogether."[45]

Other important handicraft industries were oil pressing, wine making, leather, paper, bamboo products, copper and iron utensils, timber products, silk, and so forth.[46] All these trades had their own streets and their own independant guild regulations. After the tobacco industry, the most flourishing were the copper and bamboo products, and leather trades. Next came the condiment works and the liquor brewers.[47]

The copper trade was divided into two main groups, the copper- (*hong-tong*) utensil makers and the white-brass (*baitong*) utensil makers.[48]

The copper-utensil group was further subdivided into specialists in basin making, cooking-pot making, copper-hook making, and the making of miscellaneous everyday items, as well as furnace-bellows making. The white-brass makers were also specialized, some making tobacco pipe bowls, others making head ornaments, and so forth, each group with its separate workshops and retailers. Each of these specialized crafts had its own apprentices and set up its own guild. The most important products of the bamboo-goods manufacturers were agricultural implements, such as rakes, sieves, brooms, baskets, hampers, fishing pots, and punting poles used by the boating industry, and everyday items, such as chopsticks, baskets, mosquito-net ribbing, and so on.

The leather trade was divided into the hides guild and the leather-goods guild. The hides guild procured the skins of oxen, sheep, donkeys, dogs, and so forth, and tanned them for use by the leather-goods guild, who then made equipment such as harnesses, whips, straps, and all sorts of leather goods used by the peasants.

Clearly, the market for the various products outlined above was Jining's rural hinterland. In line with traditional practices in this area, the everyday copper and bamboo products were mostly sent to Juye, Heze, Jiaxiang, Yutai, and Shanxian, where they were retailed. The leather goods were mainly marketed in the Tai-an, Ningyang region. Tanned hides were not only sold locally but were also shipped for sale all over the Yangzi provinces.

The owners of the various handicraft industries, apart from those such as wine making, oil pressing, and tobacco processing, which required rather large capital investments, were mainly peasants who had lost their land and moved to the city. Right up until 1956, on the eve of the cooperative movement, these indepen-

dent small handicraftsmen were the typical manufacturers with
their workshops and retail store in one and the same building. They
themselves made their goods, and they themselves sold them.
Including apprentices, these workshops usually contained no more
than 2 to 3 or 3 to 4 workers. As far as we could ascertain, wage
labor was very rarely employed; most were "father and son
together" or "husband and wife shops." Most of the apprentices,
too, were "nephews following in their uncles' footsteps." They
were usually apprenticed for five years, during which time they
received free food but no clothing or wages. By the end of the Qing
period, some of the handicraft workshops had grown quite large,
even to the extent of the manufacturing and retailing sides becoming
separate. For example, the Yuantai bamboo-goods store employed
19 mastercraftsmen in the workshop and had opened a separate
retail store. The whip shop on Wucheng street employed 11 or 12
mastercraftsmen who produced over 100 different items. On our
visit we met an old mastercraftsman (76 sui) of the copper-beaters
guild on Tax Station Street named Zhu Zhuang-yan, who told us,
"When I was young, there was a copper-utensil shop in Bamboo
Rod Passage specializing in making Yunnan brass tobacco-pipe
bowls, white crane's feet hubble-bubbles, and all kinds of head
ornaments. The owner was called Wang, and the business had been
passed down from generation to generation for two or three hundred
years. Their trade mark was 'Wang's Yunnan brass.' They employed
70 or 80 assistants. It used to be said that it was Wang's ambition
when he got a hundred employees to have a stage set up and cele-
brate with theatricals. But he never was able to get a hundred
employees."

In some of the trades described above, absolutely no division
of labor took place; one craftsman was responsible for the production of an item from beginning to end. But in other trades there was
considerable division of labor. Judging from information such as
that supplied by Zhu Zhuang-yan, we can be fairly certain that
some of Jining's handicraft industries had, in the Qing period,
already moved from the stage of small commodity production to
the stage of simple capitalist division of labor.

Conspicuous Consumption

As Jining's commercial economy developed, the lifestyle of its exploiting classes became ever more corrupt. A Jining man, Qiu Xin-ni, writing in the latter half of the seventeenth century, says: "In our town of Jining, articles of clothing and food, and ceremonial occasions such as marriages and funerals in particular, daily became more extravagant. In the old days palls were made of paper. Before long cotton gauze was being used, and then silk gauze, and now finally satins and brocades are used. All the strange and rare plants, the glittering and dazzling displays, the square buildings and the round pavilions, the splendid phoenixes and ornamental birds cost several tens or several hundreds of strings of cash and require a small army of craftsmen to carve and incise and many months to paint and embellish."[49]

By the first half of the nineteenth century, this extravagant style of living not only showed itself in the marriage and funeral ceremonies of the rich but also in their everyday lives. The Prefect of Jining, Xu Zong-gan, wrote in his 1844 "Exhortation to the people to reform their ways" that, "in our Jining for several decades now, evil customs are ever more apparent . . . prices are going up . . . extravagance is the order of the day . . . in the old days, farmers, scholars, and merchants all wore simple cotton clothes; even the rich would only wear tussore or silk cloth closely woven on western looms; now (c. 1830) it is common to see Huzhou crepe silks and fine worsteds, and people go in for tasseled official hats, satin boots, turquoise and jet black outer robes, all just so. As for women's ornaments, they carry former styles to excess."[50] Comments such as these suggest that the greed of the wealthy classes received added impetus from the growth of a commodity economy and showed itself in luxurious spending habits. It had reached the stage where even some of the die-hard preservers of the traditional feudal attitudes of despising merchants were beginning to hurry to "abandon the life of a scholar and become merchants."

1.3 Zhoucun

Zhoucun is situated between Yidu (in ancient times Qingzhou) and Jinan. In the old days, it was within the boundary of Chang-shan district. During the Qing period, it was a commercial and handicraft center for its surrounding hinterland.

The materials we have been able to collect suggest that Zhou-cun had become as important as Jining by the eighteenth century and may even have surpassed Jining.

It had never been an administrative center, and it was never the seat of a district magistrate's yamen. Yet, at the same time, land-lords and officials did gather there. Unlike many other market towns, it had already become something of a trade center by the mid-dle of the seventeenth century. One source records, "On the ninth day of the tenth month of 1650 'bandits' from Yixian and Tengxian districts took Zhoucun and made it a center of trade to which mer-chants came as numerous as raindrops."[51] The sources do not reveal anything further about these events.

During the latter part of the sixteenth century, Li Hua-xi, a high official from Zhoucun, undertook to pay the trade taxes on behalf of the merchants, and the town was officially changed into a private market (yiji).[52]

According to a stele erected in 1812 in front of the former Beiji pavilion recording a request to continue the town's tax-free status, "The market town of Zhoucun in Changshan district became a private market when Minister Li, the guardian of the heir apparent, contributed its taxes in lieu of further payment . . . since then over a hundred years have passed and the town has throughout continued to be a private market." Next to this stele is a fragment of an octagonal stele "expressing gratitude for imperial favor." The char-acters have become undecipherable with age, but, according to people in the town, it was erected at the time of the original tax exemption and was called "no tax today stele." By the early eighteenth century, the town's trade appears to have been flourish-ing. In the biography of one Li Si-quan, it is recorded that, his having "continued to pay the town's tax exemption for thirty years, the merchants and traders from all the provinces erected a stele to praise him."[53]

The 1710 "Record of the Private Market of Zhoucun" refers

to the town as "a large market town to which, although it is not on a major land or water route, goods from all over the empire come."[54] The town was large enough to attract "merchants and traders from all the provinces" and "goods from all over the empire." From other sources we know that Zhoucun's own merchants went south to the Yangzi provinces to do business. For example, one of them, "when he was ten, was apprenticed to a merchant and, when he was grown up, he went every year to do business in Jiangsu and Zhejiang, and he became very wealthy."[55] Another source speaks of a "certain merchant of Zhoucun who did business in Wuhu [in southern Anhui] and accumulated a lot of capital."[56]

No sooner had Zhoucun's trade begun to develop than middlemen and brokers who "fixed market prices" and collected brokerage and trade taxes for the officials began to appear. If the declared taxes they collected are considered as evidence, the town's trade in the early seventeenth century cannot have been very large. Even as late as 1734 the markets at Changshan and Zhoucun together were only assessed an annual "14.58 taels for trade tax, 0.62 taels for brokerage tax, and 3 taels for ox and donkey tax."[57] The total came to less than 20 taels. The sources of this period do not contain any mention of individual trade guilds in Zhoucun.

It was only in the late eighteenth and early nineteenth centuries that Zhoucun became a fairly substantial commercial center. According to the 1774 "Record of the Tianhou Pavilion," "Zhoucun market town in Changshan district is a place where merchants gather in large numbers and *the goods of each of its guilds all come from the southern provinces.* Its trade and transport all go very smoothly."[58] In a 1798 stele recording the repair of one of the town's bridges, we find the following description: "The inhabitants of Zhoucun live crowded together in great numbers, and money flows freely in the town which they call a dry wharf (*han matou*). A wharf is a stopping point for merchants by the waterside, like Hankou, Fatshan, Jingdezhen, or Zhuxianzhen.[59] But those trading centers that have no water transport, or great ships, or favorable winds are distinguished by being called dry wharfs . . . The Xingxiang bridge is built against a steep incline and serves all the merchants for the street to which it leads which contains the temple inns and the markets and stalls. The coolies and pack animals who cross it every day are numbered in the thousands. It is one of the most important bridges in the town."[60]

In his *Grand Canal Diary* of 1829, Bao Shi-chen compared Jining with Jinan and Zhoucun as follows: "The major market centers along the Grand Canal from the point where it enters Shandong at Taizhuang in the south to the point where it touches the border of Hebei province are Xiazhen, Nanyang, Jining, Zhangqiu, Acheng, Dongchang, and Linqing. Of these, Jining is especially large, being comparable to Jinan and Zhoucun in Changshan."[61] If the author of the stele commemorating the repair of the Xingxiang bridge in Zhoucun quoted above made an indirect comparison of the town with the largest commercial centers in the empire, Bao Shi-chen unequivocally compares it as a center of trade with the provincial capital of Shandong, Jinan, and with Jining. Clearly, by the nineteenth century, Zhoucun had overtaken most of the trading points on the Grand Canal. Right up to the end of the Qing period, people described Zhoucun as being "a flourishing trade center with goods of all sorts coming in, Shandong's leading market center."[62] According to another source, "The economy of Shandong at the end of the Qing period was well developed, the people were prosperous, there was an abundance of goods, and trade was especially flourishing. The main commercial centers of the province at this time were Yantai, Jiaozhou, Zhoucun, and Weizhou."[63] There is no doubt that, by the end of the Qing period, Zhoucun had become one of the most important if not the most important market center in all of Shandong.

Handicrafts

The handicraft products of Zhoucun included tussore (pongee), coarse cloth, silk thread, gauze silk, silk cloth, damask, copper utensils, mirrors, wood combs, bamboo combs, brass buckles, leggings, felt caps, wine, spirits, firecrackers, glue, *materia medica,* and so forth.[64] The most important of these were tussore, coarse cloth, silk cloth, and copper utensils.

Zhoucun's economic development was no accident but was closely connected with the development of its surrounding rural hinterland. We know that there was a mountain cocoon and tussore production area centered at Yeyuan market town (Linqu district) to the southeast of Zhoucun. Tussore is the silk cloth woven from the "wild" silk of mountain cocoons. Mountain cocoon (*shanjian*) is the general term for the cocoons of wild silkworms nourished on the leaves of mountain pepper (*jiao*), *cedrala odorata* (*xiangchun*), *ailantus glandulosa* (*shu*), wild mulberry (*zhe*), oak-shrub (*zuo*), *quercus dentata* (*hu*), and so forth. The various types of tussore were named after the trees whose leaves the silkworms fed on, but the general terms for them all were wild silkworm cloth (*jianchou*) or tussore (*mianchou*). According to the *Gazetteer of Qingzhou Prefecture,* "There are three types of tussore in Boshan district, *cedrala odorata,* pepper, and *ailantus glandulosa* tussore, the last being the most common." In Linqu district "the local people wove tussore, mountain silk cloth, and gauze." Oak tussore was produced in the "southwestern hills" of Anqiu district. In the "Wulian hills of Jiuxian district, *quercus dentata,* oak-shrub, and *cedrala odorata* tussore were as good as a close smooth-textured silk." The tussore of these districts was mainly "marketed at Yidu, but the buyers sold it as far afield as Peking." Apart from being used as clothing material, it was made up into silk scarfs, sashes, tassels, and girdles. These goods were sold over a wide area.[65]

Since Zhoucun was an important entrepôt on the way to Peking, we may suppose that it acted as a buying center for the Qingzhou mountain tussores. Certainly the sources speak of large quantities of mountain cocoons being sold in Zhoucun and its neighborhood. According to the *District Gazetteer of Zichuan,* "People of this district are now making *quercus dentata* tussore but, since the cocoons are not produced here, the peasants have a new side industry producing *quercus dentata* leaves for the silk worms."[66]

The *Gazetteer of Jinan Prefecture* under the sections on customs of Changshan district also says, "The people engage in silk weaving and are good at spinning the thread from mountain cocoons. The cocoons are not produced in this district . . . to the south of the district town in the neighborhood of Zhoucun people are mainly engaged in trade."[67] Zichuan and Changshan are neighboring districts, and Zhoucun served them both alike as a center of commerce. In Section 4.2 we discuss a silk-weaving works employing nearly one hundred weavers operated by a managerial landlord about ten miles from Zhoucun whose business had begun as an individual weaver making tussore for a Zhoucun merchant.

The districts to the north of Zhoucun lying along the southern bank of the Yellow River (Qidong, Gaoyuan, Boxing) were one of the main cotton-producing areas in Shandong. Qidong, the most important cotton center, was about twenty-three miles north of Zhoucun. A late-seventeenth century magistrate of the district described it in the following terms: "The land of Qidong is very barren and barely produces enough grain to feed its people. Everybody has to borrow money to pay taxes and to meet the expenses of marriages and funerals. They depend heavily upon cotton spinning and cloth weaving, which are the only occupations apart from agriculture. Both men and women are engaged in these night and day. Big merchants come from afar, bringing large amounts of capital to buy the cotton here, and this provides a living for the people of Qidong district town."[68]

In his "Record of the Cotton Cloth Market," another district magistrate of Qidong, Zhou Yi-xun, wrote in 1798: "Throughout the length and breadth of Qidong, the customs are restrained and the people virtuous. They work hard at spinning and weaving. They roll up the finished cotton in bolts ready for the market, which takes place five or six times a month. When they have finished their business, they leave. It is called the cotton-cloth market and draws people from as far as Guandong [i.e., northeast China]. By the end of the year, several hundred thousand taels' worth has been sold. The people of Qidong depend on the cotton market for a living and it also brings in a large number of merchants."[69]

We know that, in fact, Zhoucun was the collection and distribution center for the coarse cotton cloth produced in Qidong and the neighboring districts. The merchants from northeast China would go to Zhoucun to make very large wholesale deals. In Section 4.3

we describe in detail a rentier landlord operated cotton company about twenty-six miles from Zhoucun which had begun in the business by buying cotton from local weavers along the Zhangqiu, Qidong borders and selling it at its own shop in Zhoucun.

About twenty-three miles to the south of Zhoucun is Boshan, the old Yanshen market town. From the end of the Ming era, Yanshen was a center of coal, porcelain, pottery, and black and white bowl production. The "pitchers, bowls, earthenware jars, dishes, and jugs in use in the prefecture" were all produced here. To the south of Yanshen, there are many hills and only one road leading through them. As a result, Zhoucun to the north became the collection and distribution center for all the Yanshen handicraft products. Without doubt, the development of Yanshen spurred on the growth of Zhoucun. Below we discuss the course of Yanshen's development in detail. (See Section 1.4.)

Mulberry silkworm production was also widespread in the districts around Zhoucun. In Qingpingxiang, which was in the northeast corner of Zhangqiu district and next to Zhoucun, "mulberry silkworm cultivation, spinning, and the production of lusterings were the dominant occupations." Laiwu, Zouping, and Zichuan districts all traditionally raised mulberry silkworms. The following figures of households engaged in silkworm rearing in Shandong at the beginning of the Republic give some idea of its extent. Only six districts in the province had more than 8,000 households engaged in rearing silkworms. The six were Zichuan (11,052 households), Changshan (8,436), Laiwu (18,500), Linxian (11,200), and Linqu (30,450).[70] All of these districts historically had more or less close trade relations with Zhoucun. Indeed Zhoucun became the trade center for all the silk-producing districts. Wang Zhao, in his *Diary of an Itinerant Priest in Shandong* (written in 1900), records that a "carter by the name of Zhang" told a spy monk from Japan that "Zhoucun is the *main collection point for silk in the whole province; every day* the ox carts which had taken silk *from Zhoucun* to the provincial capital return empty."[71]

Quite apart from its important position in the silk trade of the province, Zhoucun produced copper utensils, iron implements, and wooden goods for the villages of its hinterland and for the neighboring districts.

Given the start sketched out above, Zhoucun clearly had the possibility of great development in the future. However, with the economic invasion of foreign imperialism in the late nineteenth century altering the normal course of development of a national commodity market in China, and with the destruction brought in 1916 by the warlord Wu Da-zhou, Zhoucun was unable to continue developing into a large flourishing city.

1.4 Yanshen (Boshan)

Yanshen market town (today Boshan sub-district, *qu,* of Zibo city) was originally attached to Yidu district. In 1734 it was made into Boshan district (*xian*), and Yanshen market town was made into the seat of the district yamen and its name changed to Boshan. Already in the seventeenth century the town had been well known for its black porcelain products and coal. The *Gazetteer of Yanshen Market Town* of 1670 records a long list of textile handicraft products made within the town, including *cedrala odorata,* pepper, *quercus dentata* tussore, silk, cotton cloth, and so on. Of these, "only Yanshen *quercus dentata* tussore was of a very high quality"; the potteries included black porcelain kilns, earthenware cooking-pot kilns, brick and tile kilns, *liuli* glass works, and so on;[72] the mining industries included coal, lead, white alum, black alum, coke, white lead, red ochre, and so forth.

Yanshen's coal miners, smelters, and glass workers had accumulated considerable technical knowledge and skills as is shown, for example, in the following passage describing the techniques used in the coal-mining industry. It was written by a seventeenth-century scholar-official from the town named Sun Ting-quan and can be found in his *Miscellaneous Records of Yanshan:*

> In order to get at the coal it is necessary to sink pits, which sometimes have to be sunk deeper than one hundred chi. When the coal is reached, lateral tunnels are cut. Depending on the coal face, tunnels can be twice as high as a man, or only up to

a man's thigh. If the coal is cut by a man in the standing position, it can quickly be transported back down the tunnel; if it is cut in the sitting position, then it has to be hauled back in a bent-over position; if it is cut lying flat, then it has to be dragged back down the tunnel in a crawling position. The shaft has to be straight and accurately cut ... when the seam is suddenly blocked by some huge rock and the tunnel has to be cut around it, it is called "snaking around the rock." When the seam varies constantly between thick and thin, now bunched together, now straggling away, or there are thick quickly exhausted parts called "chicken coops," both are indications that the pit is finished. When one goes along the tunnels, the hand is held out in front so that the lamp goes ahead. The pit is like night and the lamp is like the sun. In winter, air collects in the tunnels and, as a result, the lamp flame burns high. In summer, the air is full of positive elements, and the lamps go out. For this reason, shafts should be sunk in twos and tunnels cut in pairs to allow for the air to circulate. Then the cutting and tunneling can go in deep, and excellent results are obtained. Such pits are called air pits.

Sun also gives a very detailed description of the different types of coal mined at Yanshen and their different uses:

Of the coal found in the mountains, two types known as "dead" and "living" can be distinguished.[73] The seams of the "dead" coal are close to the surface and very abundant. The color is dull, it doesn't smell, and it burns with a soft patterned flame. It is suitable for household use. The seams of "living" coal are narrow and deep below the surface. It is bright colored and has an acrid smell and burns with a sharp bold flame. It is used for forging metals and for firing pottery kilns. It is called either *mei* or *tan*. Briquettes made from this coal are called either *gong* or *zha* and produce only a small fire.

The solid substance left when the volatile parts have been distilled from the coal is called coke (*jiao*). It is as hard as rock and heavier than iron. It has a green flame and an acrid smell. The part left after the coal has been mined is used for burning alum and is called "cupriferrous shale" (*tonqqi*). Coke is extracted from coal and yet it is stronger than coal; cupriferrous shale is left over from the coal and yet it is more precious than coal."[74]

One of the side products of the coke process at that time was "black alum" (*heifan*), whose production required considerable technical knowledge.

Mining of iron ore took place in the nearby Hei Mountains. There is a description of the industry in the 1753 edition of the *District Gazetteer of Boshan:*

> At first the local people did not know how to set about it. But in 1663, Sun Ting-quan had some people familiar with iron-smelting techniques come from Shanxi. The quality of the ore differs: the best comes in soft lumps, next best is in hard stone. The ore is pounded into fragments and then combined with coal and loaded into tube-like crucibles (*dong*); these are placed in a square furnace which is surrounded with a coke fire. The first firing does not produce iron yet. The ore is pounded again, the crucibles and the furnace are changed, and a big fire is built up. For every dan of iron ore, two dou of cast iron are produced. The worse quality is separated out and placed in a round furnace over a wood fire. One man holds a long hook and uses this to stir the iron into lumps. The resultant wrought iron is half the quantity of the original cast iron.[75]

The Boshan coal industry provided favorable conditions for the growth of various handicraft industries in the area, notably the pottery and glass industries.

The pottery and porcelain industries were highly specialized in their products as the result of local variations in the quality of the clay. The 1859 edition of the *Gazetteer of Qingzhou Prefecture* in the entry on Boshan district of the "Local Products" section records: "Pottery is made at Beiling, Shantou, Wudian, Yaoguang, Badou, and Xihe. The products include bowls, earthenware basins and jars, vases, fish globes, pickling vats, pots, and ceremonial vessels." The commentary adds: "Outstanding clays are found in Boshan of many different kinds. In Wudian, it is firm and suitable for making vats and basins; . . . in Shantou, it is light colored and excellent for bowls and smaller pieces; in Badou, it is hard and ideal for earthenware jars and vases."[76]

Techniques in the Yanshen glass-making industry are described in Sun Ting-quan's *Miscellaneous Records of Yanshan,* attesting to a considerable knowledge of chemistry:

> As to glass, stone is the fundamental ingredient, saltpeter is used to fuse it, coke is used to melt it, and copper, iron, cinnabar, and lead are used to alter it . . . When it is as white as dew and its corners are smoothed off and it is square, it is called horse-tooth stone. When it is violet like the setting sun and twinkles, it is called ruby stone. When it is knobbly and like the crust of a gem, it is called *lingzi* stone. The white is hard, the purple soft, and the *lingzi* bright . . . Saltpeter produces a soft fire and is used to combine the inside; coke has a fierce flame and is used to temper the outside . . . In mixing colors, five parts white and one part violet with twice as much *lingzi* as ruby stone give crystal. If the violet is increased and the white decreased and the *lingzi* stone is removed, you get pure white. With three parts white and one part violet and equal amounts of *lingzi* and ruby stone, with a little added copper and a touch of iron, you get plum red. Three parts white, one part violet, with no *lingzi* stone and increased copper, and yet get blue; . . . you get autumn brown; . . . you get sapphire blue; . . . you get ivory white; . . . you get green; . . . you get goose yellow.[77]

Although techniques used in the iron-smelting, ceramics, and glass industries of Yanshen did not show any advance on those used previously in other places, their wide application in Yanshen itself is of considerable interest and certainly was of comparatively recent origin in the seventeenth century.

As to the organization of these industries, we have been able to piece together the following picture for the coal-mining industry. According to the 1753 edition of the *District Gazetteer of Boshan:*

Fertile land is scarce in Boshan and the people are poor. Most of them make a living digging mine shafts and tunneling for coal . . . a crowd of penniless workers gathers in the mining area. *Their chief is called a shaft head* (jingtou); *those who go down to oversee the miners are called tunnel heads* (dongtou); *and those who receive and pay out the cash are called accountants* (zhangfang). These three types are the most powerful. *The man who supplies and shares out the money is called the head of the mine* (gongzhu). As soon as the coal has been found, they cheat the head of the mine, using the excuse that the coal is difficult to get at, and, since it will be a complicated and expensive operation, they ask for an advance. The head of the mine is ready to make a small sacrifice for what he hopes will be a big profit, and so he gives them the advance. *Without any outlay at all, therefore, the shaft head and the tunnel head* make a great deal of money. Several days pass and the head of the mine gets suspicious and begins an investigation. However, the accountant has falsified the books and, as a result, the head of the mine eventually pours all his money into the mine and goes bankrupt, and *the owner of the land where the mine is situated* (shanchang yezhu) *has no means of paying his taxes.*

Three types of people were involved in the mining operation: 1) the miners themselves; 2) the shaft head who acted as manager, the tunnel head who acted as overseer, the accountant and the head of the mine (who put up the capital); and 3) the landlord who owned the land where the mine was situated. According to the description of the "head of the mine" as "sharing out the money," the miners were paid wages. The "power" of the shaft and tunnel heads and the accountants was presumably derived from the fact that they had direct control over the miners. Although these production relations strongly suggest slave labor, nevertheless they possess certain capitalist elements new to China's feudal society.[78]

The more the local mining and handicrafts industries grew, the more the commodity markets of the area flourished. Large number of streets in which merchants specialized in the same type of merchandise began to appear in Yanshen, and the market area was enlarged. In the latter part of the seventeenth century, there was a big 3-8 market [that is, meeting on the 3rd, 8th, 13th, 18th, 23rd, and 28th of the lunar month] in the western quarter of the town; a medium 1-6 market [that is, meeting on the 1st, 6th, 11th, 16th, 21st, and 26th of the lunar month] by the east gate and a small 4-9 market [that is, meeting on the 4th, 9th, 14th, 19th, 24th, and 29th of the lunar month] by the west gate. There was a glass market on West Mine Street, and on Tax Station Street there was a pottery market. There was another pottery market at Shantou Inn. "Salt stores, tanneries, cotton shops, elm-bark shops, charcoal shops," and so forth were set up along the streets. Outside the town, there was a medium 2-7 pottery market [that is, meeting on the 2nd, 7th, 12th, 17th, 22nd, and 27th of the lunar month] at Xihe and an iron market at Shima near Badou. The business conducted at the markets is described as follows in the local gazetteer: "Grain is brought from every direction to the markets to exchange for utensils and tools, including the products of Yanshen's pottery industry."[79] During the agricultural slack season, peasants from Boshan, Zichuan, Zhangqiu, Laiwu, and other districts would frequently go to Yanshen to work as pole-carrying or wheelbarrow porters peddling pottery or glass in the surrounding areas or simply working as transport hands for the Yanshen merchants. In the late seventeenth century, the heavy coarse black pottery produced in Yanshen for the everyday use of the peasants was marketed for "upwards of eighty miles around."[80]

The conditions of work for the ordinary workers in Yanshen's industries were extremely unhealthy. According to the *Miscellaneous Records of Yanshan,* "Most of the glass workers have eye diseases; the coal miners are frequently suffocated or drowned; the alum makers mostly have poor eyesight; the cinnabar and mercury pulverizers fear internal disorders." According to the local gazetteer: "Black alum . . . is produced by heating the stones with coke. The smoke is extremely noxious and, as a result, the workers usually develop incurable diseases." Clearly occupational diseases were widespread in these industries. In view of the risks and dangers they had to work with, the workers received totally inadequate wages. On the other hand, the managers of the iron foundries, coal

mines, and so forth made very large profits. The local gazetteer
remarks on the iron industry, "During the last dozen or so years,
the profits have been very high indeed," and in the coal-mining
industry, "without any outlay at all therefore, the shaft head and
the tunnel head make a great deal of money."[81]

Both workers and exploiters in Boshan district had to "rely
on neighboring districts for their food grains," since there were
"no crops" in Boshan itself. As a result, exchanges were increased.

Already in the late seventeenth century the style of life of the
townsfolk of Yanshen was different from that of the people in the
surrounding villages. The upper strata of the townsfolk were trying
to live as luxuriously as the great gentry landlords. The local
gazetteer remarks: "Today . . . customs are ever more lavish, no
expenses are spared on rituals and ceremonies, and huge amounts
are spent on food and clothing," and continues, "The ordinary
people of the villages off the beaten track carry on simple and
unostentatious lives, the men farming and the women weaving.
Those *living close to the town,* however, go as far as to wear long
robes and white silken breeches. Scholars' caps are seen on *commoners' heads;* festal boards groan with delicacies, and even servants eat and drink like lords. You have to spend lavishly to acquire
any standing here."[82]

Clearly the lifestyles and spending habits of the new urban
classes were already breaking down the restrictions and sumptuary
regulations of the old feudal landlord class.

Several characteristic features are shared by the four towns
described above. 1) Each had developed its commerce and handicrafts in very close contact with its surrounding hinterland, and,
indeed, had become the economic center for its area. The result
was that the towns had come increasingly to affect every aspect of
the rural sector. 2) Each had broken out of the isolation typical of
the old-style town and developed very extensive markets with commercial relations throughout the country. Each had become an
important link in the structure of the national market. 3) The
handicraftsmen in each of the four towns were typically small

commodity producers but, because of the enlarged markets and increasing commercialization of the economy, these small producers were already tending towards the phase of simple capitalist division of labor. 4) Most of the population of these towns were merchants and handicraftsmen. The big gentry, landlords, and officials who in the past had played the dominant role in the towns were now gradually being thrust to one side, and their values and way of life were ignored by the new urban classes. 5) The upper strata of the urban classes broke the old sumptuary regulations while doing everything they could to imitate the lavish style of life of the old gentry landlords.

Chapter 2

THE COMMERCIALIZATION OF AGRICULTURE

In this chapter we briefly examine the commercialization of agriculture which was spurred on by the growth of the urban economy.

The development of a commercialized agriculture is an extremely persuasive piece of evidence that the society of Shandong had already reached a new stage during the Qing period. Although we have not been able to find any statistics on agricultural production for the market, we have, nevertheless, been able to collect some accounts in contemporary sources of the development of commercialization in the agricultural sector.

We begin with the commercialization of food grain production. As the new towns developed, so their populations grew, and the supply of adequate grain for the market became an increasingly important problem. In the past in Shandong, the old towns were administrative centers and seats of local gentry landlords. The grain they consumed was usually supplied directly to them by the peasants who delivered it to their granaries.

From the mid-Ming period on, as the new handicraft trade towns began to emerge, the marketing of grain to feed them became a matter of constant concern, as is expressed for example in this passage from the gazetteer of Yanshen:

In the past it was considered that, in order to have virtue in public life, it was necessary to secure adequate supplies of food production and, to secure that, hard work and frugality were required. In Yanshen, however, although there are pottery and mining industries, there is no crop farming. *All the food for the town comes from neighboring districts.* If there is a famine and a prohibition on the import of grain to Yanshen, how can we cook and fill our bellies with lead, iron, glass, cinnabar, and alum?[1]

In 1776 Linqing's reliance on food imported from considerable
distances was described in the local gazetteer as follows: "Linqing
is an important commercial center. Local supplies of grain are insufficient, and consequently the town *depends upon merchants.* The
grain brought down the Wei River on sailing boats comes mostly
from Henan; glutinous millet comes upstream from Tianjin. Most
of the grain coming up the Wen River comes from around Jining."[2]

The 1833 edition of the *District Gazetteer of Zhangqiu* remarks
that those engaged "in secondary occupations [in trade, for example]
have increased by over 60 percent" and, as a consequence, although
the district had plenty of good farming land, "in bad years, grain
has to be brought from Liaodong and, even in good years, it comes
mainly from Yizhou and Yexian."[3]

So much for the reliance of the towns on imported grain. We
get some idea of conditions in the areas whose grain exports were
increasing from a memorial by the district magistrate of Yexian,
Zhang Si-mian, who was writing in the 1750s on the prohibition of
grain exports by sea from Laizhou prefecture:

> The districts in this prefecture that lie beside the sea (Yexian,
> Changyi, and Jiaozhou) and have large harbors are prohibited
> in the regulations from exporting any rice, wheat, or other
> food grain with the exception of legumes. Dishonest merchants,
> intent only on profit, defy the law, however, and, when they
> spy out an area where the grain is cheap, they snap it up for a
> song and monopolize the market. Worst of all are those who
> ship it out to sell in other districts. For example, Xiaying, a
> harbor in Changyi district where many merchant ships gather,
> is a long way from the district town and just on the border of
> Yexian district. If grain is smuggled out of Xiaying, Yexian's
> grain prices soar.

The memorial continues: "Grain markets were originally for the
use of individual buyers, but now there are crowds of petty merchants and peddlers who load up the grain on mules and ship it off
until there is nothing left. This is the reason why market prices
soar." Zhang also complained of the "rich people and big merchants

who, when the buyers come, secure their profits by hoarding and refuse to let their grain be shipped out, preferring to wait until prices rise."[4]

The following passage describes the situation in Yidu district:

> There is not enough to feed everyone in our district, so we have to buy large amounts from other districts ... canals connect through neighboring districts such as Yangjiaogou through Shouguang and Junzhen in Xincheng. Bulk grain cargoes shipped by the sea route come by these canals. The grain that comes by land routes by way of Weixian, Anqiu, Zhucheng, Yishui, Yingzhou, and other districts is mainly collected from individual peasants selling small quantities ... it comes in without a hitch.[5]

This indicates that a commercial network was gradually developing in Shandong with grain flowing toward the new commercial and handicraft centers and their hinterlands. Not only food grains moved into the towns but also the unprocessed grains and crops used in the manufacture of wine, oil, sweetmeats, and so on. Food grains were also required by the poor peasants and laborers who had lost their lands as a result of the growing commercial land market. It seems highly probable that the demand for food grains greatly stimulated the planting of crops intended for the market. The main areas of food grain production in Shandong at this time were the southwest part of the province around Jining and the southeast part around Yishui and Yingxian.

Cotton

Turning now to the commercialization of cotton production, we note that the planting of cotton is recorded throughout Shandong from very early times. In the past, cotton was as essential a part of the self-supporting economy of every family as any other crop. The amount grown was decided by each family's direct need, and a small amount of land was put aside for this purpose. Gradually cotton production began to become commercialized, a process which had long since been under way by the sixteenth century. In his *Comprehensive Treatise on Agriculture* (1639), Xu Guang-qi writes: "Northern cotton comes from Hebei and Shandong. It is soft and fine-textured, ideal for spinning and weaving. The cloth made from it is slightly on the light side." He also says: "When people in Hebei or Shandong plant cotton, they ridge the soil and then plant the seeds, one every three feet. After the shoots have grown, they put down dry fertilizer, keeping an eye open for the thin ones which they quickly bank up. Normal yield per mu is two to three hundred jin." He adds that "raw cotton is cheap in the north, but cotton cloth is expensive. In the south it is the other way round. Northern raw cotton is shipped to the south and southern cotton cloth is shipped north."[6]

In the 1601 edition of the *District Gazetteer of Linyi* edited by Xing Dong, we find the comment that "the production of cotton in Linyi is second to no other district. *It pays the taxes and provides the people's livelihood.* Most of it is shipped to other areas."[7]

In order to "provide the people's livelihood," the cotton would first have to be sold either in its raw state or as cloth. In order to "pay the taxes," it would have to have been one of the most important crops sown in the district. In his collected works, Xing Dong enlarged on the subject, saying that, in 1622, "there was a particularly fine cotton harvest [in Linyi district]. Several tens of million jin were harvested. As much lay scattered about as could be stored in the granaries and pens. Buyers came from every direction."[8]

The 1685 edition of the *District Gazetteer of Qidong* contains the following comment: "The rich of the district store up raw cotton and grain, buying and selling according to the market price. The poor ditch the fields and do the ploughing. Their women, apart from rearing silkworms, are mainly engaged in weaving cotton. All taxes and end-of-year expenses are met by the profits made from selling the cotton cloth."[9]

In his *Zhaoyu zhi,* Gu Yan-wu remarked: "Traders from the south set up business in Gaotang, Xiajin, and Enxian to buy the raw cotton of these districts. The local people get rich on the proceeds."[10] The *Imperial Encyclopaedia* comments on the cotton industry of Dongchang: "The six prefectures of Shandong all grow cotton, but more is grown in Dongchang than in the others. Merchants come from every direction to buy, and the people make their profits from cotton."[11]

The 1736 edition of the *Provincial Gazetteer of Shandong* records that, "in Yuncheng district, there is plenty of fertile land ideal for cotton cultivation. Merchants sell it in the south and special markets are set up."[12]

The 1842 edition of the *Comprehensive Gazetteer of the Empire* says under the entry on Dongchang prefecture: "Cotton is produced in each of its districts . . . and bought by the merchants from the Huai and Yangzi valleys, which trade has made the local people rich."[13]

A prefectural magistrate of Jining in the first half of the nineteenth century pointed out that "in Zhazhou (Gaotang) district, *more land is planted to cotton than to food crops.* The rich are not in the habit of putting away large stores, while the poor have to rely on wages. As soon as there is a natural disaster, they have no recourse. This spring, for example, there was a sudden drought, and everybody was thrown into confusion. The poor had nobody from whom to borrow, and the rich feared they would be robbed; demands for equal distribution of available grain began to be heard on all sides, and there was unrest throughout the district."[14]

The 1859 edition of the *Prefectural Gazetteer of Qingzhou* says under the section on local products of Boxing district that "raw cotton and spirits are the most common products . . . to the north of the district town, the soil is both sandy and fertile and, as a result, well suited to growing cotton. Merchants and traders make a good living from the cotton trade." In the 1846 edition of the *District Gazetteer of Tengxian,* we find the following story about a cotton merchant of the mid-eighteenth century:

> Lü Fu-ru's family had for generations lived in Ge village in the western part of Tengxian. They had always been poor. Lü was serving as a peddler's assistant, carrying the baskets and rattling the hand drum. Toward the end of the year 1736, he was traveling north and was staying at Dongchang (present-day

Liaocheng). Now it happened that there was a guest riding a
fine horse with heavy saddlebags who stopped at the same inn.
Toward evening the guest saddled up his horses and set out at
a brisk trot. When Lü went out he came across a saddlebag
which he picked up and took back to the inn and looked after
as he stood by the door waiting. Eventually the guest came
back saying he had lost some silver. Lü asked him "How
much"? "Eight packages with a total of 400 taels" was the
reply. "Don't worry," said Lü, "I have the silver here." The
guest was greatly relieved, and they ended by becoming sworn
brothers. When it was time to part, the guest grasped his hand
and said, "I am from Gaotang district, and my family are
cotton merchants. Should you, my elder brother, ever have
the time, I hope you will pass our way" ... Several years later
Lü was on his way through Gaotang on a business trip and, on
the spur of the moment, looked up his friend. They spoke
together for a long while, and then his friend said, pointing to
several bales of cotton: "I want to use the proceeds from
these to build a country villa in Tengxian. Will you help me
to sell them for that purpose"? Lü agreed and, with the price
he got for the cotton, he bought 100 mu of land. He made
out a receipt showing how much he had made on the deal and
went back to the cotton merchant who said, "The price of the
villa is no more than the interest on the silver you returned to
me."[15]

This story about Lü Fu-ru was told as hearsay on good author-
ity in an official source and should be considered more reliable than
fiction. At any rate, the story indicates that the scale of operation
of a Shandong cotton merchant in the eighteenth century was
already quite large. In the story, the merchant travels with the considerable sum of 400 taels of ready money, which represented only
part of his liquid assets. Later in the story, we find he has enough
cotton in store to fetch the price of 100 mu of land.

Although the above sources do not all date from the same
period, they suffice to indicate conditions in the four main cotton-
producing areas of Shandong during the Qing period. These areas
were along the southern banks of the new course of the Yellow

River with Qidong as center, along the northern banks of the old course of the Yellow River with Linyi as center, in northwest Shandong with Liaocheng as center, and in southwest Shandong with Yuncheng as center. Each of these areas had gradually come to specialize in cotton production. Naturally, most of the cotton produced was not for home consumption but for sale on the market.

Cash Crops

Another aspect of the commercialization of agriculture was the appearance and steady increase of new cash crops. One source, for example, records conditions under which tobacco was grown in Jining prefecture and what effects its increasing production had upon the cultivation of food crops:

> The methods used in growing tobacco in Jining prefecture are modeled after the method of squared crop and fallow areas (*qutian*). The rich soil is reserved for the tobacco, and the food grains are planted on poorer soils. Tobacco is a poisonous weed, whereas crops nourish man. Can thirst for profit reach the point when such a fundamental truth can be forgotten? In the eastern sub-district, an old man surnamed Zang belongs to a family which, for generations, has combined study with farming. Zang himself is a particularly skillful farmer who has recently turned over acreage previously sown with tobacco to maize. He says that he got about 3,000 tobacco plants per square mu, and that now he can get the same number of maize plants to the square mu. In terms of yield and prices, each mu averaged 500 jin of tobacco at 15 cash per jin while maize yields are 6 dan per mu at the medium price of 1,500 cash per dan. There is no doubt, then, that maize is the more profitable. A further consideration is that sometimes tobacco cannot be sold quickly, but maize can be sold at any time. The costs of tobacco farming are as high as 75 percent of returns, while the equivalent figure for maize is only 20 percent. Tobacco requires twice as much care and labor as maize does. How could Zang not prefer maize?[16]

The 1785 editon of the *Gazetteer of the Independent Sub-Prefecture of Jining* contains the following comment on tobacco production:

Take those who grow tobacco in the prefecture; the work involved is the same as for the method of squared crop and fallow areas (*qutian*), but they care nothing for the hardship, thinking only of the profit... *Danbagu* (an early Chinese phonetic loan word for tobacco) began to be cultivated during the Ming dynasty. At first it was only cultivated in out-of-the-way places, but now it has spread throughout the empire, and Jining's production is second to none.[17]

The *Imperial Encyclopaedia* contains the following interesting passage on tobacco cultivation in Ziyang district:

The tobacco leaf is also called *nian*. In the old days it was never cultivated in Ziyang. Its cultivation was started in 1647 in the villages of Yancundian and Shijiazhuang some ten miles west of the district town. Now it is grown *throughout the district*. Every year a steady stream of *merchants come from Peking* to buy up the tobacco and they have set up tobacco guilds in many places. It serves for profit rather than nourishing the people.[18]

According to this passage, the cultivation of tobacco was fairly widespread in the Jining-Yanzhou area. Moreover, from the beginning, it was planted as a cash crop for profit. Its increasing cultivation is, therefore, an indication of the greater commercialization of agriculture in this area. It also affected the cultivation of other crops. The passage quoted above about Zang Xian's raising the yield of maize per unit of land so that it was as profitable as growing tobacco indicates the increasing commercialization of grain crops.

Another cash crop, peanuts, presents an interesting example, although its introduction was comparatively late. The 1904 edition of the *District Gazetteer of Yixian* contains the following comments:

Along the western borders of the district by the hilly banks
of the Bin River, the soil is very sandy and stony. On investigation, it was found that this soil is ideal for the growing of
peanuts, and that the people who live there are very skilled
in cultivating them. Annual yield per mu is over ten dan. The
crop is always bought at good prices by merchants from the
Yangzi valley. People all over the district have now switched
to peanut cultivation. The buyers come in ever larger numbers,
and the local people do very well out of this crop.[19]

The rapid spread of a new cash crop such as peanuts came
about in response to the growing demand furnished by an expanding market and commodity economy.

There are also many indications that there was a development
in the technical processing of agricultural produce during the Qing
period and, as Lenin pointed out, "This growth represents one of
the forms of the development of commercial farming."[20] Take, for
example, the diffusion of grain liquor brewing. In Shandong, for
the most part, liquors were brewed from kaoliang, though occasionally fruits were used. An early nineteenth-century source contains
the following details of the industry in Tengxian district at that
time: "Big brewers have several tens of brewing vats, while small
brewers own three or four. In one day a single vat takes 1.2 dan of
grain, For every community of ten families, there is bound to be
a brewery, while even tiny village [literally three-family villages]
have a liquor store. Twice as much grain is used for brewing as is
ever eaten."[21]

The same source has a passing reference to a certain eighteenth-
century military officer (*jinshi*), Hu Yan, who "brewed liquor and
traded in it between Yixian and Ningyang."[22] The *Prefectural
Gazetteer of Qingzhou* records under the section on trade goods
that *baigar* liquor was "the most common."

Not only was liquor brewing very widespread; its sale increased
the links between markets. Fermentation of the liquor, of course,
required large quantities of yeast, which in Shandong was customarily made from wheat. The same source also contains the comment

that "in Tengxian . . . inferior quality land is sown to wheat, and merchants buy it for making yeast for fermenting liquor. When they keep the buying price down, the peasants suffer."[23]

Clearly, the yeast manufacturing industry was also widespread at that time.

There are also records of the commercialization and expanding market in fruit. The *Imperial Encyclopaedia* comments about Yixian: "The district produces peaches, apricots, persimmons, chestnuts, and walnuts. It produces an especially large amount of pears and jujubes which are sold in advance to merchants from elsewhere who sell them in the Yangzi valley at a great profit."[24]

A similar passage appears in the 1904 edition of the *District Gazetteer of Yixian*. "The soil is very suitable for fruit growing. Most famous of the fruits of Yixian district are the jujubes, pears, persimmons, and haws. They are marketed thousands of li away in the Yangzi valley. The people of the mountain villages of the district make a living by growing them."[25]

The 1846 edition of the *District Gazetteer of Tengxian* comments: "In the mountainous areas of the district, jujubes are grown but, since Yan jujubes (from around Peking) have recently begun to be grown in the Yangzi valley, merchants cannot get the same profits from Tengxian jujubes."[26]

The sources show that jujube production around Tengxian and Yixian districts was very extensive, as was the area in which they were marketed. Moreover jujube production was sufficiently advanced for there to have appeared "contract" merchants (*baomai shang*) who would "buy in advance," and Tengxian and Yan jujubes were in competition on the market. In Dong-a district, "the land was very suitable for jujube cultivation, and many sold them in the Yangzi valley."[27] Yidu district in central Shandong produced a great quantity of persimmons and walnuts. "*Hetao* (walnuts) are also called *hutao*. The persimmon produces a great deal of fruit and many are grown; they are dried and then sold with the walnuts in Jiaozhou and Jimo. They are also shipped as far south as Jiangsu and Hunan and even to Fujian and Canton. The local people make a great profit from this trade."[28]

Local specialization in the various agricultural products outlined above or the development of commercialized agriculture had gradually become accepted parts of agricultural production to a degree that varied according to the area. Everywhere such developments went hand in hand with the growth of new market towns and commercial centers. In this way the groundwork for a capitalist national market was laid. The old self-sufficient economy was about to be replaced by a commodity economy, and indeed it had already entered into the process of self-generated disintegration.

Chapter 3

THE DIFFERENTIATION OF THE PEASANTRY

In this chapter, we turn to the differentiation of the peasantry in Shandong during the Qing dynasty. In Chapters 1 and 2, we have given an account of the economic development of four commercial and handicraft towns—Linqing, Jining, Zhoucun, and Yanshen—and of the development of commercial agriculture in Shandong. We believe that these changes cannot be regarded as having no influence on class relations in the surrounding economic regions. On the contrary, the characteristic of the development of a commodity economy in the towns and countryside during the Qing period was that, in the process of undermining the self-sufficient, natural economy of the villages, the existing relations of production were destroyed. In "The Chinese Revolution and the Chinese Communist Party," Comrade Mao Ze-dong points out: "China's feudal society had developed a commodity economy, and so carried within itself the seeds of capitalism."[1] This certainly was the basic trend of the landlord economy. In order to better understand the new situation in the agrarian economy of the Qing period, and before discussing the differentiation of the peasantry, we shall first give a brief account of the old class relations.

According to the *Provincial Gazetteer of Shandong*, there was a total of 994,459 qing of cultivated land in the province in 1735. This land we divide into the three categories of government-owned land (*guantian*), corporately owned land (*gongtian*), and privately owned land (*sitian*). Government-owned land included imperial estates (*guanzhuang*), military settlement land (*tuntian*), and all other types of land not classed as either corporately or privately owned. Ownership of government land was directly vested in the court. Corporately owned land included land belonging to schools (*xuetian*), shrine land (*jitian*), land held by kin groups (*yitian*), cult land (*shetian*), temple land (*sitian*), and so forth. . . . In name, such lands were publicly owned by the corporate group as a whole,

88

but in practice their control rested with the powerful landlords in such bodies. Private land, also called people's land (*mintian*) or hundred surnames land (*baixing tian*), included all land owned by owner-peasants and landlords.[2]

The basic relations of production on both government land and on corporate land were feudal tenurial relations.[3]

Neither government nor corporate land comes within the main theme of this study; our focus is on private land.

Private land, as has already been pointed out, belonged either to landlords or to peasants. Relations of production on landlord-owned land were of two different types, depending on how it was managed. 1) If most of the land was farmed by tenants, then the basic relations of production were clearly tenurial relations. 2) If most of the land was directly farmed by the landlord using hired labor, then the relations of production were hired-labor relations. To judge from the written sources, both forms of production relations had been in existence for a considerable length of time in Shandong, and they were mutually exclusive. Right at the beginning of the Qing in the second half of the seventeenth century, the renting out of land to tenants was firmly established as the most important method of landlord farming. Yet, even then, it faced a serious threat, as can be seen in the words of an edict issued in the eighth month of 1703, on the occasion of the fourth eastern tour of the Kangxi Emperor:

> We have now passed through Shandong four times, and we are thoroughly acquainted with the lives of its people. It is a province different from all the others in that, in the rural areas, *the small people make their living by ploughing and sowing for the wealthy. In good harvest years the wealthy do well, but the poor people's share is very small.* As soon as there is a bad year the poor people, since they have no land, migrate if they are strong, or if they are weak they die along the roadside . . . There is not much that can be done to mitigate the results of a bad year, but, if it were possible *to reduce the rents and each landlord to aid his tenants, this would not only ease the lot of the poor but it would also ensure that your lands did not become abandoned.*[4]

This shows that, as a rule in Shandong in the early Qing period, landlords managed their lands by letting them out to tenants, and that, because rents were so high, tenants frequently abandoned their lands and fled, leaving the landlord with uncultivated land. Tenants fleeing the land was a serious problem for the landlords in the seventeenth and early eighteenth centuries in Shandong. In an imperial edict of 1707, the Kangxi Emperor declared: "On the inspection tour beyond the borders of China in the northeast [that is, in Manchuria], *we saw people from Shandong everywhere, some hundred thousand living as merchants or working on the land.*" Another edict a few years later in 1712 stated: "There must be over 100,000 people from Shandong who have gone to open up new land in the northeast."[5]

The problem of tenants' fleeing the land continued well into the eighteenth century, as is attested by, for example, the Qianlong Emperor's comments in an announcement made in the second month of 1748 on the occasion of his return from a tour of inspection:

We have recently personally examined local conditions among our people, and we have seen with our own eyes their manners and customs. Should the harvest fail, the country people would have nothing to keep themselves alive. Our tour took us both to the south and to the northeast beyond the pass . . . there were some who had been unable to support themselves as tenants and who were even unable to provide for their own livelihood. They uprooted themselves and fled . . . *Since those who flee are numerous, there is a dearth of tenants and, as a result, the land returns to weeds because the rich cannot plough it by themselves . . .* Yesterday we happened to meet with Wang Rou who had memorialized that, in the past, poor people in Shandong had borrowed from the rich and, although the interest was as high as 40 percent or 50 percent per annum, they were still willing to repay their loans. This shows that, as long as poor people can obtain loans, they will not leave their homes and flee the land. Now, although the interest rates are at 20 percent or 30 percent, if a loan is not repaid and the creditor takes the case to the officials, they do not hear the case because it is a private debt. Families with a surplus fear that they have no recourse for securing repayment and therefore avoid making loans. They have no interest on their money, and the poor people and those who have fallen on hard times have nobody to borrow from. Their only way out is to go begging in other areas. In this way the rich gradually become poor and the poor ever poorer.

The Qianlong Emperor saw things from the landlords' point of view and suggested that "rich and poor cooperate with each other" or "rich and poor maintain each other" in order to prevent the tenants' fleeing the land. In fact, the government began to legislate at this time against people leaving Shandong. The *Qing Code*, for example, contains the following regulation: "In Penglai and the neighboring districts of Shandong, there are licensed boats; should any of these boats smuggle vagrants without passports to Fengtian, the precedent governing unlicensed boats carrying vagrants is to be applied to the captain of the boat, the punishment being reduced by one increment to 90 strokes of the heavy bamboo, exile for 2½ years, and confiscation of the boat by the officials."[6]

Such a heavy punishment shows that the government took this matter very seriously. The fundamental reason why tenants fled the land at this time, however, was that the landlords made the rents unbearably high. Rent was usually a minimum of half the crop, which had to be delivered in kind directly to the landlord. Tenants were frequently unable to bear this burden, as even the Kangxi Emperor realized when he said: "If it were possible to reduce the rents and each landlord to aid his tenants, this would not only ease the lot of the poor but it would also ensure that your land did not become abandoned." In a memorial of the third month of 1749 the provincial director of education for Shandong, Li Tian-pei, broached the fundamental causes of the tenant problem and suggested with considerable vigor that, at the time of the autumn harvest, the emperor should "issue an edict, ... exhorting the landlords to divide grain equally with the tenants." The Qianlong

Emperor, as spokesman of the landlord class, immediately repri-
manded Li in the following terms:

The tenant farmers live a life of toil from one end of the year
to the next and should therefore be pitied. If Shandong has
arrears of taxes, then we should pay special attention to
alleviating conditions there. But landowners manage their
farms and pay government taxes. They also make provision
for their own families. How can they be forced by restrictive
orders to give their proceeds to other people? Furthermore,
most tenants belong to poor, unstable elements of the population; by no means all are deserving. Even in good harvest
years they still terrorize their landlords, refusing either to pay
their rents or to pay off interest on their loans. If we were
now to promulgate an imperial edict and order the local
officials to make it known, then it would be impossible to
force the landowners to follow it, and the recalcitrant tenants
would be encouraged to resist their payments, and there
would be a situation leading to open struggle, armed fighting,
and endless litigation. The landowners would punish and
discipline their tenants and forcibly regain possession of their
land and put in new tenants, and many of the poor would lose
their land. In seeking to show consideration, you would only
be encouraging the wicked and, in trying to care for the poor,
you would simply be increasing the burdens of local government.[7]

These high-sounding phrases of the Kangxi and Qianlong
Emperors show that the court was well aware that, in order to prevent tenants fleeing the land, landlords would have to reduce rents.
But, on the other hand, in order to maintain the very basis of the
existing society, the landlords' rights had to be made secure and,
as a result, the Qianlong Emperor personally opposed the suggestion
to reduce rents. As time went by, the antagonism between the landlords and the tenants grew ever sharper. Tenants continually either
defaulted on rents or refused to pay them to such an extent that it
had to be put in black and white in that instrument for protecting

the privileges of the landlord class, the *Qing Code:* "Should a deceitful tenant cheat his landlord and default on his rent, he is to receive *80 strokes of the heavy bamboo and the amount of rent outstanding is to be paid to the landlord forthwith.*"

Clearly, "cheating of landlords," "defaulting," and refusal to pay rents must have been extremely common phenomena for such a law to be included in the *Code.*

In the last resort, the antagonism between landlords and tenants arose out of the insurmountable class contradiction at the very heart of the tenancy relationship. Eventually, in order to secure their rights and prevent their lands from falling to weeds as a result of the tenants fleeing, the landlords, especially medium and small landlords, began to adapt to the changing economic situation. Taking advantage of the increasing development of a commodity economy and a commercial agriculture, they began to switch gradually from tenant farming to direct management and in this way to raise yields and to produce commercial and cash crops.

It was against this background of change in the landlord economy that the differentiation among the peasantry was beginning to take place. Lenin has drawn attention to the fact that, "in capitalist production, the basis for the formation of a home market is the process of the disintegration of the small cultivators into agricultural entrepreneurs and workers."[8]

This observation of Lenin's can serve as a pointer in our research on the early development of capitalist relations of production in China. In Shandong, the growth of a commodity economy and the appearance of commercial centers continued a trend already begun in the late Ming period. One of the consequences of this trend was for monetary relationships to enter the villages and contribute to the dissolution of the old feudal relationships there. In particular, the differentiation of the peasantry into two widely differing groups became ever more marked. This is not to say, however, that Shandong in common with the rest of the country was not still a basically feudal society.

It is our opinion that the increasingly common use of hired labor in directly managed landlord estates in Shandong during the

Qing period is evidence of the continuing process of differentiation among the peasantry. We have gathered together scattered data from local gazetteers and occasional writings and observations of literati that would seem to lend support to such an assertion.

The *Imperial Encyclopaedia,* for example, contains an excerpt on a Shandong prefecture which gives the following definitions: "Those peasants who have no land and who work for others are called long-term laborers (*chang-gong*); those who work temporarily for others are called 'busy-season laborers' (*mang-gong*); if there are many fields and few laborers and a laborer is invited to help out, he is called a 'helping-out laborer' (*ban-gong*)."[9]

The *Imperial Encyclopaedia* also contains references (under Yanzhou prefecture) to practices followed by laborers leaving work. In Ciyang district, "On the first of the tenth month, the farmers provide wine and food and feast the laborers," or in Ningyang district, "On the first of the tenth month . . . on leaving the farms, the laborers are treated to a feast," or in Zou district, "On the first of the tenth month, the landlords provide food and wine and feast the laborers." It was also the practice in Yizhou sub-prefecture "for the landlords to provide food and wine and feast the laborers . . . on the first of the tenth month, which practice was called 'leaving the fields.'"[10]

The 1833 edition of the *District Gazetteer of Zhangqiu* contains the following story in the section on outstanding personalities: "Jiao Yu-rui became a *jinshi* in 1647. His son was drowned while crossing the river Yi. At that time *his* son (Jiao's grandson) was eight years old . . . for more than ten years there was no news of him . . . when he grew up *he worked as a laborer for a rich family and saved enough money* to have a coffin made for his father . . ."[11]

The *Miscellaneous Records of Yanshan* tells how "in 1663 there were many thunderstorms and a man was struck dead by lightning in Shentou (a village near Yanshen market town). The villagers said that on this particular day *he was taking food to the laborers in a field* which he had had made by leveling over his ancestors' tomb mounds."[12]

Another source mentions a certain Liu Xiu-cheng, "who worked as a laborer for the family of Liu Du-cheng in Ling district."[13]

The 1859 edition of the *Prefectural Gazetteer of Qingzhou* records that the district magistrate of Zhucheng in 1743, Wang Zhi-zeng, "went out into the fields and found eight or nine peasants resting their heads on their hoes taking a noontime nap. He questioned them and found that they were *hired laborers* loafing. Zhizeng then told them that they were not farming on their own account, *they were taking another person's money and food and were idling on the job.*"[14]

The *District Gazetteer of Qingping* records that Lin Mao of Huli village "founded the family's fortunes on agriculture"; that Zhao Kun of Lijia village started out *as a laborer* and made *a certain amount of money,* all of which he gave to his mother"; that Yu Wan-gui of Youji village "was exceptionally strong and *hired himself out as a laborer* and was able to save unusually *large amounts of money* and make his family modestly well off"; that Jiang Ren's wife of the same village "hired herself out as a laborer and was hardworking and conscientious in the hundred and one things she did, whether it was gathering firewood, fetching water, grinding flour, or washing clothes, and certainly did not *"calculate the cost";* that Geng Wang-you's wife of Cangshang village, on the death of her husband, was left with two mu of poor land and, when her son had begun to grow up, they both "hired themselves out as laborers and with their wages she was able to support her mother-in-law."[15]

These excerpts from the *District Gazetteer of Qingping* must serve as an example of the very large number of references to hired laborers in local gazetteers during the Qing period. Similar references are also found in the novels of the time as, for example, in the novel *A Marriage to Awaken Men,* in which there is a character called Yan Lie-suo from Mingshui market town, Zhangqiu district, "whose own living was made as a small merchant but who, during the busy agricultural season, *would hire himself out as a short-term laborer.* When he had saved up a few taels of silver, he was able to marry the daughter of a farmer."[16]

In our opinion the data quoted above suggest the following points: 1) that in the seventeenth and eighteenth centuries in the Shandong villages mentioned above, there was a tendency for the peasantry to become polarized (on the one hand, some became rich peasants or managerial landlords and, on the other hand, some became hired laborers, both short- and long-term); 2) that there was a division of labor among the agricultural laborers with the men working in the fields and the women mostly doing domestic work; 3) that in the area of Yizhou sub-prefecture (Ningyang, Zouxian, and Ciyang districts), it was the practice for long-term laborers to stop and start work on the first of the tenth month; 4) that the long-term laborers had already basically become a land-less rural proletariat; and 5) that the basic production relationship between hirer and hired was already a monetary wage relationship. Naturally, monetary wages were not found in every part of Shan-dong. Particularly in the early stages of the emergence of the new employment relations, the wages of long-term laborers were fre-quently paid partly in kind. Indeed the written sources indicate that the payment of wages in money occurred earlier in the case of short-term laborers.

In *A Marriage to Awaken Men,* long-term laborers (*mihan*) are quite frequently said to have been paid entirely in kind while short-term laborers were paid in cash only. For example, in Chapter 26 the author says: "Those laborers (*mihan*) who hire themselves out to work for other people constantly complain of the food they get and are always making difficulties. If it has been agreed that they are to receive wheat and green beans *as wages* (*gongliang*), next they will be wanting millet, and then after that they perversely want a dan of soy beans, and, should they find any sorghum stalks or black beans amongst the grain, they say: 'How can you give men food only fit for animals?'" The author continues to malign the laborers, saying, "If they don't kill your oxen on purpose, then they injure your mules and horses, ruin your tools and implements, and start joining together with the tenants and even your own household to rob you of your crops." In Chapter 54, the author alludes to "two wage-laborers who worked for someone in his orchard. They were not only provided with meals in the hirer's house but they were also given a total of *three dan of various grains* every year." The cook in Hu Chun-yuan's household got "*four dan of grain per year as wages,*" as did the cook in Master Di's household. In Chapter 26, there is the following interesting passage on "short-term laborers (*duangong*) who work for others:"

> When it comes to the hot season and it is necessary to work under the blazing sun, those with money do not consider it excessive to give more *cash* to the short-term laborers. What is hateful is that the laborers gang up and make as many extortionate demands as they can, and when they get to the fields their hoeing is not even good and their reaping is badly done. Should the meal arrive slightly late in the fields, all the laborers will put down their tools and sit around. If you let them off this time, they will still want to argue and dispute ... you give them good wages in cash and they deliberately find fault and, given half a chance, they slip you bad cash in return for your good cash.

The sixth and final point suggested by the data above is that the long-term laborers in those places had a fairly high status. At the start of work at the beginning of the contract year and again at the conclusion of the contracted time, the managerial landlords had to invite them to take a drink with them. This certainly does not mean, however, that their status was very high. In fact, there are many examples of landlords maltreating and maligning their laborers, both in literary works and in the local gazetteers. For example, in Chapter 68 of *A Marriage to Awaken Men,* we find the following: "Elder sister Su wanted to go to Taishan to make an offering of incense, and Master Di's laborer led the mule. *Master Di whipped off the laborer's head towel with one crack of the whip* and shouted to Di Xi-chen to lead the mule."

Pu Song-ling in his *Cibei qu* also shows how farm hands were treated by their masters. In Chapter 4, which describes how Zhang Na had encountered a tiger while out cutting firewood and was now returning to his dwelling, he writes: "When he came in, he prepared to lay out the bedding, but the ground had only just been swept. The windows were unpapered and there was a great deal of dirt and innumerable cobwebs on the walls. It seems that the contract was only drawn up when the laborer started work and he wondered how badly the master would treat the servants."

In the 1846 edition of the *District Gazetteer of Tengxian,* we find the following description of a laborer's conditions in the section on filial piety, that much-vaunted virtue of the landlord class:

> Zhang Lan's father, Meng Jian, was born in Tengxian. He died when Zhang Lan was only one year old. Zhang's mother decided not to marry again. After Zhang was over ten years old, he went out to gather firewood for his mother whenever he could, and he also did the cooking for her. He watched his mother spinning and learned how to do it and he became very expert at it. When he was old enough to work as a farm laborer, he changed his work and began working as a farm-hand in exchange for firewood and food. Whenever he sold what his mother or he had woven, he bought delicacies for her but, as for himself, he was content to eat the coarsest food. In winter he wore only a short jacket, but his mother wore a thick padded jacket, and at night he warmed up the bedding for her and added extra covers for her feet. He him-self slept under an oxhide. If his mother needed him during the night, he would get up ten times and still not feel tired. He worked not far from their home, and in the evening he always came home immediately and asked his mother if she was feeling well and had eaten. His mother died when she was sixty-three, and he was prostrated with grief. He begged wood for the coffin from his kin and he worked for them to pay for it. He carried the earth for the tomb mound and, after mourn-ing for three days, he went back to work. When he had paid back all the expenses he returned home, alone and with nothing. Night and day he wept and eventually he died of starvation. His kinsmen buried him beside his parents' grave.

So much for the life of a farm laborer!

The most conclusive evidence of the continued low status of the farm laborers comes from the laws of the ruling class in which a clear distinction is made between the "good" and the "base." Thus the *Qing Code* stipulated that, "should a hired laborer strike the head of the family or his close relatives or maternal relatives and should there be no injury, he is to receive 100 strokes of the heavy bamboo and be exiled for three years. If there is injury, no matter of what degree, then he is to receive 100 strokes of the heavy bamboo and be exiled for life to the border regions... On the other hand, should the head of the family (in other words, the landlord) strike a hired laborer of distant relatives on either the paternal or maternal side, provided there is no injury, no case is to be brought. Should there be an injury (up to grave illness) then he is to receive the same punishment as for striking an ordinary person *but reduced by one degree;* if he has struck a hired laborer of close relatives, then the punishment is to be *reduced by two degrees.*"[17]

The Imperial Encyclopedia (under "Customs of Qingzhou Prefecture") notes that in Anqiu "base people work as serfs" (*sujian nuyong*). Indeed this continued right up to 1949 as is shown by Comrade Ge Maochun who quotes an example of "a big landlord in Anqiu whose hired laborers worked for him on a hereditary basis. An ancestor had sold his own and his descendants' labor to the landlord and, ever since, generation after generation, they had had to work for him. The landlord had erected a stele with the name of the original laborer carved on one side and his oath of fidelity carved on the other."[18]

While saying that the status of long-term laborers had risen from what it had been in the past, we must at the same time recognize that all areas had not reached the same level of development. Even in those areas where the status of laborers was relatively high, it was in no sense on an equal footing with their employers'. But what is clear is that the long-term laborers' relations with their employers were different from the previous tenurial relations in that, as a rule, they were no longer characterized by personal dependence.

In discussing the differentiation of the peasants, we should also draw attention to increasing sales of private land and houses in response to the growing commercialization of the economy as a whole. Again *A Marriage to Awaken Men* contains some interesting material. In Chapter 25, for example, Professor Xue is having a leisurely discussion with the family head, Master Di, about Mingshui market town as it had been in the past and as it was then:

Professor Xue . . . said, "Mingshui really is a splendid place, the land is fertile, the people contented, and the local manners and customs perfect." Master Di replied, "What you say, sir, about our poor town would have applied very well to it as it was in the past. But conditions here have gradually changed since then. The new generations of recent times have none of the simple integrity of their forebears." Professor Xue said, "Although it may not compare to what it was in the past, it is certainly superior to other places. My own humble birthplace, for example, has become worse and worse. Do many people from other areas come through your honorable town?" Master Di replied, "We do not take advantage of strangers here because *there simply is no land for sale; everybody follows in his father's footsteps from generation to generation.* But, on the main prefectural road, there is plenty of business to be done apart from agriculture. Here we are completely lacking a cloth store, so if we want to buy cotton cloth, we have to go all the way to the prefectural town or to the district town, which is extremely inconvenient." Professor Xue commented, "Or is it that there is no sale for cotton cloth here? Otherwise why hasn't somebody opened a shop by now?" Master Di answered, "Our own people only understand how to farm a few mu, they have no idea how to manage a business and make money. How could you expect people from other places to be willing to come and open a store here? Take this inn that I run, for example. I don't try to make a profit on the catering side, but in return for the water for the draft animals I get their manure to take to the fields. I only supply very coarse food and fodder at just over their cost price and provide a lodging for the carters." Professor Xue said, "No wonder I felt like stopping here yesterday after 20 hard miles although it was only noontime." . . . Professor Xue went to Qingzhou where he was in office for a while . . . toward the new year . . . he sent a member of his family, Xue San-huai, to take 20 jin of sugar balls, two bolts of lustrous local gauze silk and a thank-you letter to Master Di. Di entertained Xue San-huai for a couple of days, replied to Professor Xue's letter, and wrapped up 2 bolts of home-woven tussore and 2 hams as a return present and also gave Xue San-huai 3 small pieces of silver . . .

Later when Professor Xue returns to Mingshui in order to set up business there, Master Di says to him, " 'Since you really seem to like this place, then why not register here permanently? Things are very different from what they used to be. Everybody is selling land and houses. I'll ask the agent tomorrow to come and tell you if he knows of any suitable houses for sale.' "

Clearly, Mingshui market town was undergoing considerable change. In common with other places, the "simple integrity" of the old self-sufficient economy was being penetrated by the new commodity economy. In previous years there was "simply no land for sale," and "everybody followed in his father's footsteps." Now "everybody is selling land and houses." Moreover an "agent" has appeared who is accustomed to handling property sales. In the past there had been no cotton cloth store in Mingshui itself, and people had to go to the prefectural or district town if they wanted to buy cloth. The local people were not skilled in commerce, and they regarded trade as serving agriculture, as in Master Di's description of his inn. When Di had sent his present to Professor Xue, he had sent "2 bolts of *home-woven* tussore." But, in only a short time, the ex-scholar businessman Professor Xue had arrived from Linqing selling cloth and established a branch cloth store in Mingshui.

Another source, in describing the luxurious customs and spending habits of the "rich" (*fujia*) living in Tengxian district along the Grand Canal, says they "buy building materials from Henan and Hebai and build high pavilions and spacious banquet halls, they have splendid carriages and marvelous mounts, the cost of one saddle can be as high as 100 taels. They save nothing and, *in less than a year or two, the pavilions and halls, the saddles and the horses have all changed hands.*"[19]

One of the effects of the growth of a commodity economy was to spur on the conspicuous consumption of the landlord class, but at the same time it also broke up the old pattern of each generation following its predecessor's occupation.

The differentiation of the peasantry in Shandong during the Qing period had gone far enough to produce two hostile classes. On the one hand, there was gradually appearing a class of wage laborers who had broken away from farming the landlord's land or had been forced to sell their own land and hire themselves out. On the other hand, there was the class of managerial landlords who amassed land they farmed directly using the products of the surplus labor of the long- and short-term wage laborers, as well as running handicraft industries and making high-interest loans. The managerial landlords either rose out of the ranks of the peasantry or had once been rentier landlords. The number of managerial landlords was very small in comparison with the total number of peasants, but the number of owner-peasants who lost their land and became wage laborers was constantly growing.

In the following chapters, we turn to the problems of the extent, scale, and nature of the managerial landlord farming operation. Qing historical and literary sources do not contain sufficient materials to enter into these problems in any detail. To make up for this deficiency, we undertook a field survey in the course of which old peasants and laborers were interviewed and account books and other private documents were collected. The materials gathered in our field survey form the focus of the following chapter.

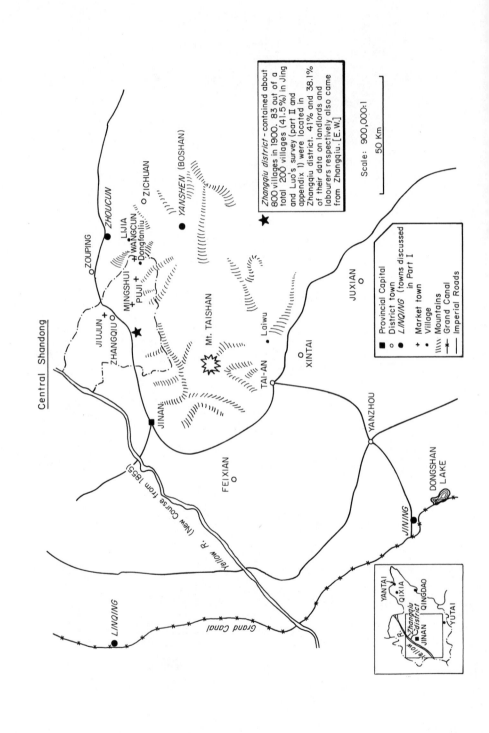

Central Shandong

Zhangqiu district - contained about 800 villages in 1900. 83 out of a total 200 villages (41.5%) in Jing and Luo's survey (part II and appendix 1) were located in Zhangqiu district. 41% and 38.1% of their data on landlords and labourers respectively also came from Zhangqiu. [E.W.]

Scale: 900,000:1

50 Km

■ Provincial Capital
○ District town
LINQING (towns discussed in Part I)
+ Market town
• Village
))))) Mountains
⁂ Grand Canal
— Imperial Roads

ZHOUCUN
ZOUPING
YANSHEN (BOSHAN)
ZICHUAN
LIJIA
WANGCUN
Dongfanliu
MINGSHUI
PUJI
JIUJUN
ZHANGQIU
Mt. TAISHAN
Laiwu
TAI-AN
XINTAI
JUXIAN
JINAN
YANZHOU
FEIXIAN
Yellow R. (New Course from 1855)
JINING
DONGSHAN LAKE
LINQING
Grand Canal

YANTAI
QIXIA
QINGDAO
Zhangqiu district
JINAN
Yellow R.
YUTAI

Part II

MICRO STUDIES OF THE MANAGERIAL LANDLORD
ECONOMY IN SHANDONG DURING THE QING PERIOD

In the previous chapters, we indicated the main outlines of the
development of the regional economy of Shandong during the Qing:
the growth of market towns, increasing commercialization of agriculture, and, under these conditions, the differentiation of the
peasants. In this chapter we turn to the development of the managerial landlord economy as seen in our field data.

Chapter 4

FIELD DATA ON THREE TYPICAL
MANAGERIAL LANDLORDS

4.1 The Taihe tang Li Family[1]

The Taihe tang Li family were fairly large landlords of Dong-fanliu village (Zhangqiu district).[2] Dongfanliu is about 30 miles east of Jinan [the provincial capital], 6 miles to the south of Puji market town, 4 miles to the south of Wangcun market town, and about 14 miles to the west of Zhoucun. To the south of the village is the hilly area along the borders of Zhangqiu district. In the days before the Jiaozhou-Jinan railway line was built [in 1904], this had been the site of an important east-west pass through the Bo Mountains. The village had had a 5-10 periodic market [that is meeting on the 5th, 10th, 15th, 20th, 25th, and 30th of the lunar month] for many years which served as the node for several dozen mountain villages in the southeast and eastern parts of Zhangqiu and Zichuan districts respectively.

The Taihe tang Lis, from their rise in the eighteenth century down to the early twentieth century, had amassed 472 mu of arable land, and they also managed a wine shop, a miscellaneous goods store, a pharmacy, a shop for lending ritual paraphernalia, and various other small stores. In addition, they also lent money in about twenty of the neighboring villages.

The Process of Land Accumulation

During our field research we found the receipt stubs of Taihe tang land deeds (*wenqi cungen*) covering the years 1761 to 1905. We have divided the process of Taihe tang's land accumulation into three periods on the basis of the names of the purchasers for the family:

1) 1761–1790—Li Ke-shi (Li Fang-cai's grandfather) was left 175.72 mu when the family property was divided in 1792. The land had been accumulated between 1761 and 1790, as

106

recorded in 36 deeds. An average of 5.46 mu had been added each year during this period.

2) 1793-1868—Li Ke-shi and Li Yong-qing bit by bit bought for Taihe tang a further 164.68 mu, as recorded in 29 deeds, giving an average of 2.2 mu per year.

3) 1870-1905—Under Li Fang-cai's management, Taihe tang bought 175.37 mu, as recorded in 40 deeds, giving an average of 5.01 mu per year.

The following three tables [2, 3, and 4] show the amounts of land bought annually and the prices paid. The tables are based on the receipt stubs of the Taihe tang land deeds.

Up to 1905, Taihe tang had accumulated 515½ mu of land, of which 43½ mu were in other villages and 472 mu were in their own village. This amounted to just over 1/6th of the cultivated acreage of the village. [See Table 5.]

Their lands were mainly bought by Taihe tang from peasants in Dongfanliu or in neighboring villages who urgently required money to meet the expenses of illnesses, marriages, funerals, or other such needs. A few had contracted debts at Taihe tang's shops and been forced to sell their land. From Table 5 below we see that, at that time, peasants owning between 1–30 mu made up the large majority of the households in the village. These poor and middle peasants had a very low standard of living; if they met unexpected calamity, they would often have to send people out to work as laborers, and to borrow money and sell their crops in order to conserve their land. In the process of land accumulation (because it was not easy to buy land, or because there was serious competition between Taihe tang and other landlords and rich peasants), every rising landlord (Taihe tang included), as well as rich and middle peasants, frequently used to use the local lineage, clan and gentry power rights of proximity and other means to buy land.[3] For this reason Taihe tang had not infrequently to struggle to buy land near Dongfanliu village at comparatively high prices.

Farm Management

Apart from the 43½ mu of land rented out in neighboring

Table 2

Accumulation of Taihe Tang's Lands, 1761–1790

Year	Amount of land (in shimu)	Price
1761	3.3	28 taels
1764	2.4	25 taels
1767	3.2	20 taels
1770	1.8	22 strings
1770	1.5	22 strings
1771	6.0	30 taels
1771	3.0	20 taels
1772	11.6	50 taels
1772	9.1	43 taels
1774	6.17	20 taels
1774	2.1	8 taels
1774	4.3	14 taels
1774	4.58	---
1774	2.23	---
1775	1.5	30 strings
1776	9.0	110 strings
1776	9.0	129 strings
1776	4.5	57 strings
1778	6.0	32 strings
1778	11.3	123 strings
1778	6.0	22 taels
1778	3.75	60 strings
1779	3.75	60 strings
1779	3.45	69 strings
1779	8.25	80 strings
1781	3.15	44 strings
1783	3.0	15 strings
1783	3.0	41 strings
1783	3.75	33 strings
1786	3.0	42 strings
1787	4.5	74 strings
1787	6.0	50 strings
1787	5.84	90 strings
1790	9.0	209 strings
1790	6.9	50 strings
TOTAL	175.92	

Note: Original acreages given in damu have been converted to shimu. This table does not include building and orchard lands. The original materials record that, on the establishment of Li Ke-shi's family in 1792, he received 132 mu of the above land.[4]

Source: Receipt stubs of Taihe tang land deeds.

Table 3

Accumulation of Taihe Tang's Lands, 1794–1868

Year	Amount of land (in shimu)	Price
1794	3.4	32 strings
1810	6.0	105 strings
1813	3.0	47 strings
1813	1.05	195 strings
1814	0.11	60 strings
1815	8.9	300 strings
1815	3.66	100 strings
1816	7.2	100 taels
1822	2.4	38 strings
1823	0.3	5 strings
1824	6.0	230 strings
1824	2.0	20 strings
1825	3.6	75 strings
1834	3.0	143 strings
1837	2.7	---
1854	2.4	47 strings
1857	4.5	110 strings
1857	0.78	20 strings
1857	6.0	148 strings
1858	7.5	240 strings
1859	2.46	80 strings
1860	7.5	240 strings
1861	3.6	140 strings
1862	3.3	92.2 strings
1867	4.2	33 taels
1867	4.02	177 strings
1868	30.0	240 strings
1868	30.0	---
1868	5.1	190 strings
TOTAL	164.68	

Note: See note to Table 2.

Source: Receipt stubs of Taihe tang land deeds.

Table 4

Accumulation of Taihe Tang's Lands, 1870–1905

Year	Amount of land (in shimu)	Price	
1870	1.5	57	strings
1871	0.93	---	
1871	3.0	16	taels
1873	5.7	44	taels
1877	1.8	40	strings
1877	5.1	100	strings
1877	4.26	14.5	taels
1877	5.16	17.2	taels
1878	2.7	70	strings
1878	3.0	17	taels
1878	3.6	60	strings
1878	0.963	52.5	strings
1878	0.15	3.5	strings
1879	7.5	2.5	taels
1879	9.0	375	strings
1879	2.7	100	strings
1879	3.0	82	strings
1880	12.0	400	strings
1880	3.6	63	strings
1885	2.1	10.5	strings
1886	9.9	330	strings
1887	0.9	60	strings
1888	3.3	14	taels
1888	5.7	190	strings
1890	4.2	11.5	taels
1890	3.0	405	strings
1891	6.891	132	strings
1892	6.3	280	strings
1892	1.8	60	strings
1893	3.0	122	strings
1893	2.022	108	strings
1894	3.45	162	strings
1894	6.0	---	
1894	4.5	---	
1899	2.4	70	strings
1900	2.4	145	strings

Table 4 (cont.)

Year	Amount of land (in shimu)	Price	
1901	19.8	706	strings
1903	3.0	107	strings
1904	6.0	180	strings
1905	3.0	70	strings
TOTAL	175.326		

Note: See note to Table 2.

Source: Receipt stubs of Taihe tang land deeds.

Table 5

Land Ownership in Dongfanliu Village c. 1906

Owners	Taihe tang	Other landlords	Rich peasants	Middle peasants	Poor peasants	Totals
Amount of land (shimu)	472	60–150	31–59	15–30	less than 15	2,640
Number of households	1	6	4	63	46	120

villages, Taihe tang managed its remaining 472 mu *using wage labor.*

Around about 1904, Taihe tang annually hired about 13 long-term wage laborers, including one foreman who was responsible for helping the landlord plan the amount of crop seed needed, decide where to plant which crops as well as on the amount of fertilizer to be used, and on the times of ploughing. In addition, he went to the short-term labor market to hire hands and apportioned them to work under the subforemen in the fields. There were six subforemen who led the hired hands to the fields and worked together with them. There were also two herdsmen who took charge of the pasturing of oxen and sheep, gathering their feed, and making up the dung heap. Two farm boys ground the grain, fetched water and firewood, and took food to the hired hands in the fields. Two female cooks prepared the food for the wage laborers. Apart from the 13 long-term wage laborers, Taihe tang frequently employed between 20 and 40 short-term laborers and 3 to 5 laborers on monthly wages, to plough, dig ditches, saw wood, cut grass, carry fertilizer to the fields, and do other similar types of work. It was the custom at that time in that part of Shandong for long-term laborers to be introduced by personal contacts (usually through other farm hands), and they were directly hired by the landlord of Taihe tang. Short-term laborers were hired at the short-term wage-labor market.

The short-term wage-labor market opened in the busy agricultural seasons. In this locality it was situated in Dongfanliu village. Poor and destitute peasants would often go to this market before sunrise carrying their own tools. Some would even go the night before and sleep out in the open.

There was frequently a fixed market price for wage labor, which was decided by the hirer and laborers, the demand depending on the season involved, and so forth. The price, however, was invariably shouted out, having been fixed by a few of the big hirers who were usually able to control it.

In the busy seasons, there were two or three hundred laborers waiting for the hirers. Taihe tang was the biggest single hirer coming to the market.

As to implements, so far as we could ascertain, Taihe tang owned 9 ploughing oxen, 4 mules, 4 donkeys, 2 4-ox ploughs, 1 large 2-wheel cart, 2 large wheelbarrows, 8 small wheelbarrows, a complete set of saws, spades, ploughs, cutting implements, and other farm tools, and 14 pig sties. Apart from using the manure of the oxen, donkeys, and mules, Taihe tang also raised over 100 sheep and 40 pigs, and in an average year was able to collect over 5,000 cartloads of fertilizer.

Labor on Taihe tang was comparatively plentiful and production techniques were comparatively complete, which gave it a decided advantage. For example, most peasants in that locality had to borrow ploughing oxen from rich peasants or otherwise use their neighbors' oxen with their own to form a team, each team consisting of 3 oxen.

Taihe tang had 9 oxen and used 4 to a team, so that it could set up 2 teams and have 1 replacement ox. Ordinary peasants ploughed to a depth of about 3 inches (cun), while Taihe tang ploughed to a depth of half a foot (chi). Ordinary peasants used 3 to 10 carts of fertilizer per mu (these were small carts holding about 400 jin). Taihe tang used 10 to 20 carts per mu (putting more fertilizer on some fields than others and not limiting the manuring to one application). Since Taihe tang used grain left over from brewing as pig feed and had a large number of animals, the quality of the fertilizer was far superior to that of the peasants. Apart from that, Taihe tang was able to use much more labor for such tasks as ploughing, sowing, hoeing, and reaping and, as a result, was able to get things done in time and much more thoroughly.

The different crops planted by Taihe tang and the acreage of each were as follows:

1. Wheat	180–240 mu
2. Kaoliang	100–150 mu
3. Millet	70–120 mu
4. Maize	150–180 mu
5. Others (beans, sesame, etc.)	30–60 mu

Note that, because wheat cultivation required a lot of labor, most peasants were able to plant only about 20 percent of their land to it. Since Taihe tang had a lot of labor, its wheat fields amounted to about 50 percent of its acreage. Wheat prices were usually twice as high as those of the coarser grains. Furthermore, after the wheat harvest, second crops such as maize could be planted. In this way, the area of double cropping could be extended.

Thanks to the superiority of Taihe tang's production methods and ploughing arrangements, the yield for all the above crops was

Table 6

Estimates of Annual Totals Harvested by Taihe Tang
and Proportions Consumed and Marketed, c. 1904 (Unit = 100 jin)

Annual Harvest	Wheat	Kaoliang	Millet	Maize	Others (legume, sesame, etc.)	Totals
	260–345	360–480	330–360	500–630	28–42	1,480–1,850

Distribution	For consumption				For sale
	Landlord family dependants	Farm hands and day laborers	Shopkeepers	Others	
	172.8	172.8	60.48	72	1,002–1,380

Notes: Calculated on the basis of 48 people each eating 30 jin per month. — Calculated as 14 farm hands and 3,600 working days (day laborers each eating 60 jin per month). — Calculated on the basis of 14 people each eating 36 jin per month. — Includes chance passersby and the costs of the animals, etc. — The proceeds from the sale of this amount in the local market were used for wages for the farm laborers, buying land, repair of farm buildings, making clothes, or directly used for business or usury.

Source: Oral interviews.

more than twice as great as that on the ordinary peasants' land.
(This point is expanded in Section 7.1, where the progressive nature
of managerial landlords is discussed.)

On the basis of oral interviews, we were able to draw up
Table 6 showing the annual amounts harvested by Taihe tang and
how they were disposed of. Clearly this is not an exact table, but
it represents estimates that cannot be too far from the realities of
the time.

Conditions of Hired Laborers

Most of the short-term farm hands (both day laborers and
month laborers), employed by Taihe tang were laborers with a
small parcel of land or otherwise poor peasants or even middle
peasants. When they were hired and were not busy on the farm or
at the times when they were not hired, most of the short-term
laborers would peddle earthenware pots or sell firewood in an effort
to support their families. The wages derived from selling their labor
were by no means their main source of income. They had not funda-
mentally changed their original status as small freeholders.

The status of long-term wage laborers also requires considerable qualification. Using the wage labor account books of Taihe
tang we have recorded the actual dates on which the long-term
laborers went to work and left work [Table 7].

Table 7 reflects two phenomena worth noting:

1) Out of the 33 long-term laborers employed in the course of
these two years, 15 worked for less than 100 days (46 percent of
the laborers). Only 11 worked for between 100 and 200 days (33
percent of the laborers). And only 7 worked for more than 200
days (21 percent of the laborers).

2) Although it was the custom at that time to stop work on
the eighth of the twelfth month (*in the slack season*), nevertheless
many of the laborers stopped work *in the busy season.*

The *main* reason for this was that the long-term laborers
wished to become short-term laborers during the busy season when
their wages were much higher. Most of them owned small amounts
of land, but this was cultivated by the other members of their
families.

Table 7

Dates on Which Taihe Tang Long-Term Laborers
Started and Stopped Work, 1908–1909

Name	Busy Season Yr/Mo/Day	Off Season Yr/Mo/Day	Busy Season Yr/Mo/Day	Off Season Yr/Mo/Day	Days Worked
Feng Ba-Zi		1907/12/8		1908/12/8	360
Qiu Si-Zhang		1907/12/8		1908/12/8	360
Wang Wei-ming		1907/12/13	1908/2/10		57
Gong Gou-zi		1907/12/8		1908/9/28	280
Gu Jiu-ren		1907/12/19		1908/8/22	243
Wang Ye-zi		1907/12/22		1908/1/15	23
Jie Jing-rui		1907/12/22	1908/3/15		83
Han Fa-ming	1908/1/14		1908/3/14		60
Dong Shui-zi	1908/2/21		1908/4/4		43
Meng Xian-gui	1908/3/27			1908/6/22	85
Zhang De-xiang	1908/3/27			1908/12/8	250
Zhang Wai-zi	1908/4/8		1908/5/15		37
Gao Pu Ji-zi	1908/5/28		1908/7/21		53
Wang Sui-zi	1908/7/28			1908/11/8	100
Liang Seng-zi		1908/9/13		1908/10/20	37
Li Gui-liu		1908/9/18		1908/12/8	80
Wang Zuo-fan		1908/10/1		1909/3/27	173
Wang Jiu-fa		1908/11/7		1909/6/21	223
Yang Dao-chu		1908/11/3	1909/5/14		181
Zhang De-xiang		1908/12/8	1909/4/1		112
Qiu Si-zhang		1908/12/8	1909/5/24		166
Wang Gui-zi		1908/12/25	1909/4/13		108
Sun Huo-ji	1909/2/6		1909/4/15		70
Li De-xiang	1909/5/3			1909/12/8	215
Sun Hui-zhong	1909/5/7		1909/5/12		5
Li Ke-chang	1909/5/7		1909/6/12		35
Wang Sui-zi	1909/5/25		1909/7/23		59
Dong Wan-zuo			1909/8/20		50
Bi Xi-cheng				1909/12/28	175
Wang Ri-hong				1909/12/15	158
Liu Feng-shen				1909/12/25	168
Yan Shou-li				1909/12/25	168
Li Zhen-qi	1909/7/30			1909/12/13	134

Notes: 1. It was customary at that time in that part of Shandong for farmhands to start and stop work on the eighth day of the twelfth month.
2. The slack season was customarily from the middle of the sixth to the middle of the seventh month and from the beginning of the tenth month to the beginning of the first month of the following year.
3. The above dates are all in the lunar calendar.

Source: Taihe tang wage-labor accounts.

Table 8

Wages of Taihe Tang Long-Term Laborers, 1908–1909
Unit: cash (1 string = 1,000 cash)

Name	Annual wage	Daily rate
Feng Ba-zi	29,700	82.5
Qiu Si-zhang	21,000	58.33
Wang Wei-ming	13,968	38.8
Gong Gou-zi	6,480	18.0
Gu Jiu-ren	28,980	80.55
Wang Ye-zi	25,500	70.833
Jie Jing-rui	22,500	62.5
Han Fa-ming	19,200	53.33
Dong Shui-zi	17,861	44.614
Meng Xian-gui	25,200	70.0
Zhang De-xiang	25,920	72.0
Zhang Wai-zi	17,064	47.4
Gao Pu Ji-zi	16,560	46.0
Wang Sui-zi	15,228	42.3
Liang Seng-zi	13,622	37.84
Li Gui-liu	11,250	31.25
Wang Zuo-fan	7,200	20.0
Wang Jiu-fa	27,684	76.9
Yang Dao-chu	14,040	39.0
Zhang De-xiang	23,976	66.6
Qiu Si-zhang	21,000	58.33
Wang Gui-zi	25,248	71.8
Sun Huo-ji	22,396	63.6
Li De-xiang	28,465	79.07
Sun Hui-zhong	23,998	66.66
Li Ke-chang	22,320	62.0
Wang Sui-zi	18,857	52.38
Dong Wan-zuo	21,600	60.0
Bi Xi-cheng	30,600	85.0
Wang Ri-hong	28,800	80.0
Liu Feng-shen	27,000	75.0
Yan Shou-li	27,000	75.0
Li Zhen-qi	18,806	52.24
AVERAGES	21,200	59.0

Note: Some of the daily rates were recorded in the original sources, some were calculated by the authors.

Source: Taihe tang wage-labor accounts.

Table 9

Wages of Taihe Tang Short-Term Laborers, 1908–1910
Unit: cash (1 string = 1,000 cash)

Name	Daily wage	Calculated for a month	Notes
Liang Shu-he	140	4,200	(Wage at autumn harvest, 1909)
Liang Peng-lin	90	2,700	(Wage at busy season, second month 1910)
Wang Yue-zhi	80	2,400	(Wage at summer busy season 1910)
Zhang Wai-zi	60	1,800	(Wage at fourth month busy season 1910)
Zhang Wai-zi	40	1,200	(*Light work* wage, fourth month busy season, 1910)
Zhang Wai-zi	100	3,000	(Wage at summer busy season 1910)
Zhang Wai-zi	240	7,200	(*Heavy work* wage at summer busy season, 1910)
Zhang Wai-zi	360	10,800	(Wage at autumn *busiest* season 1910)
Zhang Wai-zi	140	4,200	(Ordinary wage before autumn harvest, 1910)
Liang Ba-zi	360	10,800	(Wage at autumn *busiest* season 1910)
*Bi	37.14	1,114	(Wage at winter slack season 1908)
*Chen	37.14	1,114	(Wage at winter slack season 1908)
AVERAGES	124	3,720	

*Month laborers.

Note: Short-term laborers' wage rates fluctuated very widely according to the farming season and they could even change from one day to the next. The wages included in this table are typical of the different seasons. All dates are given in the lunar calendar.

Source: Taihe tang wage-labor accounts.

At that time the actual wages of both long-term and short-term laborers were very low as can be seen in Tables 8 and 9.

From these two tables [8 and 9] we can see that the long-term laborers' average wage at this time was 21,200 standard cash, while the daily wage of short-term laborers was 124 standard cash. When we calculate how much these sums were in terms of grain prices, we see just how shockingly low they were!

Using the same account books, we have calculated that, in 1908, the price of one dou (55 jin) of kaoliang was 3,600 cash. A long-term laborer's annual average wage would only have bought 5.89 dou (324 jin)! A short-term laborer's average daily wage would only have bought 0.35 sheng (1.92 jin)! Compared with 1957 prices in the same village, kaoliang was 7.5 fen per jin, so that a long-term laborer's annual wage would only have been worth 24.30 RMB! A day laborer's wage would have only been worth 0.14 RMB!

Apart from this, Taihe tang's method of payment still retained elements of payment in kind as shown by the fact that: 1) while on the job, both long-term and short-term laborers had their food supplied by Taihe tang; 2)the shepherd's wage was paid in wool (the shepherd was a long-term laborer); 3) among the records of payment in the wage labor accounts are found the following type of entry—"1907, Qiu Si-zhang (long-term) took one sheng of millet reckoned at 400 cash; 1908, Feng Ba-zi (long-term) took two sheng of wheat reckoned at 1,120 cash, one dou of kaoliang reckoned at 3,600 cash; 1908, Feng Peng-lin (day laborer) took five sheng of millet reckoned at 1,900 cash.

This shows that, aside from the shepherd, both long-term and short-term laborers were at times paid in kind instead of in money.

Commercial Activities

During the last half of the nineteenth century and at the beginning of the twentieth century, under the management of Li Fang-cai, Taihe tang at one time or another operated a wine shop, a miscellaneous goods shop, a pharmacy, a paraphernalia lending store, and other shops in the village of Dongfanliu with its less than 150 households. Everything that a peasant needed from the cradle to the grave, including daily necessities, agricultural tools, and food, could all be bought from the shops operated by Taihe tang. Taihe tang itself was able to supply most of its own needs.

We give the details of the management of some of its most important stores.

Wine shop. Opened in about 1874, this shop was operated on the largest scale and for the longest time of all Taihe tang's stores. They brewed their own *baigar* liquor, *huangjiu*, and vinegar. They brewed once a month, producing roughly 3,000 catties. Five persons were employed in the shop: a sales clerk, three assistants, and an apprentice. They also combined with a number of other wine shops to hire a master brewer and, when the time came to brew the wine, they hired two or three extra hands who would leave the shop when the brewing was finished (it took about 7 days). As far as we could ascertain, at the end of the year, after accounts had been settled and wages and all incidental expenses subtracted, Taihe tang was left with a profit of 2,000–3,000 strings of cash [one string = 1,000 cash].

Miscellaneous goods shop. The goods stocked included wine, vinegar, sesame oil, tobacco, scythes, saws, writing brushes, ink, paper, incense, sugar, tea, and so forth. Aside from the wine, vinegar, and sesame oil, which they manufactured themselves, all the other goods were bought in Zhoucun. From what we were told, people in villages within a seven-mile radius all bought their goods at the Taihe tang miscellaneous goods store. The store employed four assistants.

Pharmacy. Around about 1894, Taihe tang withdrew its shares from the Dehe tang's pharmacy in Wangcun and set up the "Hall of Accumulated Virtue Pharmacy" in Dongfanliu village. Two assistants were employed; one, Wang Chuan-jin, doubled as sales clerk and doctor, while the other, Wang Shu-zhan, mixed the medicines. Some of the medicines were bought from a big pharmacist in Jinan; some were made up from materials bought from the neighboring mountain regions. The operating capital of the shop was about one to two thousand strings. In 1938, as there was not enough capital, the doctor was too old, and there was nobody to carry on the business in the family, the shop was closed down.

Paraphernalia lending shop (Linhuo pu). This type of shop was found in the village in the old days for lending out the paraphernalia needed for marriages, funeral processions, and celebrations. Taihe tang had bought several sedan chairs, as well as lanterns, balustrades, flags, cymbals, parasols, fans, and so forth, and these it let out. The shop had connections to a greater or lesser extent with the villagers in many of the surrounding villages. Whenever the shop let out goods, it would frequently hire one to three short-term laborers and sometimes would send one of its own long-term laborers or servants to accompany the paraphernalia.

From what has been said about these shops, we can see that, although they were not large, they fitted in well with the needs of the small consumers' market of the village. On the busy days of the periodic market, the shops didn't attract much attention but, on the days when the market did not meet, they were the few shops of which Dongfanliu could boast.

Usury

In the latter part of the nineteenth and early part of the twentieth centuries, Taihe tang engaged in wide-scale moneylending activities, whether in the form of direct loans or through loan societies (*suihui*).

Just in the years 1906 to 1908, according to the "External Loan Books," 12 village-level local organizations, 3 religious societies, and 38 businesses *borrowed from or deposited funds* with Taihe tang. During the same period, Taihe tang made *loans* to 456 individuals.

Apart from the transactions with the various local organizations, societies, businesses, and emergency loans, most of the loans were to peasants who borrowed money from Taihe tang on occasions such as marriages, funerals, and illnesses. In order to secure repayment of loans to villagers in outlying villages, Taihe tang always acted through a third party, usually medium or small landlords.

There was no special organization for the moneylending business. It was done using the operating capital of the wine shop.

Loans were made at the wine shop and deposits were all kept there. As a result many of the village organizations and businesses withdrew their deposits in kind, taking goods instead of cash. The annual interest rates at that time were between 10 and 30 percent. The borrower always had someone act as go-between to set up the loan and then found a guarantor, wrote out the contract, and collected the money.

At the end of the nineteenth century, mutual savings societies (*qinghui*) in the neighborhood of Dongfanliu village were very popular. Taihe tang was not short of cash so did not have to use such societies, but contributed money and accumulated interest.[5]

Conspicuous Consumption

We learnt from our investigation that, between 1870 and 1911, Taihe tang built 13 courtyard houses (comprising more than 30 two-storied halls and over 130 rooms with roof-tiles). Among these, the eastern and western wings of a courtyard built in 1875 required 4,000 man-hours to build. At that time an artisan earned 400 cash a day and unskilled building hands earned 60 cash a day, so that the wages alone for these buildings cost more than 750 strings of cash. (We arrived at this figure by reckoning that the work required 1,500 skilled man-hours and 2,500 unskilled man-hours.)

The expenses for marriages, funerals, and anniversaries were also very great. As soon as a child was fourteen or fifteen, he was married, and the expenses ranged from one to several hundred strings of cash. At fifty years of age, special congratulatory celebrations were held, and thereafter, every ten years, there were large celebrations, and every single year a small celebration. At about the age of sixty and in some cases slightly earlier, preparations were made for constructing a grave and burial goods and special grave clothes and all the necessary paraphernalia for a proper "reception" prepared. Between 1860 and 1911, Taihe tang conducted 14 full-scale funerals and 19 marriage congratulatory celebrations.[6] As far as we could ascertain, an ordinary Taihe tang funeral cost over 200 strings of cash; for an old and senior member of the family, it could cost as much as 2,000 strings. *"To spend seven years constructing the grave," "to conduct a seven-day funeral"* to hold magnificent banquets for a thousand guests were in those days considered "correct behavior" and matters which "brought credit" to one's family.

In the broader society, in pursuit of hollow glory and to raise its social status by using "voluntary grain contributions to the court," Taihe tang collected the following honorary titles: one Guiwenge Recorder (Rank 7a), one Grand Guestmaster (Rank 6a), one Expectant Prefectural Magistrate (Rank 5a) and four Imperial Academy Studentships.

In 1907, the internal antagonisms of the clan began to appear. The Lis of Taihe tang split into one major branch and two minor branches. The land was divided up equally and the businesses managed jointly. Next, several of the younger generation lived degenerate lives and, after receiving their share of the property, quickly wasted it. Several of those who had managed the farming, usury, and businesses died. Finally the lands, which had taken so long to accumulate, became even more broken up because of equal inheritance.

Li Fang-cai and his successors of that generation began to pay more attention to the businesses and, apart from trying to hold onto the already shrinking number of shops they already had, they opened an old-clothes shop, a pawnshop, a money shop, and a salt shop, all of them small-scale. This was the last resurgence of the Taihe tang economy. After 1928, apart from one or two households who still held on to comparatively large amounts of land and lived off the exploitation of others, the remainder of the clan had practically all fallen to the level of small owner-peasants.

4.2 The Shujing Tang Bi Family[7]

The Shujing tang of Lijia village, Zichuan district, were managerial landlords who also ran a silk-weaving works.[8]

Lijia village is about 10 miles to the west of Zhoucun and 30 miles to the east of Jinan. To the north lies Mt. Baiyun and to the south lies Mt. Sigai, both about 6 miles away. Lijia village lies on a fairly open small plain. In 1840, Bi Yuan-rong (1814–1896), the head of the Shujing tang at that time, inherited his father's patrimony and set about extending it until he was managing about 900 mu of land besides running the Hengsheng silk-weaving workshop in addition to a felt-cap works. At its peak the family regularly employed 300 hired laborers (over 100 each in the silk workshop and in the cap works and about 70 or 80 on the farm).

The Process of Land Accumulation

From what we gathered from interviews, we understand it took four generations for the Shujing tang to accumulate 900 mu. In the early eighteenth century, they only had about 30 mu. During the late eighteenth century under the management of Bi Feng-lian (1754–1840), this had grown to more than 100 mu. His son Bi Ning-jie (1773–1840) increased this to 300 mu. The most successful manager in the family was Bi Ning-jie's son, Bi Yuan-rong, who built up the lands to over 900 mu. Around about 1904 [see Table 10], there were over 80 households and about 3,000 mu of land in Lijia village. At that time the Shujing tang owned about 600 mu of land or just less than one-fifth of the cultivated land of the village.

The Shujing tang's land accumulation was latterly **rather rapid**, and this was because the two handicraft workshops it operated steadily expanded and were closely integrated with the management of the farm.

Farm Management[9]

The Shujing tang rented out 300 mu in other villages, but it farmed the 600 mu of its land in Lijia village using hired labor.

Around about 1894, the Shujing tang hired over 30 long-term laborers, including a foreman and 20 subforemen, a herdsman, a shepherd, a swineherd, and 3 (female) cooks. In the busy seasons of spring, summer, and autumn, they hired an additional 50 or so short-term laborers and, at particularly busy ploughing or harvesting times, they would hire up to 120 short-term laborers.

The Shujing tang had comparatively complete production and transportation equipment.

Table 10

Landownership in Lijia Village, c. 1904

| | Landlords | | | | | |
	Shujing tang	Others	Rich peasants	Middle peasants	Poor peasants	Totals
Amount of land (in shimu)	600	50+	30–50	15–30	>15	3,000
Number of households	1	3	2	17	57	80

Source: Interviews.

Because they had sufficient capital and adequate labor, they could afford to spend over 20 work days on the cultivation of one mu, whereas ordinary peasants could at the very most only afford 15 work days. As far as we could ascertain, Shujing tang could accumulate annually over 200 cartloads of big manure (human excrement). Their 20 pigs, 10 oxen, and 100 sheep produced 7,000 cartloads of manure (each cartload weighing 400 jin). Since they had adequate supplies of manure, they were frequently able to make three applications: before the sowing they would put down a "bottom application," at the time of sowing they would put down a "furrow manure" (covering the seeds with fertilizer), and before the sprouting of the ears, they would put down a top dressing known as "encouraging the sprouts manure." They would use 10 or 15 cartloads of manure on each mu, while ordinary peasants were only able to use 5 to 6 cartloads.

Because of these advantages, the Shujing tang were able to plant 300 of their 600 mu to kaoliang, 200 mu to millet, and more than 80 mu to beans, and so forth. Furthermore, they were able to plant about 300 mu of wheat as a second crop. At that time, ordinary peasants in Lijia village had insufficient fertilizer and irrigation to be able to plant wheat. Yields per mu for the different crops on the Shujing tang lands were as follows: wheat, 300 jin;

kaoliang, 600 jin; millet, 600 jin; and beans, 300 jin. These yields were about twice as high as those on ordinary peasant lands. Using these yields, we can calculate roughly that, in an ordinary year, Shujing tang's agricultural production was 90,000 jin of wheat, 180,000 jin of kaoliang; 120,000 jin of millet, and 24,000 jin of beans, giving a total of 114,000 jin of fine grains (wheat, beans) and 300,000 jin of coarse grains (kaoliang, millet).

In those days, the price of fine grains such as wheat was more or less the same as the price of coarse grains such as kaoliang between the spring and autumn harvests. After the autumn harvest and before the spring harvest the price of fine grains was twice as high as that of coarse grains. Grain prices were comparatively low in autumn and winter and high in spring and summer. There was always at least a 100-percent difference between the year's highest and lowest prices. Apart from the grain that Shujing tang put aside for its own consumption, for the laborers, for seed-grain, and for animal feed, all the rest under normal conditions was sold at the Wangcun market in seasons when prices were at their highest. Here again, Shujing tang was able to make a larger profit than the peasants who were unable to sell their grain at the most advantageous times.

Conditions of Hired Laborers

Most of the Shujing tang short-term laborers were poor peasants owning between 3 and 7 mu of land. The laborers went to work with their own scythes, hoes, and so forth. Those whose tools were inadequate for the hirer's requirements had to use the hirer's tools at no reduction of their wage. The laborers relied mainly on the cultivation of their plots to support their families. Hiring themselves out as laborers in the busy seasons or acting as porters, selling fruit, and so on, were only secondary sources of income.

Some of the long-term laborers were members of the rural proletariat with no land at all, but some had become laborers because their family land was small and there was surplus labor. The long-term laborers always used Shujing tang's implements.

Table 11

Wages of Shujing Tang Laborers, c. 1904

Long-term laborers	Annual wage in cash	Equivalent in kind	Notes
Foreman	32,000	4 dan	The equivalent in kind
Subforeman	24,000	3 dan	in this table is worked
Herdsman	20,000	2.5 dan	out on the assumption
Shepherd	----	----	that one dou of *kaoliang*
Swineherd	8,000	1 dan	was worth 800 cash, 10
Muleteer	20,000	2.5 dan	dou to a dan, there being
Farmboys	4,000	0.5 dan	55 jin to a dou.
Cooks (female)	8,000	1 dan	

Short-term laborers	Daily wage in cash	Equivalent in kind	Notes
Day laborers	200	2.5 sheng	Same as above.

Source: Interviews.

They were free to start work and stop work as they chose, except in the busy seasons when the hirer would usually be unwilling to let them go.

The food of both long-term and short-term laborers was provided by Shujing tang and, in addition, their wages were sometimes paid in kind. Because wages, whether in cash or in kind, were so low [see Table 11], they were only enough to support the individual laborers, who were often unable to support a wife or children. Many never married because they were too poor.

The Hengsheng Silk-Weaving Workshop

The silk-weaving workshop managed by Shujing tang had gradually developed from a cottage side-industry into a handicraft factory. The course of this development was protracted and complex.[10]

As far as we could ascertain, about the middle of the eighteenth century a considerable number of "small-loom households" (independent weavers) had begun to appear around Lijia village. At that time Bi Yuan-rong's grandfather, Bi Feng-lian, was still a medium-sized, self-cultivating peasant, owning something less than 30 mu of land, from which he derived his main source of income. Seeing that the "small-loom households" were making quite a profit, Bi Feng-lian went one slack season to a nearby village and learned how to weave silk. Next he set up a "wooden loom" in his own household.

He had no workers helping him at this stage. The small quantities of silk cloth he was able to produce he carried to the market at Zhoucun and sold bit by bit to one of the silk piece-goods shops. There were lots of these shops in Zhoucun specializing in buying up the output of the "small-loom households." [See Chapter 1, Section 3 on the development of Zhoucun.]

We heard that, in order to get a good price for his goods, Bi Feng-lian would always carry his tussore to the market himself and go from door to door of the silk shops at the Zhoucun market, stopping outside each to shout at the top of his voice whether or not they were prepared to offer a better price. If there was an answer, he would go in, show the counterhand his cloth, and then begin to bargain about price.[11]

The business grew, and before long he had added a few more looms and was employing some workers. In the first half of the nineteenth century, he and his son Bi Ning-jie continued to operate the silk-weaving business until, by 1840, the year in which father and son both died, the Hengsheng silk-weaving workshop had 20 looms.

Thereafter, under the energetic management of Bi Yuan-rong over the course of the next sixty years, the business developed into a handicraft factory with 72 looms in 26 rooms employing over 100 workers and producing 300 bolts of silk per month.

The raw silk was mainly bought at Zhoucun where the oak-fed "wild" silk, produced in the districts of Tai-an, Feixian, Laiwu, Juxian, and Qixia could be bought. Of these, Tai-an silk was fine and suitable for the warp while that of Feixian district was somewhat coarse and suitable for the woof. The weavers of the whole district of Zichuan preferred these silks, and Hengsheng was no exception. If there was a shortage of silk at Zhoucun, they would sometimes go directly to Tai-an or Feixian to buy it. At the height of its prosperity, Hengsheng would buy over 360 bales of raw silk (each bale weighed 8 jin), and only then could uninterrupted production be assured.

After the raw silk was bought, it had to go through the four process of sorting (*xuansi*), spinning (*luosuo*), stretching (*qianshua*), and reeling (*raosui*) before it was ready for weaving. In order to produce its characteristic dyed tussore, Hengsheng also had a dye works attached.

At the height of its prosperity, Hengsheng employed 72 weavers, 22 workers for sorting, spinning, stretching and reeling, and 3 buyers. Monthly production depended on the skill of the weaver. An experienced weaver could produce one bolt in 3 days where an ordinary weaver would take 4 days. Less skilled workers might take 5 days. Since there were 72 weavers working on 72 looms, monthly production can be roughly calculated at about 300 bolts (each bolt was 5.6 zhang long and 1.6 chi wide).

In about 1894, the production costs of one bolt of silk were as follows:

Raw material	1,700 cash
Sorting (2 workers)	160 cash
Spinning, stretching (1 worker)	80 cash
Reeling (half a day's labor)	40 cash
Weaving (4 weavers)	500 cash
TOTAL	2,480 cash

Since the market price of one bolt at that time was 3,000 cash, there was a profit of 500 cash per bolt. [Estimated monthly profit, therefore, was around 300 X 500, equals 150 strings of cash (1 string = 1,000 cash).]

Most of the 97 workers at the Hengsheng silk workshop were

poor peasants from within a one-mile radius. Some were from families who had lost all their land, some had only 2 or 3 mu. The process of starting work was very simple. After an introduction by one of the old workers or a relative and acceptance by the manager, it was possible to start without any form of written contract. The head of the workshop had no personal hold over the workers, and there were no regulations in the workshop.

In the workshop, the weavers were called master, the young workers were called apprentices. With the head of the workshop's consent, master weavers could take on their own relatives as apprentices. There were no regulations regarding treatment of apprentices and no limit to the term of apprenticeship.

The owner did not provide food for the workers. Those who lived outside the village brought grain with them, and those who lived in the village went home to eat. At New Year's and festival times, the owner would invite the workers to have a drink. It should be noted that, although the agricultural laborers and the weavers were in the same economy, the laborers were paid cash wages in addition to their food, while the latter were paid entirely in cash.

In order to have a concrete understanding of the status and economic conditions of the workers at Hengsheng, we introduce the life of Nie Xing-de who worked there as a weaver for more than forty years.

Nie Xing-de was born in Hengsheng village in 1877. His family consisted of his mother and father, two elder brothers and their wives, two sisters, and one nephew, altogether no less than "a family of ten." They had only 1.8 mu of rented tomb land to culti-vate. In good years, they could harvest one dan (roughly 550 jin) of food grain; in ordinary years, just over half a dan; and in bad years, nothing at all.

Rent was one-half the amount harvested so that, in an ordinary year, his family was left with 3 or 4 dou of grain after paying the rent. Adults and children both consumed one dou of grain a month so that his family exhausted their total grain for a year in half a month. As a result the family could not rely on income from agri-culture but relied on working as laborers outside the family.

His father, himself, and his two elder brothers all worked at the Hengsheng silk works. His elder brothers wove 6 and 10 bolts a month respectively, and he wove 7 bolts. His father was skilled at stretching silk yarn and could prepare enough for 2 bolts a day. The wage for weaving one bolt was 500 cash and for stretching enough for one bolt, 80 cash. So the whole family earned roughly 15 strings of cash per month.

During the busy farming seasons, a day laborer could earn 70 or 80 more cash per day than a weaver, so the four of them would frequently go to a neighboring landlord and work as day laborers during the busy season.

At that time in the Hengsheng silk works, pay was according to the piece-rate system. So much cash for weaving one bolt, so much cash for stretching the silk yarn for one bolt, and so on. In addition, whenever a merchant buyer placed a large order with Hengsheng, the head of the works, in order to complete the order by the agreed time, would frequently spur on the weavers by offering "bonus money." Every worker who completed his fixed quota in advance would receive a certain amount of "bonus money" for each day saved. The weavers would often work the whole day without a rest, and, to gain the bonus, they would weave on into the night by the weak light of vegetable-oil lamps.

A weaver took 4 days to weave one bolt of silk for which he received 500 cash, so his daily wage came to 125 cash. The women silk-sorters took 2 days to sort the silk required for one bolt for which they received 160 cash (or 80 cash per day). It took half a day to stretch the silk yarn required to weave one bolt for which the workers received 80 cash (or 160 per day) and it took half a day to reel the silk required for one bolt for which the workers received 40 cash (or 80 cash per day).

The prices of grain and daily necessities at that time were 1,200 cash per dou of wheat, 900 cash per dou of *kaoliang,* 700 cash per dou of millet, 64 cash per jin of pork, 28 cash per jin of beancurd, and 67 cash per chi of coarse cloth.

If we take the Hengsheng weavers' highest possible earnings and compare them with the above commodity prices, we find that the price of their labor was very low. A weaver's daily wage was only the equivalent of 7.6 jin of kaoliang (taking the price of kaoliang in the same village in February 1957 of 8 cents per jin, they would have received 60 cents a day in present-day money), or the equivalent of 1.8 chi of coarse cotton (taking the February 1957 price in the same village of 22 cents a chi, they would have received a wage of 41 cents a day in present-day money). A woman silk-sorter's wage would have bought 5 jin of kaoliang (equivalent to 40 cents in today's money) or 1.2 chi of coarse cotton (equivalent to 26 cents in today's money).

4.3 The Jinxiu Tang Meng Family[12]

The Mengs were one of the large clans of Jiujun market town, Zhangqiu district. In 1369, their ancestors migrated here from Zaoqiang district in Hebei. By 1892, this clan had grown to include 308 constituent families. By calculation from the stele which recorded contributions to the repairing of the Meng ancestral hall, the clan included at least 90 poor tenant families, 140 middle peasant families, 40 rich peasant families, over 20 small- and medium-sized landlords, and 10 large landlords. At the end of the Qing era when people referred to the "Mengs of Jiujun," they were usually referring either to the Jinxiu tang or to the Jinshu tang, both of whom were reckoned among the 10 big landlords of the clan.

Besides possessing large amounts of land, Jinxiu tang and Jinshu tang also ran a number of businesses with the word "xiang" in their names which were famous throughout the country. Both families were typical large merchant landlords. We begin by introducing the data we gathered on Jinxiu tang.

Land Accumulation, Farm Management, and Yields

From the beginning of the eighteenth century, Jinxiu tang had specialized in agriculture at the same time as running businesses. There were five generations between Meng Yu-qi and Meng Zhao-bing, and the family properties had passed from single son to single son in each generation. At the beginning of the twentieth century, Jinxiu tang possessed 1,050 mu of land, of which there were 600 mu in Jiujun and more than 300 mu in Shunguan village (about 13 miles away), as well as over 150 mu in Shuizhai market town (about 2 miles away), and other villages.

Most of their land in Jiujun was farmed with hired labor (450 mu). The remaining 150 mu as well as their land in other villages was let out to tenants. At the beginning of the twentieth century, Jinxiu tang employed 37 long-term laborers, who were responsible for transport of rent crops and firewood, the rearing of farm animals, the supervision of the short-term laborers, and so forth. In the busy farming seasons, they often hired over 50 short-term laborers. They had all their own farm implements as well as 6 heavy carts and more than 70 mules and horses which were used for ploughing, transport, manure, and mounts. They did not keep pigs, oxen, or sheep. They had plenty of fertilizer, every year collecting over 1,000 cartloads of mule and horse dung (each cartload weighed 2,000 jin).

On the lands cultivated by Jinxiu tang using hired laborers, the yields per mu were higher than those of the average poor tenant, as can be seen in the following table:

Table 12

Comparison of Yields on Jinxiu Tang Land
and on Poor Tenant Land, c. 1904
Unit = jin per mu

	Wheat	Kaoliang	Millet	Maize
Jinxiu tang	200–230	200–240	330–400	170–230
Poor tenant	80–100	120–170	170–230	120–135

Source: Interviews.

Laborers and Tenants

The wages of the laborers were very low. Their wages apart from food are shown in Table 13.

The condition of Jinxiu tang's tenantry may be seen in the

Table 13

Annual Wages of Jinxiu Tang Laborers, c. 1904

	Foreman	Sub-foreman	Farm boy	Female servants
Long-term laborers	24 strings	16 strings	8 strings	6 strings
Equivalent value in *kaoliang*	1,015 jin	677 jin	338.5 jin	253.8 jin
Short-term laborers' day wage	500 to 1,000 cash (standard wage in the busy season)			1,500 cash (highest wage in busy season)
Equivalent value in *kaoliang*		21.15 to 42.3 jin		63.45 jin

Notes: 1) Long- and short-term laborers received their daily food from Jinxiu tang. The short-term laborers were given three meals a day. At each meal they got 5 biscuits, one bowl of cereal (always coarse grains), and half a bowl of vegetables. Breakfast and lunch were eaten in the fields, and the evening meal was taken in the stable yard. After the evening meal they received their cash wages.

2) The *kaoliang* equivalents in the table have been worked out on the basis of the 1904 price of 1,300 cash per dou (55 jin).

Source: Interviews.

example of Gao Qing-yu (1910). Since his arrival at the age of twenty-nine in Jiujun he had been a tenant of Jinxiu tang's for forty-one years and had rented 18 mu of land (12 mu of good land and 6 mu of swamp land). Rent was payable after the wheat harvest in the fourth or fifth month and in the autumn. The rent for the good land was 74 jin and for the swampy land 54 jin, roughly 40 percent of the crop. He grew 6 mu of maize, 6 mu of *kaoliang,* 4 mu of millet, and 2 mu of beans and other crops. In the summer, he planted 6 mu to a second crop of wheat. There were two people in his family. To start with, he had no implements and had to borrow, but he was gradually able to save and buy his own tools, and keep an ox which he shared for ploughing with others. When he had any free time, he hired himself out as a short-term laborer. In good years he was just able to keep from starving, but even this was not guaranteed in bad years.

Both short-term laborers and tenants were only barely able to provide for one person. Despite the fact that the farm laborers raised the yields on the landlord's land, their wages remained very low, which shows that the landlord appropriated the product of their surplus labor, quite apart from eating into their subsistence. As for the tenants, they had no means of increasing the yields on their land because of the high rents they had to pay. The rents received by the landlord here too represented the extraction of the product of the surplus labor of the tenants as well as of the product necessary for survival.

Business Activities

The businesses with the word "xiang" [good fortune] in their names included "Qianxiang," "Longxiang," "Hongxiang," "Liuhexiang," and so forth. They dealt mainly in silk and cotton, tea, and glassware.

There was a story in the village that the Peking branch of the Qianxiang store had opened in the Kangxi period [1662–1722] that the Kangxi Emperor himself had gone to the second floor of the shop to buy goods, and that after this event the store had become very famous and had constructed a stairway for imperial use; so everyone said that the "power of Qianxiang reaches as high as heaven."

Another story had it that the **Qianlong Emperor** [1736–1796] was out on an inspection, that all the shops had closed up their store fronts according to the regulations for the imperial passage, but that the Qianxiang shop had not yet closed up by the time the emperor passed it. When the emperor noticed, he merely said, "What a magnificent store." From that time on, when the emperor went on inspection, Qianxiang was excused from closing up shop.

While not completely reliable, these stories at least show that, already in the Kangxi period (1662–1722), Qianxiang had established a branch in Peking and that, by the eighteenth century, the store had grown considerably.

Qianxiang had originally begun business in Zhoucun and had then gradually established branches throughout the country until, by the early twentieth century, it had a wholesale branch in Jinan, two retail stores in Peking, two in Tianjin, three in Hankou, and one in Qingdao. It had also set up a wholesale foreign goods store in Shanghai as well as ordinary wholesale stores in Maozhou, specializing in Tianzi and Dizi range coarse cotton. The scale of Qianxiang's stores was very large as is shown by the fact that the three Qianxiang Hankou branches employed 200 shop clerks in the west store, 100 in the Hengji, and 20 in the Lao wholesale store. It was said at the time (1900) that the daily takings of the Qianxiang businesses were over 1,000 dollars.

During the same time period, Longxiang silk cloth company established three retail stores in Jinan, and the Hongxiang Tea Company had two branches in Jinan and one in Zhoucun.

Conspicuous Consumption

At the beginning of the twentieth century, there were only 4 people in the Jinxiu tang family but they lived in 6 spacious courtyards. Apart from agricultural laborers, they employed 3 bookkeepers, 3 cooks, 8 carters, 8 serving women, 8 maids, 3 gardeners, 2 doctors of Chinese medicine, 5 carpenters, 1 barber, 1 tailor, and 8 guards and escorts, for a total of 54 people.

They had set up a pharmacy in Jinan, and the Hongxiang Tea to prepare medicine for the family.

They had also established a large private park in Jiujun in which were kept peacocks, cranes, Mongolian larks, monkeys, and so forth, and in which were cultivated many rare and precious plants and flowers.

Apart from the birthday celebrations of each of the four members of the family, each Chinese New Year they celebrated with the managers and shop assistants from all of the "xiang" chain of businesses together with the household servants. These celebrations would continue for four or five days and would include all varieties of regional theatricals. The scale of the family's waste became even larger under the Republic. In 1924, they installed a diesel electric generator and other electrical equipment exclusively for family use.

Chapter 5

FIELD DATA ON TWO RENTIER LANDLORDS

In order to provide some means of comparison with the managerial landlords, we investigated the economic and social conditions of two rentier landlord families. One were the Jinshu tang Mengs of Jiujun market town in Zhangqiu district (like the Jinxiu tang Mengs they were counted among the ten big landlord families of the Meng clan), and the other were the Yu tang Suns (owners of the Yu tang Condiment Works in Jining).

5.1 The Jinshu Tang Meng Family[1]
The Jinshu tang had originated at the division of the Qiangxue branch of the Meng clan. It was in 1854 that the Qiangxue had divided into four families (one of which was the Jinshu tang) and each family had received 240 mu (including 6½ mu with buildings on them). Between 1854 and 1911, the Jinshu tang had bought up a large amount of land, totaling 2,140 mu of which 2,095½ mu were cultivated and 44½ mu were uncultivated land. Of these, 1,140 mu were cotton fields within the boundaries of Zouping district, which had been acquired just after 1898 in 7 or 8 villages around E village. [The course of accumulation of these lands is not tabulated in the original.] The remaining 1,000 mu were in Zhangqiu district (450 mu in Jiujun market town and the remaining 550 mu in neighboring villages). Their acquisition is shown in Tables 14 to 17. After 1912, Jinshu tang acquired a further 162 mu in Zhangqiu district [see Table 18] as well as 10.8 mu of non-cultivatable land [see Table 17].
Apart from the considerable amounts bought from landlords such as Ansu tang, Legeng tang, Chengshun tang, and others who had fallen on hard times, the greater part of all of this land was bought from owner-peasants who were in difficulties.

Estate Management
Except of a small amount of the land in Jiujun market town that was planted to vegetables for family consumption and farmed

138

Table 14

Accumulation of Jinshu Tang's Inherited Land, 1718–1850

Date of acquisition	Original owner	Acreage (shimu)
11/1718	Meng Ke-ren Meng Ke-jing	1.625
12/1731	Meng Sheng-ce	1.154
5/1736	Meng Shang-zhao	1.848
7/1838	Zhao Ke-lian	9.391
7/1838	Zhao Ke-lian	9.000
11/1842	Zhenxiu tang Li	5.296
1/1843	Lejing tang Meng	14.329
2/1843	Kunliu tang Zhao	2.127
11/1843	Ansu tang	15.291
10/1845	Meng Zhao-hui	13.985
3/1847	Li Zhao-ji	1.718
3/1847	Li Zhao-ji	1.456
3/1850	Zhao Bing-yi	3.148
SUB-TOTAL		80.368
3/1756 (outside of Jiujun)	Meng Shi-xiang	7.872
3/1764 (outside of Jiujun)	Meng Ke-lian	15.970
1/1843 (outside of Jiujun)	Jide tang	14.951
--- (outside of Jiujun)	---	37.867
--- (outside of Jiujun)	---	approx. *78.000
SUB-TOTAL		154.660
GRAND TOTAL		235.028

*Original source gives no details of where this land came from but, according to Meng Guang-he, this represents ¼ of 320 mu of inherited land.

Source: Jinshu tang land accounts.

with hired labor, Jinshu tang's 2,140 mu were all rented out.

According to the details recorded in Jinshu tang land account books, we find that its land was situated in the following villages around Jiujun market town (distance from Jiujun given in parenthe-

Table 15

Jinshu Tang Land Accumulation (in Jiujun), 1854–1911

Date of acquisition	Original owner	Acreage (shimu)
2/1854	Zhensi tang Liu	3.870
12/1858	Meng Ji-wan	16.697
3/1871	Li Yi-qing	1.705
12/1879	Zhao Wen-jin Zhao Wen-quan	1.316
12/1879	Renshu tang Shoushan tang	1.500
12/1879	Meng Pan-shi	2.790
1879	---	18.538
9/1883	Li Jia-dong	1.871
5/1885	Li Wen-xiang	1.890
6/1885	Meng Ji-quan	1.489
12/1894	Meng Qing-shui	7.083
1/1896	Qiru tang	1.036
9/1899	Li Xi-xing	1.357
9/1899	Li Wen-ming	0.499
9/1899	Meng Xuan-mu	3.915
12/1899	Li Jeng-zhi etc	0.467
4/1900	Zhunzhen tang Meng	3.475
11/1900	Zhao Yan-wu	2.163
12/1900	Bureau of Public Safety	2.455
12/1901	Li Shu-yü	0.468
4/1906	Hui Yu-xing	6.372
10/1907	Qiu Tian-yuan	2.896
TOTAL		83.852

Source: Jinshu tang land accounts.

ses: Xin (1 mile), Qianjing (13 miles), Mingshui (15 miles), Sunguan (13 miles), Zhangqiu district town (6 miles), Wangsi (1½ miles), Zhangjia (3 miles), and in Zouping district, E (10 miles) [In the translation I have not given the exact location of each piece of land, which information the authors included in Tables 14 to 18.]

Table 16

Jinshu Tang Land Accumulation (outside Jiujun), 1854–1911

Date of acquisition	Original owner	Acreage (shimu)
10/1857	Zhao Wen-shi	5.974
10/1857	Zhao Wen-shi	26.484
12/1901	Xinyi tang Lü	9.767
10/1904	Li Ma-hou etc	1.738
2/1908	Leyu tang	3.276
2/1908	Leyu tang	35.348
2/1908	Leyu tang	145.299
2/1908	Leyu tang	3.307
2/1908	Leyu tang	9.857
2/1908	Leyu tang	19.313
2/1908	Leyu tang	5.614
1909	Jiao Qi-sheng	3.000
1909	Ci Yong-han	3.640
1909	Wang Ji-gong	2.401
1909	Zhao Jun-cheng	4.353
1909	Gao Yu-kun	3.467
1909	Liu Guang-sheng	4.349
1909	Gao Nai-zhu	8.938
1909	Hu Ji-jin	5.933
1909	Shi Si-bao	3.000
1909	Zhao Zhen-yuan	3.318
1909	Qiao Nian-jiao	4.559
1909	Qiao Nian-jiao	3.094
1909	Qiao Nian-jiao	4.453
1909	Xinshang tang Hui	6.724
1909	Guo Tai-wu	3.036
1909	Lü Shan-yi	11.744
1909	Chengshun tang	21.980
1909	Chengshun tang	24.364
1909	Chengshun tang	8.449
1909	Chengshun tang	51.505
1909	Chengshun tang	105.759
1909	Chengshun tang	4.400
1911	Qiao Fang-zhao	12.526
1911	Qiao Fang-zhao	5.964

Table 16 (cont.)

Date of acquisition	Original owner	Acreage (shimu)
1911	Qiao Fang-zhao	4.455
1911	Liu Chang-ling	3.495
1911	Kejian tang Gao	25.858
TOTAL		610.741

Source: Jinshu tang land accounts.

Rent was paid according to fixed quotas in kind; tenants paid in wheat, millet, kaoliang, corn, beans, or rice or cotton depending upon what they planted. Rent in food crops was mainly used by Jinshu tang for family consumption, while the cotton was sold as a commercial crop.

The amount of rent was fixed according to the quality of the land and varied between one and two dou per mu (1 dou = 54 jin). It was payable in two installments, spring and autumn. Brushwood and hay were equally divided between landlord and tenant. Rent on cotton fields was 50 percent of the crop, cotton stalks being retained by the tenant. In this period in this region of Shandong, average yield of cotton per shimu was 100 to 130 jin, and so the annual rent came to approximately 50 to 65 jin. The state land tax was payable by Jinshu tang.

After the autumn harvest, Jinshu tang's accountant would go round the fields of the tenants farming food crops and collect the rent. To collect the rent of those tenants farming cotton in Zouping district, Ruifuxiang Company and Quanxiang Company of Jinan would send employees out to set up a "rent collection hut" in the fields where they would assess the rent according to the size of the harvest.

According to a document of c. 1900 recording subscriptions to a dike works, lands let out by Jinshu tang in Jiujun were as follows in Table 20.

When he rented the land, a tenant had to show "submission" to the landlord's accountant before the signing of the contract. The

Table 17

Jinshu Tang Land Accumulation
(non-cultivatable lands, that is orchards, building land, etc.)

Date of acquisition	Original owner	Type of land	Acreage (shimu)
3/1844	Huaide tang	Orchard	0.817
3/1844	Meng Ji-zou	Vegetable garden	1.633
5/1846	Meng Ji-zou	Building land	1.746
12/1846	Legeng tang Meng	Gardens	2.313
Sub-total			6.509
3/1858	Meng Qing-du	---	0.380
3/1874	Meng Zhao-cheng	Building	2.082
2/1875	Meng Zhao-xian's wife	Building	1.773
11/1879	Meng Ji-shi	Vegetable garden	5.462
11/1879	Meng Ji-shi	Hut	0.275
8/1888	Cheng Dian-wu	Building	0.355
8/1888	Fushou tang Li	Recreation park	0.518
12/1888	Li Shu-nian	Gardens	1.427
11/1891	Li Shu-wang	Vegetable garden	0.784
7/1894	Li Nai-fang	Building	0.391
12/1899	Shigu tang Meng	Building	1.166
11/1905	Meng Xuan-rao	Vegetable garden	4.529
6/1911	Meng Guang-long	Vegetable garden	0.844
7/1903	Huairen tang Zhang	Shop building	1.003
3/1911	Chenshun tang	House	6.961
Sub-total			27.950
3/1916	Juye tang	Recreation garden	1.662
11/1918	Leying tang	Recreation garden	2.280
6/1919	Qiru tang	Building	0.480
12/1920	Meng Zhao-le	Recreation garden	2.448
3/1921	Meng Xuan-xing	Building	0.896
12/1921	Liuye tang	Building	2.502
9/1922	Huairen tang Zhang	Shop building	0.577
Sub-total			10.845
TOTAL			45.304

Source: Jinshu tang land accounts.

Table 18

Jinshu Tang Land Accumulation (after 1912)

Date of acquisition	Original owner	Acreage (shimu)
2/1916	Li Fu-hou	4.874
2/1916	Zhenyu tang Kang	1.505
2/1916	Guoren tang Kang	7.341
2/1916	Guoren tang Kang	2.877
10/1915	Yang Mian-ting	9.325
4/1920	Liuye tang	17.376
9/1920	Jingde tang Ma	4.012
9/1920	Jingde tang Ma	3.763
2/1924	Ligeng tang	3.881
10/1927	Juye tang	39.559
11/1931	Hong Xiang	11.307
3/1935	Gongshu tang	34.870
8/1935	Chengyi tang Cheng	14.946
8/1935	Chengyi tang Cheng	7.007
TOTAL		162.673

Source: Jinshu tang land accounts.

Table 19

Landownership in Jiujun in 1912[2]
(Unit = shimu)

	Landlords		Rich peasants	Middle peasants	Poor laborers	Total
	Jinshu tang	Others				
Amount of land (shimu)	450	60–450	45–60	15–45	>15	11,400
Number of households	1	99	100	400	700	1,300

Source: Interviews.

Table 20

Land Rented by Jinshu Tang Tenants in Jiujun, c. 1900

Place	Area (shimu)	Tenant
Jiujun market town	28.0	Yan Qing-mao
Jiujun market town	8.0	Li Xu-kang
Jiujun market town	18.5	Li Shu-ying
Jiujun market town	16.5	Li Jia-zhi; Li wen-cheng; Meng Zhao-xing
Jiujun market town	3.5	Meng Lang-mo
Jiujun market town	7.0	Guo Yan-ling
Jiujun market town	3.0	Li Jian-tai
Jiujun market town	6.0	Yu An-zhi
Xin village	15.0	Wang Guang-rong
Xin village	30.0	Guo Siqian; Guo Han-biao; Wang Ting-fang; Wang Xi-tai
Wangsi village	37.5	Guo Feng-ming
Jiujun market town	4.0	Que Wan-tong

contract stipulated the amount of rent and the date by which it had to be paid. Once the rent was fixed, the tenant had to produce that amount by the stipulated time whether or not there were natural or man-made disasters and whether or not he had a good harvest. There was no limit to the amount of land let to any one tenant; he could cultivate it himself or cultivate it with someone else. The tenant provided his own implements and was responsible also for providing fertilizer.

Jinshu tang's tenants were mainly former small owner-peasants who had fallen on hard times. Others had been long-term laborers for Jinshu tang and, having come to some arrangement with the accountant, they would borrow tools, seeds, animals, housing, and land from the landlord and become tenants. Still others were small owner-peasants whose land was too small to support them. As a result, they rented land from Jinshu tang while still retaining their own land. They thus had dual status as tenants and small owners.

On the production side, a single farmer, given the conditions of the Jiujun area and given support from his family with cooking, rearing pigs, collecting manure, and so forth, working full-time could cultivate about 15 mu. But most tenants did not rent this much. Because of the exploitative rents and such factors as inadequate fertilizer and lack of animal power, which led to poor yields, the standard of living of the tenants was shockingly low. As far as we could ascertain, the yields on the lands rented by tenants for dry-land cultivation were as follows:

Maize	110–135 jin per mu
Kaoliang	110–165 jin per mu
Millet	165–230 jin per mu
Beans	110–135 jin per mu
Cotton	35–135 jin per mu

It can be calculated that, if each tenant owned 5 mu of his own and rented a further 10 mu, then he could harvest between 2,000 and 3,000 jin of food crops. From this would have to be subtracted between 550 and 850 jin for rent, 150 jin for seed grain, 50 jin for repairs and purchase of tools, and so on. This would leave an actual income in food grain of between 1,250 and 1,950 jin. Taking an average family as having five members, each eating 30 jin a month, such an income would be inadequate to feed the family, let alone leave enough over to meet the expenses of clothes, housing, education, medicine, marriages, funerals, and so forth.

If the tenant rented 10 mu and harvested 1,330 jin every year, paid 550 jin in rent, laid aside 100 jin for seed, 200 jin for fertilizer, 35 jin for repairs of tools, and so forth, and 360 jin for his own consumption while working in the fields, then the exploitation ratio of the landlord can be worked out as follows:

$$\frac{550}{1,330 - 100 - 200 - 35 - 360} = \frac{550}{1,330 - 695} = \frac{550}{635} = 86.6\%$$

Under these conditions, it was extremely difficult for the tenant to increase his production.

Commercial Activities

An earlier generation of Jinshu tang had already, in the first
half of the eighteenth century, set up two miscellaneous goods
stores in Laiwu district town (Zhengxiang and Chengxiang were
their respective names) and at the same time had also set up a
miscellaneous goods store in Xintai district town called Ruilinxiang.
At the very beginning of the nineteenth century, before the division
of family property, Qiangxue tang had set up a miscellaneous goods
store in Peking and Jinan called Ruishengxiang, another called
Qingxiang in Jinan and Tianjin, and a cotton cloth store in Jiujun
market town called Hongji with a branch in Zhoucun, specializing
in the buying and selling of the rough cotton cloth of Zhangqiu,
Zouping, and Qidong (usually called Zhaizi cotton cloth after the
main production center). In the mid-nineteenth century, the
manager of Jinshu tang, Meng Ji-sheng, withdrew his capital from
Shengxiang and Qingxiang stores and set up Ruifuxiang silk
cloth store and Quanxiang tea store in Jinan. Later Ruifuxiang
opened two branches in Jinan, three branches in Tianjin, two in
Peking, and one each in Yantai and Qingdao. The family also opened
a wholesale goods store in Shanghai specializing in foreign cloth and
silk piece-goods. It was said that the annual net profit of Ruifuxiang
was in the region of 3 million taels. During the same period, the
Quanxiang tea store set up two branches in Jinan and Tianjin and
one each in Peking, Yantai, and Qingdao. In addition, a special
wholesale buying branch was established in Fuzhou. Of the "xiang"
companies set up by Jinshu tang, the Ruifuxiang and the Quanxiang
were the most profitable. At the end of the Qing period and the
beginning of the Republic, feudal warlords and officials deposited
the cash and silver they had squeezed from the people with the
Ruifuxiang, because of its "deep roots" and "reliability" (*xinyong*)!
As a result, the Ruifuxiang set up a banking department specializing
in deposits from warlords and officials. Using these as capital, they
began to deal in gold in Peking and Shanghai. During the 1914–
1918 war when the price of gold fell to 18 dollars an ounce, Meng
Ji-sheng seized his chance and bought gold as fast as he could. After

the war the price of gold rose again and Meng was able to sell at over 50 dollars an ounce, making a tremendous profit of 160,000 dollars.

Political Life

One of Jinshu tang's most important managers, Meng Chuan-shan (born 1820), had bought the title of Expectant Secretary of the Imperial Patent Office, Additional Grade Three. His eldest son, Meng Ji-fu, had purchased the title of Expectant First Class Sub-Prefect, Additional Grade Five. His next son, Meng Rui-zhen, had bought the title of Salt Controller with the Rank of Expectant Prefect, Additional Grade Five. His fourth son, Meng Ji-sheng (1851–1937), had bought in 1893 the title of Expectant Daotai of Jiangsu with Button of the Third Rank. In 1912 he had been made head of the Jinan merchant guild with a monthly salary of 600 dollars. In 1915 he had been very active in support of Yuan Shi-kai's restoration of the monarchy. It was said that the imperial coronation robes Yuan had worn when he made himself emperor were a gift from Meng Ji-sheng.

Although they had bought a few so-called "honors," in practice the Mengs were only concerned with commerce and were not the slightest bit interested in study. It was said that the head of the family of Jinshu tang would brag, "There's no point in our studying; the poor kids have already done it for us."

For several decades, the large landlords of Jiujun had controlled the district government of Zhangqiu. In the early years of the Republic when a "Zhangqiu district fiscal and production area" was set up under the prefectural government, Meng sent one of his men to get control of it. At that time, Meng Hua-feng was the head of Zhangqiu district no. 2 zone and concurrently the head of the Public Security Corps. There was a jingle in Zhangqiu at the time, "Public Security Corps, Public Security Corps, Why does the whole district contribute when the money is only used to secure the private garden of the Mengs of Jiujun!"

Conspicuous Consumption

On the consumption side, there was a general accounting office in the family which calculated the interest rates of the various businesses and also directed the collecting of the rents. In addition, there were three sub-accounting offices to supervise the family income and expenditure. There was also a family office to encourage the children to study and a pharmacy to provide medicine for the family.

The family had two flower gardens covering 30 mu of land. Each of the children had his own horse-drawn sedan cart. There were large numbers of servants in the family: 6 or 7 carters, 4 or 5 stable hands, over 20 serving girls, 5 or 6 maids, 5 or 6 carpenters, several dozen masons, 3 or 4 gardeners, 4 or 5 accountants, 4 or 5 cooks, 2 doctors, a school teacher, 6 or 7 handymen, and over 20 armed guards.

Marriages, funerals, birthdays, and festivals were celebrated on an extremely lavish scale. For birthdays for senior family members, they would frequently invite a famous Peking opera company to come down to Jiujun and put on an opera in the family hall. The family itself had a large collection of theatrical properties and costumes. At one funeral over 40 bonzes were invited to see the corpse on its way and over 2,000 guests were entertained. From these and similar details, we got some idea of the scale of the conspicuous consumption of the Jinshu tang.

5.2 The Yu Tang Sun Family[3]

The Yu tang Suns were a big official landlord family of Jining prefecture during the Qing dynasty. Two members of the family were included in the *Draft History of the Qing.* One was Sun Yuting (1753–1834), who was a metropolitan graduate of 1775 and had held a series of high posts culminating in the Governor-generalship of Jiangxi, Jiangsu, and Anhui (a post he held for nine years while concurrently acting as a grand councillor). The other was his grandson, Sun Yu-wen (?–1899), who was a metropolitan graduate of 1856 and eventually rose to be the President of the Zongli Yamen and finally President of the Board of War (in 1893).

During the eighteenth and nineteenth centuries, the family owned over 30,000 mu, besides operating the Yu tang soybean products manufactory (*jiangyuan*).

Land Accumulation and Estate Management

According to the genealogy of the Suns, the family had migrated to Jining at the end of the sixteenth and beginning of the seventeenth centuries. The genealogy records that Sun Ying-zhou, towards the end of the Ming dynasty, was able to "make a contribution towards military maneuver expenses," so was already a considerable landowner. During the upheavals at the fall of the Ming dynasty, he lost all his property and fled. Later "he returned to his original home and rebuilt his house and, by using his own efforts, just managed to raise himself to the level of middle householder" (*zhongren*). In other words, the family had now fallen into the rich peasant stratum. In the mid-eighteenth century under Sun Ying-zhou's great grandson, Sun Kuo-tu, "the family became ever poorer." But, given the fact that Kuo-tu was able to "converse endlessly" with the so-called literati of the day, the family were now landlords fallen on hard times.[4] By the beginning of the nineteenth century, when Sun Kuo-tu's son, Sun Yu-ting, became a high official, the family began to accumulate land around the area of Dushan Lake and amassed 30,000 mu altogether. In the second half of the nineteenth century when Yu-ting's grandson, Sun Yuwen, was a grand councillor, they forceably bought 6,000 mu around the village of Cuijiaqiao in Yutai district.

Most of the Suns' land was bought from big landlords who had fallen on hard times. It was said that the land around Dushan Lake was of poor quality and could only support one harvest of wheat per year. Had they only bought a few mu at a time, they would have been unable to find tenants to let it to. It was only by buying huge quantities at a time that they were able to let it out and make a profit.

The Yu tang Suns' land was scattered in several districts

including Jining, Yutai, Jinxiang, and Qufu. None of it was farmed directly, all of it being rented out.

At that time, tenants had to enter into written contractual relations with landlords. Most of the tenants who first came to the Sun lands were destitute peasants, so that the landlord, apart from lending housing to the tenants, also lent them oxen, implements, and seeds in order to ensure production. All these loaned goods had to be returned, and with interest. The contract was drawn up at a time when the tenants were threatened with starvation, so they had to accept these terms.

As far as we could ascertain, the Suns exacted rents in kind which were fixed at 50 percent of the harvest.

The annual yields per mu of the tenants at Cuijiaqiao were 100 to 150 jin of wheat, and the same amounts for *kaoliang*. Out of this they had to pay between 50 to 75 jin of the spring harvest (wheat) in rent and 50 to 75 jin of the autumn harvest (*kaoliang*). They could only have made at best a precarious living out of the remainder, but they still had to pay off what they owed the landlord for the tools, oxen, and seeds. Even after a few years' labor they would still have practically nothing to support their families with.

The Yu Tang Soybean Products Manufactory

The Yu tang soy manufactory of Jining was founded in the eighteenth century. At that time it belonged to a Mr. Dai from Suzhou. It was only a temporary three-room street-front stall and was called Dai Yu tang. Shortly after its foundation, it was bought by Sun Yu-ting through the good services of a certain Mr. Leng, and it became jointly operated by the Suns and Lengs. The people of Jining referred to it as the Sun Yu tang.

At the very end of the eighteenth century, the Suns and Lengs had a capital investment of 40,000 strings in the business. By the end of the nineteenth century, this sum had risen to 100,000 strings. In the 1900s the Leng family left the business and it came into the sole ownership of the Suns. At this time it was worth 100,000 silver dollars, and by 1922 this figure had increased to 600,000 strings.[5]

The manufactory was at its most flourishing in the early years of this century, employing nearly 400 wage laborers (including masters, foremen, subforemen, temporary workers, and managers).[6] The organization was highly complex. On the management side, there was a head office, accounting office, general office, buying department, marketing and miscellaneous goods departments, sauce departments, cash departments, and so forth. On the production side, there was a soy-pickling room, salt-pickling room, hot-sauce room, liquor-fermenting room, soy-sauce room, oil room, vinegar room, and a room for making bamboo baskets.

To each room was assigned a set number of skilled workers and assistants, making each room, in effect, an independent and specialized "workshop." In the course of production, most of the workers undertook similar tasks, working interchangeably, the division of labor not being very obvious. But to a certain extent there was overall coordination of production.

In the open stock yard, there were frequently as many as 5,000 vats of pickled vegetables. More than 16 types of wine and 68 types of pickled vegetables were produced. They were marketed not only throughout Shandong but also in Henan, Zhili, Anhui, Jiangsu, and other provinces.

In the first decades of this century, the Yu tang manufactory annually bought over 5,000 dan of grains (1 dan = 550 jin), 400,000 jin of vegetables, 300,000 jin of eating salt, and 200,000 jin of coal. Total outgoings were 200,000 dollars. After all expenses were deducted, there was an annual profit of 40,000 to 50,000 dollars. There was a saying in the district: "Sell soy if you want to get rich or turn stone to gold and open a pharmacy." The Yu tang soy manufactory was clearly a profitable business!

Status and Wages of Yu Tang Workers

The Yu tang soy manufactory's wage laborers were divided between long-term workers (masters, foremen, subforemen, and so forth) and apprentices. Most of them were landless or near-landless peasants who had come to the town and, having no other means of support, had come to work at Yu tang through the introduction of relatives or friends. Apprentices received no wages but were given food and head-shaving money (*titouqian*). Newly hired workers had to serve as apprentices for several years before being promoted to short-term laborers. These had no fixed wage but picked up the wages of the long-term laborers when they substituted for those who had not come to work. A very considerable proportion of Yu tang workers were, in fact, short-term laborers. Before becoming long-term laborers, they had to have worked for many years. Long-term laborers had a fixed monthly wage and at the end of each year also received a bonus or, as the workers themselves put it, they got "cash for the New Year celebrations."

To give a concrete idea of the origins and livelihood of the Yu tang workers, we record the results of our interviews with three of them.

1) Sun Shu-yu (born 1888), from Yutai district. At the turn of the century, his family numbered four: his father and mother, younger sister, and himself. They had no land. When he was twelve, the whole family begged for a living. At fifteen, he began working for a landlord. When he was eighteen, his father died, and his mother and sister wandered from place to place. At twenty he became an apprentice in the vinegar works of Yu tang. He had no wages and received only his food. Four years later, having become a short-term worker, he began to earn "substitute," money but he could only make 50 cash a day and was unable to support his mother and sister. At thirty, he was promoted to long-term laborer with a monthly wage of 2 strings of cash (2,000 cash). Gradually this rose to 3 strings. This was only just enough to clothe himself, and he was still unable to support his mother and sister. Because of his extreme poverty, he was never able to marry.

2) Yang Qing-yun (born 1895), from Jining prefectural town. In about 1900, his family numbered four: his mother, his wife, a younger sister, and himself. They had no land. At twenty-four, he became an apprentice in the pickling works of Yu tang. Later he became a long-term worker with a monthly wage of one string of cash which was not enough even to support himself, let alone his wife and children. They could only scrape together a meager living in the town.

3) Dong Sheng-ren (born 1895), from Jining. In about 1900, his family numbered seven people: his mother and father, his elder brother and wife, two younger brothers, and himself. They owned 10 mu of land. Since the family had spare labor, at the age of twenty he went to become an apprentice in the Yu tang liquor-fermenting works. In 1917, he was earning a monthly wage of 3 strings of cash, which was totally inadequate to support the family. At that time the family relied upon his father's and elder brother's work on their land as well as the wages they were able to earn as short-term agricultural laborers.

Map 2: <u>Regions of Shandong</u>

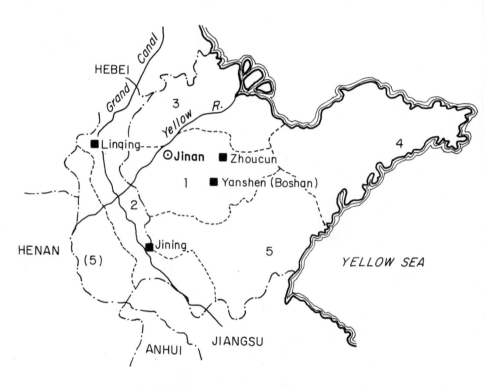

1 Jinan-Zhovcun region (central Shandong)
2 Grand Canal region
3 North Shandong region
4 Shandong promontory region
5 West and south Shandong region

Chapter 6

FIELD DATA ON 131 MANAGERIAL LANDLORDS

In order to ascertain whether or not managerial landlords similar to the Taihe tang, Shujing tang, and Jinxiu tang described above in Sections 4.1, 4.2, and 4.3 were widespread in Shandong at the end of the Qing dynasty, we collected materials on the class structure at that time of 197 rural villages in Shandong scattered in 42 of the total 49 districts covered by our survey. The names of the villages as well as the names of the districts included in the survey are given in Appendix A.

We also collected documentary data on the economic activities of 131 managerial landlords in 46 out of the 49 districts surveyed. The names of the landlords and of the villages in which they lived are given in Appendix B.

In arranging and setting forth the survey material on the class structure of the villages, we have made the assumption that it was not something that had developed overnight but, on the contrary, that it had gradually developed over a long period of time and that it had largely inherited certain special features of the class structure of these villages from the past. For this reason, we believe it is perfectly possible, on the basis of the class structure of the villages in the late Qing, to discern the broad outlines and main developmental directions of the class structure of Shandong villages throughout the Qing dynasty (1644–1911).

To facilitate comparison, the 49 districts of our survey have been divided into the following five regions:

Region		Percent
1 Central Shandong (Jinan/ Zhoucun)	(80 villages surveyed)	40.6
2 Grand Canal	(25 villages surveyed)	12.6
3 North Shandong	(38 villages surveyed)	19.2
4 Shandong promontory	(30 villages surveyed)	15.2
5 South and West Shandong	(24 villages surveyed)	12.1
TOTAL	197	100

157

The 197 villages surveyed can be divided into two main types. In the first type, in addition to agricultural laborers, tenants, and owner-peasants, both managerial landlords and rentier landlords are found. We define a rich peasant as one who employed between 1 and 3 long-term laborers, a managerial landlord as a landlord who employed over 3 long-term laborers, and a rentier landlord as one who rented out more than 50 mu of land. In this type of village, both wage-labor and tenant production relations are found. In the second type of village, the only landlords are managerial landlords, and the relations of production are solely wage-labor relations.

Our data show that villages of the first type (containing both managerial and rentier landlord relations of production) existed in all five regions of Shandong at the end of the Qing. One example of this type of village must suffice here. In Dongxiang [see Appendix A, Region 1, Feicheng district], out of a total classifiable population of 618 households, there were 4 rich peasant households (hiring between 1 and 3 long-term laborers), 3 managerial landlords (hiring between 4 and 8 long-term laborers), 2 large managerial landlords (hiring 9 or more long-term laborers), 120 households who mainly depended on hiring out their members as wage laborers, 9 landlords who rented out more than 50 mu, 180 tenant households whose main livelihood was from rented land, and 300 owner-peasant households.[1]

The data also show that villages of the second type (in which the only landlords were managerial landlords) were found in all five regions. One example of the second type of village will suffice here. In Qiaoguantun village [see Appendix A, Region 2, Xiajin district], out of a total population of 343 households, there were 20 rich peasant households (hiring between 1 and 3 long-term laborers), 1 managerial landlord (hiring between 4 and 8 long-term laborers), 50 households which mainly depended on hiring their members out as wage-laborers, and 272 owner-peasant households. There were no rentier landlords and no tenants in the village at this time.[2]

The percentages of villages of both types in each of the five regions were as follows:

Region	Villages of type 1 (containing both rentier and managerial landlord relations of production–percentage)	Villages of type 2 (containing only wage-labor relations of production–percentage)
1	56	44
2	88	12
3	42	58
4	93	7
5	92	8

These figures indicate that, by the late Qing, complex changes were taking place in the landlord economy of Shandong. The use of wage labor was no isolated phenomenon but was used by both managerial landlords and rich peasants throughout the province. In villages of type 2, landlord-tenant relations of production had been replaced by landlord-wage labor relations of production. In villages of type 1, although rentier landlords renting out more than 50 mu and peasants renting land from the landlords still formed the majority, managerial landlords and rich peasants hiring wage labor had, without doubt, come to form a stratum.

As we pointed out above, the class structure of each village had not developed overnight, but had gradually taken form, frequently and to a large extent preserving particular features of the past class structure of the villages. Starting from this point of view, we may put forward the hypothesis based on the conditions of the class structure of the villages in late Qing Shandong, namely that in the Qing period the economic forms of managerial landlords such as Taihe tang, Shujing tang, and Jinxiu tang were not isolated phenomena, but, following the development of a commodity economy, they had begun to appear in every region of Shandong.

6.1 Average Farm Size

The data summarized in Tables 21 through 27 show conclusively that the amount of land the managerial landlords cultivated using wage labor had definite limits. In general, managerial landlords only directly managed a portion of their land; the remainder (usually because it was too extensive or widely dispersed in different villages), they rented out. If they did directly manage all their land it was because they did not own very much and what they did own was all concentrated in their own villages. Not only were there definite limits on the amount of land directly managed with wage-labor by the managerial landlords, but also that amount tended to be more or less constant as is shown in the following tables [21–28].

Table 21

Amount of Land Farmed with Wage Labor
by Individual Landlords—I
(Unit = shimu)

Region	Date	Finding number for landlord's name and village (see Appendix B)	Total amount owned	Amount farmed with wage labor	Amount rented out
1	1904	46	1,000	30	970
1	1899	52	3,000	80	2,920
2	1908	53	200	50	150
2	1884	60	190	80	110
4	1894	90	3,000	80	2,920
4	1902	91	450	70	380
5	1894	125	500	50	450
5	1900	124	320	80	240
5	1896	128	2,350	75	2,275
5	c.1908	131	450	90	360

Table 21 shows that 10 of the managerial landlords (7.6 percent of the survey) farmed less than 100 mu using wage labor.

Table 22 shows that 37 of the managerial landlords (28.2 percent of the survey) farmed between 100 and 199 mu using wage labor.

Table 23 shows that 20 of the managerial landlords (15.3 percent of the survey) farmed between 200 and 299 mu using wage labor.

Table 22

Amount of Land Farmed with Wage Labor
by Individual Landlords—II
(Unit = shimu)

Region	Date	Finding number for landlord's name and village (see Appendix B)	Total amount owned	Amount farmed with wage labor	Amount rented out
1	1894	11	250	120	130
1	1894	12	300	100	200
1	1894	14	250	100	150
1	1896	15	390	120	270
1	1895	16	180	180	---
1	1896	17	180	180	---
1	1907	21	180	180	---
1	c.1908	22	150	150	---
1	c.1908	23	150	150	---
1	c.1908	24	150	150	---
1	c.1908	25	150	150	---
1	c.1908	26	120	120	---
1	c.1908	27	120	120	---
1	c.1908	28	120	120	---
1	c.1908	29	170	170	---
1	1905	37	140	140	---
1	1897	47	160	120	40
1	1896	40	240	180	60
1	1902	45	300	180	120
1	1895	48	300	120	180
1	1895	50	205	145	60
2	c.1908	58	200	140	60
2	1896	62	200	120	80
3	1894	68	320	120	200
3	1908	70	280	150	130
3	1908	71	144	144	---
3	1876	79	1,380	180	1,200
4	1881	88	720	100	620
4	1896	87	180	120	60
4	1898	93	1,000	100	900

Table 22 (cont.)

Region	Date	Finding number for landlord's name and village (see Appendix B)	Total amount owned	Amount farmed with wage labor	Amount rented out
4	1898	98	360	160	200
4	1897	102	600	100	500
4	1899	103	1,000	140	860
4	1904	104	800	150	650
5	1886	107	200	182	18
5	1899	129	1,200	100	1,100
5	1902	130	2,040	152	1,888

Table 23

Amount of Land Farmed with Wage Labor
by Individual Landlords—III
(Unit = shimu)

Region	Date	Finding number for landlord's name and village (see Appendix B)	Total amount owned	Amount farmed with wage labor	Amount rented out
1	1880	4	600	200	400
1	1884	5	360	240	120
1	1892	8	213	213	---
1	1904	20	200	200	---
1	1902	31	200	200	---
1	1875–1908	35	240	240	---
1	1894	41	300	200	100
1	1897	44	800	240	560
2	1894	55	380	230	150
2	1895	56	260	260	---
2	c.1908	57	300	200	100
3	1894	61	284	284	---
3	1904	72	480	260	220
3	1876	78	420	240	180
4	1898	92	3,000	200	2,800

Table 23 (cont.)

Region	Date	Finding number for landlord's name and village (see Appendix B)	Total amount owned	Amount farmed with wage labor	Amount rented out
4	1898	96	400	200	200
4	1897	99	750	200	550
5	1893	121	11,000	200	10,800
5	1898	108	220	220	---
5	1875–1908	123	1,000	200	800

Table 24

Amount of Land Farmed with Wage Labor
by Individual Landlords—IV
(Unit = shimu)

Region	Date	Finding number for landlord's name and village (see Appendix B)	Total amount owned	Amount farmed with wage labor	Amount rented out
1	1894	2	500	300	200
1	1876	3	360	360	---
1	1889	7	300	300	---
1	1894	9	300	300	---
1	1894	10	360	360	---
1	1897	18	360	360	---
1	1875	30	343	343	---
1	1876	31	300	300	---
1	1891	36	300	300	---
1	1875–1908	38	300	300	---
1	1899	51	1,000	300	700
1	1875–1908	61	3,800	350	3,450
2	c.1908	63	10,000	350	9,650
3	c.1908	73	300	300	---
3	1876	77	650	325	325
3	1894	82	350	350	---
3	1902	84	360	360	---

Table 24 (cont.)

Region	Date	Finding number for landlord's name and village (see Appendix B)	Total amount owned	Amount farmed with wage labor	Amount rented out
3	1897	81	420	360	60
4	1888	94	600	300	300
4	c.1875	95	800	300	500
5	1882	105	300	300	---
5	1894	109	520	300	220
5	1896	113	500	350	150
5	1879	116	2,600	320	2,280
5	1899	122	2,800	300	2,500
5	1876	127	1,500	340	1,160
5	c.1908	115	350	350	---

Table 24 shows that 27 of the managerial landlords (20.6 percent of the survey) farmed between 300 and 399 mu using wage-labor.

Table 25

Amount of Land Farmed with Wage Labor
by Individual Landlords—V
(Unit = shimu)

Region	Date	Finding number for landlord's name and village (see Appendix B)	Total amount owned	Amount farmed with wage-labor	Amount rented out
1	1901	19	400	400	---
1	c.1908	34	480	480	---
1	1894	42	400	400	---
1	1894	49	400	400	---
3	1892	66	480	480	---
3	1898	75	400	400	---
3	1900	85	460	400	60
4	c.1875	97	600	400	200
4	c.1908	100	3,000	400	2,600
5	1884	111	400	400	---
5	1894	120	6,000	400	5,600

Table 25 shows that 11 of the managerial landlords (8.4 percent of the survey) farmed between 400 and 499 mu using wage-labor.

Table 26

Amount of Land Farmed with Wage Labor
by Individual Landlords—VI
(Unit = shimu)

Region	Date	*Finding number for landlord's name and village (see Appendix B)*	*Total amount owned*	*Amount farmed with wage-labor*	*Amount rented out*
1	1897	32	502	502	---
3	c.1908	64	550	550	---
3	1897	76	500	500	---
4	1894	86	1,000	500	500
1	1894	13	600	600	---
2	1892	54	650	650	---
3	1875	83	660	660	---
4	1894	101	20,000	600	19,400
5	1894	112	1,800	600	1,200
5	1896	117	800	600	200

Table 26 shows that 4 of the managerial landlords (3.1 percent of the survey) farmed between 500 and 599 mu using wage labor and 6 of them (4.6 percent of the survey) farmed between 600 and 699 mu using wage-labor.

Table 27 shows 4, 3, and 9 managerial landlords (3.1 percent, 2.3 percent, and 6.8 percent of the survey) farmed between 700 and 799, 900 and 999, and over 1,000 mu respectively using wage-labor.

Of all the managerial landlords, 80 percent (105 out of 131) farmed less than 500 mu using wage labor; those farming between 500 and 999 mu with wage labor constituted only 13 percent of the total (17 out of 131), while only 7 percent farmed over 1,000 mu with wage labor.

Table 27

Amount of Land Farmed with Wage Labor
by Individual Landlords—VII
(Unit = shimu)

Region	Date	Finding number for landlord's name and village	Total amount owned	Amount farmed with wage labor	Amount rented out
1	1889	6	750	750	---
3	1894	74	777	777	---
4	1898	89	3,000	700	2,300
5	c.1908	114	70,000	700	69,300
1	1889	39	900	900	---
3	1890	80	900	900	---
5	1886	106	1,060	960	100
1	1894	1	1,000	1,000	---
1	1897	43	2,100	1,000	1,100
2	1879	59	13,000	1,000	12,000
3	1882	65	1,800	1,000	800
3	1896	67	2,000	1,850	150
5	c.1908	110	8,000	2,000	6,000
5	1889	119	2,400	2,000	400
5	1897	118	1,056	1,056	---
5	1875-1908	126	5,440	1,200	4,240

In our opinion, it is no accident that the amount of land directly farmed with wage labor was, in the great majority of cases, not over 500 mu for, with the level of productive forces at that time, farms of between 100 and 500 mu must have been the optimum size for operation using wage labor. This is a point we discuss in some detail in Section 7.3.

6.2 Farming, Commerce, Handicrafts, and Usury

According to the data collected in the survey, one of the characteristics of managerial landlords in Shandong in the late Qing era was their widespread involvement in business activities, handicrafts, and usury.

Table 28

Amount of Land Farmed with Wage Labor
by Individual Landlords–Summary
(Unit = shimu)

Amount of land managed with wage labor	Number of landlords	Percentage of total landlords in survey
Less than 100	10	7.6
100-199	37	28.2
200-299	20	15.3
300-399	27	20.6
400-499	11	8.4
SUB-TOTAL	105	80.1
500-599	4	3.1
600-699	6	4.6
700-799	4	3.1
800-899	0	0.0
900-999	3	2.3
SUB-TOTAL	17	13.1
Over 1,000	9	6.8
TOTAL	131	100.0

In origin, the managerial landlords had usually made their wealth in business activities, through farming, or from being officials. According to our estimates, of the 131 managerial landlords in the sample, 64 had made their money in business (49 percent), 59 through farming (45 percent), and 8 from being officials (6 percent).

Apart from these three main ways of founding the fortunes of a family, there were many others. For example, Li Jia-shu of Bu village had originally made his money in coal. Other landlords had taken advantage of the difficulties of peasants during natural disasters and bought up large amounts of land.[3]

Table 29

Origins of Landlord Wealth

Region	Original wealth from business activities	Original wealth from farming	Original wealth from being an official
1	28	20	4
2	2	8	1
3	9	12	1
4	11	6	2
5	14	13	---
TOTAL	64	59	8

Source: Appendix B.

The data show, however, that far more managerial landlords were engaged in either business, handicrafts, or usury than were not. We give five typical examples of business, handicraft, or usury activities of landlords below:

1) In 1874, a managerial landlord named Lu Guo [Region 1, Yidu district, Beiputong village, landlord no. 41, Appendix B], who had founded the family wealth through being an official, apart from farming, was also running a miscellaneous goods store, a vineyard, and an oil press as well as mking loans in his own and neighboring villages at an interest rate of 20 percent per month.

2) At the beginning of the twentieth century, a managerial landlord named Li Ling-zhou [Region 2, Liaocheng district, Zhoutang village, landlord no. 58, Appendix B], who had founded the family wealth through farming, was also running an oil press and making loans in his own and neighboring villages at a monthly interest rate of 20 percent.

3) In 1896, a managerial landlord named Wu Ji-wu [Region 3, Binxian district, Lize market town, landlord no. 67, Appendix B], who had founded the family wealth in trade, apart from farming, also managed a wine store, oil press, miscellaneous goods store, cotton cloth shop, pharmacy, and a money shop. He also made

loans in his own and neighboring villages at a monthly interest rate of 30 percent.

4) In 1881, a managerial landlord named Zou Huan-zhang [Region 4, Penglai district, Anxiangyujia village, landlord no. 88, Appendix B], who had founded the family fortune in trade, apart from farming, also managed an oil press, miscellaneous goods store, and a weaving workshop. He also made loans in his own and neighboring villages at a monthly interest rate of 15 percent.

5) In 1889, a managerial landlord named Wu Qing-rang [Region 5, Tanxian district, Cao village, landlord no. 119, Appendix B], who had founded the family wealth in trade, apart from farming, also managed a wine store, an oil press, and a miscellaneous goods store. He also made loans in his own and neighboring villages at a monthly interest rate of 30 percent.

The numbers of managerial landlords in each region who conducted nonfarming activities similar to the above examples are summarized in the following table [30].[4]

Table 30

Number of Landlords Conducting Nonfarming Activities

Region	Number of landlords conducting nonfarming activities	Percentage of total sample in each region	Number of landlords conducting no nonfarming activities	Percentage of total sample in each region
1	44	85	8	15
2	9	82	2	18
3	18	82	4	18
4	18	95	1	5
5	24	89	3	11
TOTAL	113	average 87	18	average 13

Source: See Appendix B.

The types of shops run by the landlords included the following:

miscellaneous goods	embroidery	salt	soda
wine	cooking pots	vegetables	snacks
raw cotton	tea	grain	restaurant
cotton cloth	wooden tools	coal	inn
oil	pharmacy	iron tools	old clothes
raw silk	rice	shoes	butcher
silk goods	condiments		

Of these, the most commonly found were miscellaneous goods stores, wine shops, and cotton cloth shops.

The handicraft enterprises run by the managerial landlords included liquor breweries, oil presses, flour mills, weaving workshops, dye works, felt-cap works, silk-reeling workshops, cotton-bowing works, cooking-pot foundries, water mills, and so forth

Of these, the most commonly found were liquor breweries, oil presses, flour mills, and silk-weaving workshops.

6.3 Hiring and Wages of Long-Term Laborers

The detailed findings of the survey with regard to customs relating to the hiring of long-term rural laborers are tabulated in Appendix C. Here we summarize those findings. In many areas, all that was required before starting work was a verbal agreement on hours and wages between the landlord and the worker. In some areas, a third party ("old laborer," "friend," "fellow worker," "foreman") was required to effect an introduction between the two parties. In other areas, it was customary for the landlord to give the laborer some "security money" (*dingqian*) once the verbal agreement was made to prevent "one side's eating his words." In some areas, if the landlord wished to continue to hire a laborer in the coming year, he had to decide the wage in advance in the autumn and make a definite commitment. In some areas, it was customary for the landlord to offer the laborer a bowl of wine on commencement or termination of work in a hollow show of politeness. In other areas, the laborer had to enter into a contractual agreement. Frequently the laborer had to provide a guarantor (usually a service provided by the third party who had made the introduction). In some areas, at New Year's and other festivals, the laborers had to send presents to the landlord as a token of their

Table 31

Wages of Long-Term Laborers, c. 1900

Finding number for village (see Appendix C)	Date	Male Laborers		Female Laborers		Price of wheat in cash per jin
		Annual wage (in 1,000s cash)	Equivalent in jin of wheat	Annual wage (in 1,000s cash)	Equivalent in jin of wheat	
Region 1:						
1	1894	28	933	8	266	30
11	1894	30	909	3	91	33
26	1891	30	1,111	12	444	27
43	1899	19	2,375	3	375	8
45	1895	20	400	11	220	50
34	1895	8	615	3	230	13
38	1894	18	2,250	10	1,250	8
47	1895	16	888	4	222	18
49	1895	15	441	4	117	34
AVERAGE		20.4	1,102	6.4	357	25
Region 2:						
53	1908	20	666	--	--	30
54	1892	18	1,125	--	--	16
--	1908	10	769	3	230	13
61	1908	20	666	6	200	30
65	1894	15	750	5	250	20

67	1896	36	1,800	---	---	20
68	1908	24	2,400	4	400	10
AVERAGE		20.4	1,168	4	270	20

Region 3:

69	1908	50	2,173	5	217	23
73	1894	18	1,058	10	588	17
76	1894	20	1,176	---	---	17
79	1904	21	700	7	233	30
80	1908	30	454	7	106	66
81	1898	20	606	---	---	33
89	1897	10	500	7	350	20
86	1894	30	1,250	16	666	24
90	1896	8	400	---	---	20
AVERAGE		23	924	8.7	360	28

Region 4:

---	1898	20	833	10	416	21
94	1894	15	833	---	---	18
96	1898	24	1,500	6	375	16
98	1896	30	789	---	---	38
101	1898	50	2,941	10	588	17
103	1908	40	1,250	7	218	32
104	1897	20	1,111	3	166	18
108	1897	20	1,538	5	384	13
AVERAGE		27.4	1,349	6.8	358	22

Table 31 (cont.)

Finding number for village (see Appendix C)	Date	Male Laborers		Female Laborers		Price of wheat in cash per jin
		Annual wage (in 1,000s cash)	Equivalent in jin of wheat	Annual wage (in 1,000s cash)	Equivalent in jin of wheat	
Region 5:						
111	1886	12	666	--	--	18
116	1896	8	615	--	--	13
140	1897	18	1,058	5	294	17
139	1908	24	600	--	--	40
120	1896	18	750	9	375	24
125	1898	13	1,444	3	333	9
128	1894	12	160	6	80	75
132	1896	16	533	7	233	30
AVERAGE		15.1	722	6	263	28

Note: Long-term laborers' food was always supplied by the landlord. This table shows only the monetary wage.[5]

"esteem." Sometimes the laborer had to work for a trial three days even after coming to a verbal agreement.

The dates of starting work and stopping work for long-term laborers were different in every locality, but, in general, the landlords hired at the beginning of the busy season, and agreements were terminated at the beginning of the off season.

The wages of long-term laborers in Shandong toward the end of the nineteenth and the beginning of the twentieth centuries are tabulated in Table 31.

The average annual wages and their equivalents in wheat were more or less the same for each of the five regions—all equally low! In general, wages in Region 4 were higher than those in the other regions while those in Region 5 were the lowest. That the wages were all more or less at the same level shows that developments over the whole province were following the same course. The lowness of the wages in Region 5 is a reflection of the persistence of feudal landlord-tenant relations in south and west Shandong.

Because of their low wages, rural wage laborers were as a rule unable to support wives of their own in addition to supporting their mothers and fathers. For this reason, many were unable to marry and have children. It was a problem for wage laborers just to support their own mothers and fathers, and even this in some cases proved impossible.

In the survey, we asked what the main means of support for the families of long-term laborers were. The answers to this question from laborers in 141 villages scattered in 47 districts are tabulated in full in Appendix C. In general, the means of support can be divided into three categories:

1) Complete reliance on wages: 81 villages (57.4 percent of the total sample).

2) Part reliance on wages, part reliance on farming a small privately owned plot or on farming a rented plot: 33 villages (23.4 percent of the total sample).

3) Main income from family's privately owned plot or from farming land rented from the landlord: 23 villages (16.3 percent of the total sample).

Table 32

Sources of Income of Long-Term Laborers

Region	Number of districts surveyed	Number of villages surveyed	Category 1	Category 2	Category 3	Other
1	10	52	35	12	4	1
2	6	16	8	1	7	0
3	9	23	14	7	0	2
4	9	19	9	7	3	0
5	13	31	15	6	9	1
TOTALS	47	141	81	33	23	4

Source: See Appendix C.

The breakdown by region of these three categories may be seen in the above table [Table 32].

Region 5 had the most in category 3, and, of the 9 villages in this category, 4 reported income not from privately owned plots but from plots rented from the landlord. This shows that the old tenant system had persisted longest in Region 5.

6.4 Hiring and Wages of Short-Term Laborers

The methods of hiring short-term wage laborers toward the end of the nineteenth and beginning of the twentieth centuries were more or less uniform throughout Shandong. In the slack seasons, when there was no great demand for short-term laborers, landlords relied upon "village short-term laborers." In the busy seasons, the short-term laborers would go to the labor market (usually situated in the larger villages) and wait to be hired. So far as we could ascertain, in places where the peasantry were more stratified and the managerial landlords more clustered, the wage markets were correspondingly larger. In some such markets, 50 or 60 laborers would be found, in others, as many as 1,000. In general, there were around 200. Numbers rose or fell depending on the season. All short-term laborers had to supply their own tools. The

Table 33

Daily Wages (Busy Season) of Short-Term Laborers, c. 1900

Finding number for village (see Appendix C)	Date	Daily wage (in cash)	Equivalent in jin of wheat	Price of wheat in cash per jin
Region 1:				
1	1894	60	2.0	30
11	1894	150	4.5	33
26	1891	150	5.5	27
43	1899	80	10.0	8
45	1895	500	10.0	50
34	1895	200	15.4	13
38	1894	140	17.5	8
47	1895	200	11.0	18
49	1895	120	3.5	34
AVERAGE		177	7.2	24.6
Region 2:				
53	1908	120	4.0	30
54	1887	120	7.5	16
---	c.1908	50	3.8	13
61	c.1908	200	6.6	30
65	1894	80	4.0	20
67	1896	400	20.0	20
68	c.1908	100	10.0	10
AVERAGE		144	7.2	20
Region 3:				
69	c.1908	60	2.6	23
73	1894	70	4.1	17
76	1894	300	17.7	17
79	1904	200	6.6	30
80	c.1908	100	1.5	66
81	1898	300	9.0	33
89	1897	120	6.0	20
86	1894	200	8.3	24
90	1896	240	12.0	20
AVERAGE		176	6.2	28

Table 33 (cont.)

Finding number for village (see Appendix C)	Date	Daily wage (in cash)	Equivalent in jin of wheat	Price of wheat in cash per jin
Region 4:				
---	1898	300	12.5	24
94	1894	200	11.0	18
96	1898	250	15.6	16
98	1896	150	4.0	38
101	1898	200	11.7	17
103	1908	600	18.7	32
104	1897	150	8.3	18
108	1897	120	9.2	13
AVERAGE		246	11.1	22
Region 5:				
111	1886	70	3.9	18
116	1896	200	15.0	13
140	1897	200	11.8	17
139	1908	200	5.0	40
120	1896	500	20.8	24
125	1898	150	16.6	9
128	1894	200	2.6	75
132	1896	300	10.0	30
AVERAGE		227	8.1	28

Note: Short-term laborers' food was supplied by the hirer. This table is only concerned with their money wages.[6]

Source: See Appendix C.

landlords gave them their food. Wages varied considerably depending on the area, the season, and the type of work. Data on daily wages are given in Table 33.

Highest average wages (as with the long-term laborers) were in Region 4. The lowest were not in Region 5 but in Region 3. This was because owner-peasants were still predominant in this region, and wage labor was extensively used. In the busy season, the peasants needed only a few hired hands or none at all. Demand was low and, as a consequence, so were wages.

Most short-term laborers were not members of a rural proletariat. Most still had their own small plots, and the major portion of their income did not come from their wages but from their plots. In 65 of the villages surveyed (46 percent of the total), short-term laborers owned or rented between 1 and 5 mu; in 56 villages (40 percent of the total), they owned or rented between 6 and 10 mu; in 6 villages (4 percent of the total), they owned or rented between 11 and 15 mu; and in 3 villages (2 percent of the total), they owned or rented between 16 and 20 mu. In general, of course, the more land a short-term laborer owned or rented, the less important in his total income were his wages.[7]

Working as hired laborers or cultivating their own plots were not the only sources of income for short-term laborers. They also engaged in all kinds of side occupations to supplement their income. Most important of such occupations were: 1) production of small commercial goods such as mats, hampers, reed and bamboo rain hats, straw rain coats, baskets, wooden cooking-pot lids, grass cord, straw sandals, beancurd, table salt, sugar lumps, coarse paper, cotton yarn, coarse cotton goods, tussore, and so forth; 2) peddling goods such as vegetables, fruit, sweet potatoes, peanuts, ginger, hemp, tobacco, earthenware, cooking pots, black-glazed ware, and so forth; 3) doing transport work such as carrying coal, fish, salt, tea, and so on.

They also acted as subsidiary labor for such handicraft industries as pottery, paper, alum, cotton, and others.

In Part II, we have presented and quantified the data gathered in our survey on managerial landlords and wage laborers in Shandong in the late nineteenth and early twentieth centuries. In Part III, we turn to the further analysis of the data.

Part III

ANALYSIS OF THE ECONOMIC AND
SOCIAL SIGNIFICANCE OF THE
MANAGERIAL LANDLORDS AND CONCLUSIONS

In Parts I and II, we described the development of the regional economy of Shandong and of the managerial landlords, using written and field research data. We showed that, in several important market towns such as Linqing, Jining, Zhoucun, and Yanshen, commerce and handicraft industries were flourishing and that the economic ties between local markets were very close. Spurred on by the development of a commodity economy, monetary relations began to penetrate the villages. In order to increase their monetary income, members of the landlord class concentrated their efforts on the management of commercial agriculture. New differences among strata within the villages began to appear, especially as managerial landlords such as the Taihe tang, Jinxiu tang, and Shujing tang emerged and as agricultural laborers such as Feng Ba-zi, the wife of Gong Gou-zi, and Qiu Si-zhang, began to appear in increasing numbers. Judging from the materials gathered on 131 managerial landlords from 46 districts of Shandong, covering the later nineteenth and early twentieth centuries, the emergence of these new strata was no chance phenomenon. Within the landlord economy, those who managed their lands directly using wage labor already formed a new stratum to be distinguished in management methods and other important points from those landlords who rented out their land.

In Part III, the same materials as presented in Part II are used to form the basis of an analysis of the social nature of the managerial landlord economy in Shandong from the eighteenth century onward. It goes without saying that the materials are insufficient to present a complete analysis of this problem even for one province.

Chapter 7

ANALYSIS OF THE ECONOMIC AND
SOCIAL SIGNIFICANCE OF THE
MANAGERIAL LANDLORDS

7.1 The Relatively Progressive Nature of the Production
Process of the Managerial Landlords

There were many special aspects of the production process of
the managerial landlords, and these were relatively progressive compared with the production process of the rentier landlords. They
can be summed up under the four main headings of implements,
labor, concentration of land, and high yields.

Implements

Managerial landlords were equipped with comparatively
modern implements and means of transport and all kinds of
domestic animals, as well as having adequate amounts of fertilizer.
The implements that they used were highly productive for that
time. For example, they had iron ploughs.[1] They also had seeding
drills (using one, two, or three seeding tubes, the most common
being the double-tubed seeding drill), and at harvest time they
used winnowing fans. Taihe tang had 2 4-ox ploughs and 9 ploughing oxen. They could plough deep and quickly with their iron
ploughs since they had 4 oxen to each plough. Animals were also
used to pull the seeding drills. They had a complete set of farm
implements, enough not only for the use of the laborers, but
including a reserve for emergencies.

Ploughing and sowing are two of the most important processes of agricultural production. Depending upon the economic
level, very different implements were used. Both the plough and
the seeding drill were large and complex implements in the agriculture of the old society.

As far as we were able to ascertain, the managerial landlords'
teams of 2, 3, or 4 oxen and one ploughman could plough between

181

3 and 5 mu per day to a depth of 5 cun. A seeding drill with one ox (or an ass or a mule) and 4 men could seed between 30 and 40 mu per day. We have emphasized the capacity of the landlords' iron ploughs and seeding drills because, although traction ploughs had started to come into use from the fifth century B.C. and seeding drills had already been discovered in the Han dynasty,[2] owing to the uneven development of productive forces and to the expense of these implements, they were not used by poor peasants or tenant farmers, who could not afford to buy or use such big implements. Ploughing was either done with a traction plough (using human and animal power), a shovel plough (using human and animal power), or with a cultivation hoe (using human power only). Sowing was either done with a seeding drill (using human and animal power) or with a shovel plough (human and animal power), or with a cultivation hoe (human power only). In the neighborhood of Fushanhou village (Jimo district, now attached to the suburbs of Qingdao) and in Dawa village (Xiejiadao district, Jiaozhou bay area), the middle and poor peasants and tenants used simple triangle-shaped shovel ploughs for ploughing and seeding.[3] The cutting power of the shovel plough was nowhere nearly as great as that of the ploughshare plough. Ploughing and seeding in Dawa village were still mainly done by hand, so that the shape of the shovel plough was different from that used in Fushanhou village. In Fushanhou, the plough was directed by 1 man and pulled by a team of 2 animals (donkeys, mules, or oxen) and led by another laborer. The local people called it a "donkey team." Sowing was done in the same way, with the addition that 2 further people followed behind the plough scattering the seed and spreading fertilizer. In Dawa village, the plough was called a "shoulder plough." One man directed it while 1 or 2 others pulled it. From the point of view of production efficiency, ploughing and sowing with shovel ploughs could not equal the ploughshare plough and the seeding drill. With a "donkey team" shovel plough, only 2 to 3 mu could be ploughed per day and only 10 to 16 mu (with 2 extra men) could be sown per day. With the entirely hand-operated "shoulder plough," 2 to 2½ mu could be ploughed per day and, with 2 extra

men, 5 to 8 mu could be sown. But even these implements were by
no means used by all middle, and poor peasants and tenants. Throughout Shandong, most poor peasants had only hoes with which to
dig the ground and prepare seed holes. Naturally their production
efficiency was very low. One man could dig or sow only between
1 and 1½ mu per day using a hoe. The superiority of the implements used by the managerial landlords is quite obvious.

Since the areas managed by the landlords were fairly large,
most of them had their own carts (both large and small) as well as
animals to pull them. With these, they were able to shift earth or
manure or to bring crops in from the fields to the threshing ground.
Taihe tang for example, which managed over 470 mu, owned 1
large 2-wheeled wooden cart (the only one in the village, which
was in a hilly area), 2 large and 8 small wheelbarrows and 4 donkeys
and 4 mules which were only used for haulage. Jinxiu tang owned
6 large 2-wheeled carts and over 70 mules and horses which were
used for haulage as well as for ploughing (oxen not being used in
the neighborhood). In transport, the managerial landlords had a
tremendous advantage over the poor peasants and tenants who had
to carry everything over their shoulders.

In fertilizer, the managerial landlords were able to build up
enough stocks to provide adequate amounts for each unit of land.
In agricultural production, fertilizer is the key to increased yields.
For this reason, the managerial landlords, apart from keeping
plenty of oxen, mules, donkeys, and horses for general use as well
as for their manure, also kept pigs and sheep for manure. Taihe
tang, for example, kept 13 donkeys and oxen, over 100 sheep, and
40 pigs on the public grazing grounds (there was much uncultivated
hill land) and every year gathered over 5,000 small cartloads of
manure. Jinxiu tang kept over 70 mules and horses and gathered
over 1,000 large cartloads of manure every year. Shujing tang kept
10 oxen, over 100 sheep, and over 20 pigs and gathered 7,000
small cartloads of manure annually. Our sources indicate that it
was a common practice for managerial landlords in Shandong at
this time to keep large numbers of animals for their manure. For
example, a managerial landlord named Wang Su-bo of Sulizhuang,

Zichuan district, kept 10 oxen, over 50 sheep, and over 20 pigs;
Li Yu-gui of Mazhuang, Tai-an district, kept 9 oxen, over 120 sheep,
and over 40 pigs and collected very large annual totals of animal
manure. [Appendix B, landlord numbers 30 and 43.]

Since they had adequate supplies of fertilizer, the managerial
landlords could apply a great deal more than the peasants to each
unit of land. For example, in Dongfanliu village, most peasants put
between 3 and 10 small cartloads of fertilizer on each mu of land,
while Taihe tang in the same village was able to put on between 10
and 20 small cartloads per mu, the piles being separated by no
more than a cart's length. As a further example, Shujing tang of
Lijiazhuang spread between 10 and 15 small cartloads of fertilizer
per mus, while the average peasant landholder in the same village was only able to spread 5 or 6 small cartloads per mu. The
extent of double-cropping was often decided by the amount of
fertilizer available. The usual pattern in Shandong was to harvest
three crops every two years, but many of the managerial landlords
were frequently able to harvest four crops in two years on fairly
good land. Most peasants, mainly because of insufficient fertilizer,
only planted a small area to winter wheat, if any at all. In Taihe
tang's case, 180 to 240 mu of their total of 472 mu were double-
cropped with winter wheat, while, of the 600 mu of Shujing tang's
land managed with wage labor, over 300 mu were double-cropped
with winter wheat.

Labor

The managerial landlords were never short of labor. In the
busy seasons, they could afford to hire whatever extra hands they
needed by offering high prices. As a result, they could guarantee
that the sowing and reaping would be finished on time and they
could also better arrange agricultural tasks requiring coordination.
We have seen that, apart from hiring a given number of long-term
laborers, the managerial landlords were able to hire extra hands in
the busy seasons at the short-term labor market. In doing so, they
were concerned with the overall profit, and so did not grudge
paying relatively high wages to the short-term laborers so long as

they secured adequate supplies of labor. This was obviously something the average peasant could not afford to do.

There was a clear division of labor between long-term and
short-term laborers on the managerial landlords' lands. Generally
speaking, the foreman (*da huoji*) helped the landlord to plan how
many acres to plant to each crop and where and when to plant,
how much fertilizer to use, and the amount of labor required,
besides hiring the short-term laborers at the market. The subfore-
man (*er huoji*) generally was charged with taking the short-term
laborers to the fields and working with them there. The herdsmen
and the shepherds looked after the animals, got the fodder, built
the fences, and collected the manure. The farm boys (*xiao mihan*)
were responsible for milling the grain, feeding the pigs, fetching the
water, and taking food to the men in the fields. The female cooks
prepared the food for the laborers. The short-term laborers did the
temporary work required of them by the landlords; they did not
do the odd jobs around the landlord's house.

The subforemen and short-term laborers were direct producers,
while the foremen, herdsmen, shepherds, farm boys, and cooks
were basically involved in management of production. This shows
that there was a division of labor between production and management of production. On the basis of this division, the various aspects
of production were conducted in a coordinated way. The coordination of labor was an important characteristic of the economy of the
managerial landlords and requires further discussion. It can be seen,
for example, in the work involved in the application of fertilizer.
For most middle and poor peasants, the work of shifting the
fertilizer from the manure pit to the compost heap, and from the
compost heap to the fields, and then of spreading it was done by
one or two people.[4] In between, they needed to rest or do other
jobs and, as a result, they took longer over the job. They also
tended to use the most primitive carrying tools, that is, two
baskets on a carrying pole. For the managerial landlords, however,
the work was divided so that one laborer would gather the manure
which two others would then carry to the compost heap. There it
would be the responsibility of a laborer to break it up for loading

on carts, which would be taken to the fields (two men to a cart, one pushing, one pulling) where a third group of laborers would spread it. In ploughing and sowing, middle and poor peasants usually used their own manpower to dig the fields (each mu requiring 3 complete man-days); apart from using teams (a 3-ox team could plough 3 to 4 mu per day), the managerial landlords also used extra labor to finish off the edges of the fields, fill in cart ruts, and so forth. They would often divide the labor into ploughing, care of animals, and finishing-off tasks. In scatter-sowing the seeds, middle and poor peasants would usually work with one another or scatter the seeds alone. The managerial landlords, however, would usually use a manure drill (a drill that sows seed and spreads manure at the same time) and often divide the labor so that some would lead the animals, some would follow the cart, some would lay down manure and others pack down the soil, and so on. Again when it came to summer hoeing and weeding the sprouts, although this involved no division of labor, the managerial landlords were able to apply a lot of extra short-term labor to get the work on the different crops finished off quickly. The managerial landlords also put down a further application of fertilizer at this time, again with a certain amount of division of labor. The busiest seasons were at the wheat harvest, summer ploughing, autumn harvest, and autumn ploughing, since both harvesting and ploughing had to be undertaken at the same time. No sooner was the wheat harvest in than there was a rush to sow the maize and soy beans, and no sooner was the autumn harvest in than there was once more a rush to sow the winter wheat. Division of labor in the application of fertilizer and sowing have already been discussed above. Here we are only concerned with the actual harvesting. Harvesting of most crops involved cutting the stalks, binding them up in bundles, knocking off the ears of grain, and transporting the harvest. Each of these tasks was further subdivided. For example, in cutting *kaoliang,* two people would work together, one holding the stalks ready, the other cutting them. In drying and threshing the grain, there were many tasks that could all be done at once, or consecutively, as, for example, with wheat. The managerial landlords would frequently hire a large number of women to reap, dry, turn, and roll the grain, gather up the stray stalks, and pile and winnow the grain (using either a rotary-fan winnower or relying on the wind alone). In all of these tasks, minute division of labor took place. Finally the managerial landlords were able to link together the resources of their kitchens with the labor in the fields. They provided the food for the long- and short-term laborers who, in the busy seasons, took their morning and noon meals in the fields. They were able to prepare the food and have it sent out to several dozen or even more than one hundred laborers and thereby save on work time and increase the exploitation.

If all these and many other types of coordination of effort in the production process of the managerial landlords are taken into account and compared with the uncoordinated production conditions of peasants and tenants, then it is clear that the production efficiency of the landlords was far higher.

Concentration of Land

The area of land cultivated by a managerial landlord was comparatively large and concentrated in one place, making the organization of production much more convenient. Generally speaking, most of the managerial landlord's land was concentrated in the neighborhood of the village in which he lived (unlike rentier landlords, most of whose land was scattered in different villages). The managerial landlords could make overall plans for distributing tools, dividing the labor force, deciding on field use, and arranging the whole process of production. However, the presence of small-holding peasants meant that the managerial landlord's fields could not be managed entirely as a single entity, but his production methods came near to being large-scale production methods. Taihe tang, Jinxiu tang, and Shujing tang all used large-scale production methods on their lands.

Of the total of 131 managerial landlords in 46 districts for which materials were gathered, 10 operated farms of less than 100 mu (7.6 percent of total); 37 operated farms of between 100 and 199 mu (28.2 percent); 20 between 200 and 299 mu (15.3 percent);

27 between 300 and 399 mu (20.6 percent); 11 between 400 and
499 mu (8.4 percent); 4 between 500 and 599 mu (3.1 percent); 6
between 600 and 699 mu (4.6 percent); 4 between 700 and 799
mu (3.1 percent); 3 between 900 and 999 mu (2.3 percent); 9 over
1,000 mu (6.8 percent).

Turning to rentier landlords, we find their practice was
exactly the opposite of the managerial landlords. Instead of operating single large units, they deliberately split up large stretches of
land, letting small parcels here and there, or they preserved the
original small-holders' patterns in letting land to their tenants. Take,
for example, the rentier landlord Jinshu tang; apart from the land
used for their kitchen gardens, all the rest was let out. The 177
mu in or near their own village of Jiujun, for instance, were let out
to 17 peasant families. [See Table 20.]

The rentier landlords' practice of taking large amounts of land
and renting them out in small plots according to various forms of
arrangement (letting them out in partnerships according to their
distance and quality or letting them out directly and fixing the
rents according to their quality) was naturally influenced by the
limitations of the small-peasant economy, and it was a general
phenomenon.

The comparatively large-scale and compact nature of the
managerial landlords' operation did away with wasted land in field
borders. But, most important, it allowed unified allocation of tools
and labor power and unified planning of crop acreages and production processes, enabling ploughing, ditching, hoeing and weeding,
laying down of fertilizer, irrigation, and repairing of fields, and so
forth, all to be completed on time. Labor power was economized
and production efficiency increased. It also meant that fairly large
amounts of land could be planted to easily processed and marketed
cash crops (such as kaoliang for wine-making, sesame for sesame
oil, mung beans for flour, cotton, tobacco, and so forth).

High Yields
Yield per mu on the managerial landlords' fields was comparatively high, owing to the various advantages discussed above,

and it surpassed yields on most middle and poor peasants' land, as shown, for example, in the following table [34]:

Table 34

Comparison of Yields on Taihe Tang Land
and on Peasant Land, c. 1904
(Unit = jin per shimu)

	Wheat	*Kaoliang*	*Millet*	*Maize*	
Yields on Taihe tang land	124–165	250–350	300–400	250–320	(Dry land)
Yields on peasant land	70–120	110–250	125–250	140–250	(Dry land)

Source: Interviews.

The survey materials as a whole show that, in 87 villages in 36 districts (that is, in 90 percent of the 96 villages surveyed on this point), the yields per mu for the main crops of wheat, kaoliang, and millet were higher on managerial landlords' fields than on most peasants' land.[5] The following table [35] quantifies a selection of the survey data on this point.

7.2 Capitalist Elements in the Economy of the Managerial Landlords

In the previous section, we surveyed, under four main heads, the comparatively advanced elements of the production process of the managerial landlords. The discussion continues with an analysis of the capitalist elements in that process, elements that stand out particularly clearly when comparisons are drawn with the practices of the rentier landlords.

1) There was a duality in the social status of the owners of the means of production (the managerial landlords). On the one hand, they had begun to acquire the status of rural bourgeoisie while, on the other hand, they still retained many feudal characteristics. (See Section 7.4.) Their status as rural bourgeoisie can be substantiated

Table 35

Comparison of Yields on Land Farmed by Managerial Landlords
and by Poor Peasants and Tenants, c. 1910
(Unit = jin per shimu)

Place (District/Village)	Wheat		Kaoliang		Millet		Maize		Cotton	
	Landlord	Peasant	Landlord	Peasant	Landlord	Peasant	Landlord	Peasant	Landlord	Peasant
Zichuan/Wangcun	150	100	230	200	250	230	120	100	—	—
Licheng/Laocengkou	240	200	300	250	520	480	320	290	—	—
Zhangqiu/Cuijiazhuang	220	180	250	200	260	220	215	185	130	100
Zouping/Zhangfangcun	100	100	150	150	200	200	—	—	—	—
Linyi/Dizisongcun	130	90	95	54	125	95	130	100	—	—
Huantai/Qianchencun	250	170	300	220	320	220	—	—	—	—
Linzi/Nanfengkecun	120	50	170	100	280	200	150	100	—	—
Yidu/Beiputongcun	250	150	300	200	500	300	250	150	150	100
Zhucheng/Xuejiucun	350	300	320	240	520	500	—	—	60	50
Pingdu/Baibucun	120	100	180	170	200	180	—	—	95	90
Anqiu/Yijiecun	330	230	300	215	280	184	—	—	—	—
Dexian/Fenghuangdian	100	60	200	120	200	150	220	180	—	—
Xiajin/Mozhuang	60	50	150	100	310	250	100	75	120	70
Tangyi/Dingliubazhai	120	100	160	140	160	140	110	100	70	60
Wenshang/Bonansanlilou	210	130	260	200	500	350	—	—	170	130
Dongping/Xiaoyangzhuang	180	130	250	200	550	350	250	200	—	—
Liaocheng/Qiaohuangcun	30	30	200	200	150	150	60	60	—	—
Pingying/Liusuozhuang	135	100	100	70	135	100	200	150	—	—
Dongping/Shahezhan	150	150	220	220	400	400	250	250	—	—
Juancheng/Xuzhai	80	80	100	100	—	—	—	—	—	—
Zouxian/Dahuangcun	160	140	180	170	210	200	—	—	—	—

Tengxian/Dayancun	200	150	300	200	750	500	—	—	—	—
Tai-an/Shankoucun	150	120	240	180	480	350	450	320	—	—
Xintai/Beishidian	100	80	220	180	300	200	—	—	30	20
Yishui/Xiaweizhuang	85	75	250	235	210	180	240	220	—	20
Feixian/Nanshigou	160	120	230	180	360	270	—	—	—	—
Juye/Beiganmiaozhaozhuang	120	120	240	240	360	360	—	—	80	80
Fanxian/Nanyangzhuang	180	120	220	—	500	350	—	—	100	70
Puxian/Guyunji	200	140	210	160	350	300	—	—	—	—
Jiaoxian/Tanjiacun	280	160	320	240	400	330	—	—	—	—
Zhaoyuan/Houkuangcun	110	85	250	225	270	270	300	230	—	—
Qixia/Malingzhong	200	110	400	200	270	270	300	200	—	—
Laiyang/Nanzuojiakuang	110	80	250	200	280	230	—	—	—	—
Fushan/Wangyuanwangcun	75	60	100	100	80	80	—	—	—	—
Penglai/Anxiangyujia	160	130	260	220	300	250	200	170	—	—
Yexian/Xizhangjiacun	300	200	280	200	350	300	—	—	—	—
Changyi/Beixingfucun	188	150	250	200	330	275	—	—	—	—
Zhanhua/Wanjiacun	130	120	180	175	300	285	—	—	150	130
Lijin/Daniucun	160	150	240	210	240	230	160	150	180	180
Humin/Weijicun	150	75	240	180	320	220	—	—	100	60
Binxian/Zhengjiacun	180	200	240	180	325	250	150	125	140	150

Notes: 1. The figures in the table are based on estimates made by peasants sixty years of age and over.
2. Since the conversion of old local mu to shimu differs from village to village, some of the figures may be either too high or too low.
3. There are many missing values for maize and cotton because many villages did not plant these crops.

by the following evidence. First, they did not rent out their lands but managed them with wage labor. The actual producers were not tenants but long- and short-term laborers paid a money wage. Thus, for example, Taihe tang hired 13 long-term laborers annually and between 20 and 40 short-term laborers in the busy season; Shujing tang hired 30 long-term laborers annually and 50 short-term laborers in the busy season; Jinxiu tang hired 37 long-term laborers annually and 50 short-term laborers in the busy season. The survey materials show that the employment of long- and short-term labor was a common characteristic of the managerial landlords. Thus, for example, Lu Guo of Beiputongcun, Yidu district, hired 10 long-term laborers in a normal year and 24 short-term laborers; Wang Jin-han of Xiyangloucun, Tai-an district, hired 9 long-term and between 20 and 30 short-term laborers; Li Xiao-jie of Ponansanli-loucun, Wenshang district, hired 6 long-term and 15 short-term laborers; Li Meng-yue of Xisilicun, Liaocheng district, hired 11 long-term and 14 short-term laborers; Zhou Shu-sheng of Longhe-cun, Boxing district, hired 6 long-term and 60 short-term laborers; Han Zhao-li of Wanjiacun, Zhanhua district, hired 10 long-term and 18 short-term laborers; Yang Zhong-qin of Xisonggucun, Zhucheng district, hired 21 long-term and 40 short-term laborers; Chen Mao-de of Guyunji, Puxian district, hired 6 long-term and 14 short-term laborers; Ma Zeng-shou of Qianjiazhuang, Pingdu district, hired 29 long-term and 30 short-term laborers; and Yue Zhao-xing of Beishilibao, Yexian district, hired 14 long-term and 20 short-term laborers.[6] To put it in another way, the survey materials show that the direct producers on the managerial landlords' lands were not the exploited tenants but laborers whose implements were for the most part owned by the landlords. Although the short-term laborers often brought their own small tools with them to the labor market, the evidence shows that it was common for them to rely on the landlord for larger implements such as carts, ploughs, seeding drills, and so on. Furthermore, since they were required to do a wide variety of tasks, their own tools would often be inadequate and they would use those supplied by the landlord. In *The Development of Capitalism in Russia,* Lenin pointed out: "The capitalist farming system consists of the hire of workers (annual, seasonal, day, etc.) who till the land with the owner's implements."[7] The managerial landlords' use of hired labor in agricultural production was clearly of a capitalist nature.

Second, most of the managerial landlords also engaged in handicraft industries, commerce, and usury. They had at their disposal comparatively large amounts of money. The survey materials show that they frequently set up breweries, oil presses, flour mills, weaving works, miscellaneous goods stores, and cloth stores as well as money shops, pawn shops, and so forth. (See Appendix B for a full listing of their different activities.) The various activities of the Taihe tang, Shujing tang, and Jinxiu tang have already been described in some detail (see Part II). The remainder of the survey materials tell the same story.[8] Of the 131 landlord families surveyed, 113 (87 percent) combined handicrafts and commercial and moneylending activities with their agricultural operations. There were only 18, or 13 percent, who did not engage in such activities. One result of the wide range of their activities was that this stratum had a firm hold on working capital resources. It was a wealthy, moneyed stratum. We consider that this is an extremely important point, because, as is well known, the circulation of capital starts with the appearance of money. It follows that there must be a stratum owning money before there can be the possibility of a rural bourgeoisie using money to buy labor in order to exploit surplus labor value. Naturally a rural bourgeoisie could only gradually develop from the wealthy money-owning rural stratum.

Third, the main object of the managerial landlords' production operation was not simply to provide for their own needs but to produce comparatively large amounts of different commercial crops. This can be seen very clearly from the proportion of commercial crops sold annually to the total amounts harvested by Taihe tang. [See Table 6.]

We consider that it is possible to explain how the managerial landlords were able to obtain high quotas of commercial crops as is shown in the following equation. Granted similar land areas,

194

conditions of production, and level of capital investment and production, the managerial landlords would have sold larger quantities by far than the rentier landlords.

> If: Total crop production equals 10
> Landlord family's consumption equals 2
> Laborers' food consumption equals 1 [9]
> Tenants' retained portion of crop equals 5 [10]
> Then: Amount of commercial crops available for sale by rentier landlords will be 10−2−5=3 and amount of commercial crops available for sale by managerial landlords will be 10−2−1=7. [11]

The above equation shows that, granted equal conditions for both types of landlord, the managerial landlord would have more than twice the amount of commercial crops for sale as the rentier landlord. Furthermore, compared with most peasants, the conditions of production were superior and yield per mu higher on the managerial landlords' land. This gave the managerial landlords an even greater amount of crops for sale.

In our opinion, it is extremely important to underline the object of the managerial landlords' production as being the obtaining of large amounts of grain for sale on the market. Engels pointed out in *Anti-Dühring:* "The word 'capital' in its modern economic meaning is first met with . . . at the time when the thing itself makes its appearance, when movable wealth (i.e., money) acquires, to a greater and greater extent, the function of capital, by exploiting the surplus-labor of the laborers for the production of commodities." [12]

Thus, to evaluate the social nature of the landlords, it is necessary to examine whether they exploited the labor of free laborers to produce commodities for the market, that is to say, whether they engaged in production in order to realize the augmented sum (M′) in the circuit M–C–M′ where M equals money, C equals commodities, and M′ equals original sum plus surplus value. [13]

Fourth, the managerial landlords' acquisition of land had

usually taken place gradually. In general, they had risen from middle peasant to rich peasant to landlord. Of the 131 landlord families in the survey, 64 originally owed their wealth to trade and 59 owed their wealth to farming, a total of 123 (94 percent). Only 8 (6 percent) originally owed their wealth to having been officials. This shows that the managerial landlords owed their position not primarily to feudal privileges but to their gradually accumulating the fruits of their own success as managers, though this is not to say that the managerial landlords did not use force and extortion to achieve their ends. This can be seen from the case of Taihe tang's accumulation of land. Between 1761 and 1790, they only had 175.72 mu; between 1793 and 1905, this had been increased to 515.72 mu. Particularly noteworthy is the evidence of the land account books which show that this land was accumulated in no less than 104 separate purchases over the course of 145 years. In the case of Shujing tang, in the early eighteenth century, the family owned 30 mu and they were still middle peasants; under Bi Feng-lian's management in the later eighteenth century, this had gradually been increased to over 100 mu; and in the early nineteenth century, it had risen to over 300 mu; it was only in the course of the next hundred years that it topped 900 mu. The managerial landlords gradually made their way by slowly accumulating land. In general, most had passed through the stages of being middle and rich peasants. This is an extremely important point.

The managerial landlords and the rich peasants resembled each other in respect to the nature of their operations (farming, commerce, handicrafts, and usury), except that the landlords far surpassed the rich peasants in their activities. Also, in scale of operation (both in terms of the amount of land and the exploitation of labor) the managerial landlords far surpassed the rich peasants. For these reasons, it is our opinion that, even before the Opium War [1840–1842], the managerial landlords of Shandong already possessed some characteristics of a rural bourgeoisie; they had risen from the ranks of the rich peasants and, in the course of becoming differentiated from the peasants, they employed wage labor to operate comparatively large farms, they controlled adequate sources of floating capital, and they produced for the market.

2) The direct producers who provided labor for the managerial landlords, the long-term laborers, already basically possessed the status of a free proletariat. "Free" as here used includes two meanings: a) long-term laborers were able to use their labor power comparatively freely; and b) they were basically not tied to the land.

The methods of hiring long-term laborers used by Taihe tang, Shujing tang, Jinxiu tang, and the other managerial landlords were simple. The laborer was first introduced by a middleman, and then, provided the hirer agreed, he could start work straight away, his wage having first been decided between the middleman and the landlord. Sometimes the middleman's services were dispensed with and laborer and landlord would decide on the wage directly between themselves. Payment of wages was usually in money (annual cash wage). The survey materials on 134 managerial landlords from 43 districts show broadly similar practices throughout the province as those outlined above. (See Appendix C.) The long-term laborer would be introduced by a "fellow worker," "old laborer," "friend," or "middleman"; the wage would either be decided directly between the laborer and the landlord or by the middleman. As soon as the wage was fixed, he could begin work. In some areas such as Xiyaocun (Zhangqiu district), Fenghuangdian (Dexian district), or Mazhuang (Tai-an district), after the wage had been decided, the landlord had to give the laborer an advance payment as a form of surety. In the neighborhood of Longhecun, Boxing district, the landlord had to provide a meal of "good food and wine" when the long-term laborers started work. Around Shankoucun, Tai-an district, it was the custom for the laborer and the middleman to be invited to the landlord's house on the first day of work. The landlord would exert himself to be as polite as possible to make the laborer feel obliged to him.

In practice, the dates at which long-term laborers started and stopped work were fairly flexible. They differed in different areas of the province. In the area of Dongfanliu (Zhangqiu district), Dashangcun and Dashicun (Zichuan district), and Guanzhuang (Dongping district), the date of starting and stopping work was the eighth day of the twelfth lunar month; in the area of Weizhihecun

(Dongping district), Beiputongcun (Yidu district), and Xizhangjia-cun (Yexian district), the date of starting work was around the Qingming festival (beginning of April), and the date of stopping work was around the first of the tenth lunar month.

Customary dates of stopping or starting work, moreover, did not prevent either the landlord dismissing the long-term laborer or the laborer leaving the landlord. Generally speaking, landlords did not agree to laborer leaving work in the busy season and, if a laborer tried to, there would always be conflict, the landlord frequently using his status to ensure that the laborer continued to work for him. The wage labor account books of Taihe tang record the dates, and they provide evidence of the "freedom" with which laborers began and ended their work. (See Table 7.) The table shows that, although the fixed day for starting and ending work in Dongfanliu village was the eighth of the twelfth month, many of the long-term laborers either started or stopped work in the busy season. In our opinion, the "freedom" of entering into or leaving work of the long-term laborer is a reflection of his improved status and indicates that he could "dispose of his labor power as his own commodity."

The reason that people became hired laborers was that either their families had no land or they had such a little (their own or rented) that there was surplus labor power and so one or more of the brothers were obliged to hire themselves out as laborers. Bi Xian-zhen of Zhengjia village, Zichuan district, for example, had become a laborer for this reason.

When we interviewed long-term laborer Bi Xian-zhen in 1957, he was 73 (born in 1885). In about 1900, his family had numbered five members (father, mother, two younger brothers, and himself). The family rented 2.7 mu and lived in a grass hut with two small rooms. They had one hoe and one mattock. Other tools they had to borrow. They had no pig pen for manure, so their land was poorly cultivated and not very productive. In good years, they harvested between 825 and 880 jin. After the harvest, they had to pay rent of 5 to 6 strings of cash (equivalent to over 280 jin of kaoliang or 40 percent of the harvest). What was left from the harvest only provided enough for three months' food for the family. His mother would often go begging in other villages. When he was ten years old, Bi was sent to work as a shepherd for a landlord. He looked after a flock of 36 sheep and was paid an annual wage of 2 strings of cash (equivalent to 80 to 90 jin of kaoliang), apart from receiving his food. When he was fifteen, his wage was increased to 2½ strings of cash. At that time, one jin of pork cost 60 cash and one jin of steamed bread rolls was 48 cash. A foot of coarse cloth was 59 cash, which meant that a rough padded cotton jacket and trousers cost 1,500 cash and an unpadded set cost about 1,000 cash. Given these prices, Bi's wages were hardly adequate to clothe himself. When he was sixteen, his father died and his mother was forced to make ends meet by selling shoe uppers, needles, and thread. When he was nineteen, his wage was increased to 8 strings a year but he still could not support his family and so, at twenty, he left Zhengjia village and went to Tangshan to become a black-smith.

Although his family rented 2.7 mu of land, he himself had nothing directly to do with this land, since all year round he worked as a long-term laborer for a landlord. His particular social status, therefore, was that of a free laborer who had been squeezed off the land. In the course of his analysis of the social conditions in which the owner of money turns into a capitalist, Marx clearly points out: "For the conversion of his money into capital, therefore, the owner of money must meet in the market with the free laborer, free in the double sense, that as a free man he can dispose of his labor-power as his own commodity, *and that on the other hand he has no other commodity for sale, is short of everything necessary for the realization of his labor-power.*"[14]

Clearly, the touchstone for deciding the social nature of the managerial landlords is the question of whether or not the long-term laborers were free laborers. It is our opinion, on the basis of the data quoted above, that the long-term laborers hired by the managerial landlords possessed the nature of free laborers to some extent. We turn now to the discussion of the other type of direct producers hired by the managerial landlords, the short-term laborers.

One of the characteristics of agricultural production is that ploughing, sowing, harvesting, and so forth, all have to be finished at particular seasons. The managerial landlords had no need to hire large amounts of labor all year round and, as a result, from the point of view of managerial efficiency, did their utmost to hire as few long-term laborers as possible, relying rather on hiring a large number of short-term laborers to work for them in the busy season. Generally speaking, the short-term laborers in the aggregate played a much more important part in production than the long-term laborers. The survey data show that the means of hiring short-term labor were similar throughout the province. The hirer went to the short-term labor market and directly fixed the daily wage with the laborer on the basis of the market price of that day. The short-term laborer usually carried his own hand tools such as hoe, spade, mattock, and so forth. No personal obligations were entered into; the laborers received their wages, and that was all. They were paid by the day, and the laborer could decide when he wanted to quit.

The short-term laborers were, for the most part, poor peasants or tenants with small amounts of their own or rented land. For example, the short-term laborers in the area of Xiyaocun (Zhangqiu district), Zhangfangcun (Zouping district), and Nanfengkecun (Linzi district) were mainly owner-peasants possessing between 5 and 8 mu of land, while those in the area of Liaocun (Dongping district), Baifenzicun (Anqiu district), Shiqiaocun (Anqiu district), Linchicun (Zichuan district), and Liboshicun (Pingying district) were mainly tenants renting between 1 and 10 mu. Short-term laborers relied mainly on their own or rented land to make a living; working as laborers was only one of the ways in which they supplemented their income. Depending on the local economy in which they found themselves, they undertook various side occupations, working as grass cutters, gatherers of firewood, transport coolies, mat weavers, fishermen, charcoal sellers, millstone cutters, peddlers, and so forth. The main characteristic of the short-term laborers was that they had not yet become completely separated from the land. They were not yet a completely propertyless proletariat but rather semiproletariat owners or renters of tiny plots of land. In our opinion, the short-term laborers had a dual social status. In his "How to Differentiate the Classes in the Rural Areas," Comrade Mao Ze-dong clearly pointed out:

> Among the poor peasants, some own part of their land and have a few odd farm implements, others own no land at all but only a few odd farm implements. As a rule poor peasants have to rent the land they work on and are subjected to exploitation, having to pay land rent and interest on loans and *to hire themselves out to some extent. In general the poor peasant has to sell part of his labour power*... The worker (including the farm labourer) as a rule owns no land or farm implements, though some do own *a very small amount of land and very few farm implements. Workers make their living wholly or mainly by selling their labour power.*[15]

Two phenomena in the above analysis are worth emphasizing: 1) both farm laborers and poor peasants, because of their economic position, were forced to a greater or lesser degree to sell their labor power; 2) both farm laborers and poor peasants, because of their economic position, to a greater or lesser degree *owned land.*

If these two phenomena are linked, then it becomes clear that, in China, farm laborers and poor peasants were both strata providing hired labor.

Granted the foregoing, there is nothing strange in the fact that short-term laborers combined the status of hired laborer and poor peasant. In his "Socialism: Utopian and Scientific," Engels wrote: "The first capitalists found ... alongside of other forms of labor, wage-labour ready-made for them on the market. But it was exceptional, complimentary, accessory, transitory wage-labour. The agricultural labourer though, upon occasion, he hired himself out by the day, had a few acres of his own land on which he could at all events live at a pinch."[16]

In practice, even in capitalist countries today, agricultural wage laborers frequently own their own small plots of land as a means of supplementing their meager incomes and as a last resort to fall back on when they are unable to find work. We conclude that the dual nature of the short-term laborers (part peasant, part laborer) in no way weakens our analysis of the managerial landlords as possessing capitalist characteristics.

The relationship between the managerial landlords and both the long-term and the short-term laborers was basically a monetary relationship. According to the Taihe tang wage labor account books, wages for their long-term and short-term (including year, month, and day) laborers between 1908 and 1909 were as follows.

Long-term laborer Feng Ba-zi, annual wage 29.7 strings of cash; woman worker Gong Gou-zi, annual wage, 6,480 cash; month laborer Chen, monthly wage of 1,114 cash; day laborer Zhang Wai-zi, light laborer's wage during the summer busy season of 1910, 40 cash per day and, during the autumn harvest of the same year, a heavy laborer's wage of 360 cash per day for the first three days of the ninth month. If the Dongfanliu price of one dou (70 jin) of wheat of 5,600 cash is taken as the basis of calculation, Feng Ba-zi's annual wage could only buy 371 jin and Gong Gou-zi's annual wage was worth 81 jin. If the 1908 Dongfanliu price of kaoliang of 3,600 cash per dou (55 jin) is taken as the basis of calculation, month laborer Chen's monthly wage was worth 16.9 jin of kaoliang, and day laborer Zhang Wai-zi's light laborer's wage was worth 0.5 jin and his heavy laborer's wage was only worth 5.5 jin of kaoliang.[17] These materials reflect the following conditions:

1) The variation among long-term laborers' wages was very great. Foremen's wages were in general much higher than those of the herdsmen, shepherds, swineherds, male and female handymen, and cooks. For example, foreman Feng Ba-zi's annual wage was nearly five times as high as (woman) cook Gong Gou-zi's wage!

2) The variation of short-term laborer's wages depending on the season and the work was also very great. Thus short-term laborer Zhang Wai-zi's heavy laborer's wage at the autumn harvest was nine times higher than his light laborer's wage in the summer busy season.

3) The low wages of long- and short-term laborers at the time are evident when their value is expressed in terms of food grains calculated at current prices.

7.3 Hindrances to Further Development of the
Managerial Landlord Economy

In describing the comparatively progressive nature of the managerial landlords and their capitalist characteristics, we tentatively affirm that they represented a new phenomenon within the feudal economy. We turn now to the question of whether or not there were impediments to progress on the road taken by the managerial landlords. If so, what were these impediments?

In Appendix B, the amounts of land managed with wage labor by the 131 landlords in 46 districts of Shandong included in the survey are set out. These statistics are summarized in Table 28 reproduced below. One hundred and five landlords (80 percent of the total 131 surveyed) farmed between 100 and 499 mu using wage labor. This suggests that there were certain objective factors preventing the extension of this type of farming much beyond 500 mu. The actual amounts of land owned by the managerial landlords often surpassed 500 mu. Thus, for example, Lu Zun-shu of Baibu village, Pingdu district, owned 750 mu, of which he cultivated 200 mu using wage labor, the remainder being let out; Dacheng tang of Dong-guan village, Fushan district, owned 3,000 mu, of which they cultivated 700 mu using hired labor, the remainder being let out; Chen Jia-fu of Laizhuangpu village, Feixian district, owned 6,000 mu of which he cultivated 400 mu using hired labor, the remainder being let out. [Appendix B, landlord numbers 99, 89, 120. Full details of land ownership of all 131 managerial landlords are given in this Appendix.] The figures in Table 28, it should be stressed, refer only to those lands cultivated with wage labor. The reason the managerial landlords were unable to farm all their land using wage labor was because of certain contradictions within the landlord wage labor system itself.

In the first place, there were the limitations imposed upon the landlords by the level of productive forces available to them. For example, in the case of implements, a 3- or 4-ox ploughing team could only plough about 4 mu per day. If 600 mu were ploughed twice a year, then one plough team would require 300 ploughing days. But only about 180 days a year were suitable for

Table 28

Amount of Land Farmed with Wage Labor
by Landlords—Summary
(Unit = shimu)

Amount of land managed with wage labor	Number of landlords	Percentage of total landlords in survey
Less than 100	10	7.6
100–199	37	28.2
200–299	20	15.3
300–399	27	20.6
400–499	11	8.4
SUB-TOTAL	105	80.1
500–599	4	3.1
600–699	6	4.6
700–799	4	3.1
800–899	0	---
900–999	3	2.3
SUB-TOTAL	17	13.1
Over 1,000	9	6.8
TOTAL	131	100.0

Source: See Appendix B.

ploughing. Consequently the landlord would have to keep at least 6 to 8 ploughing oxen and 2 plough sets in order to cultivate 600 mu. With so many oxen, just the provision of fodder would become a major problem. For, if each ox required 10 jin of fodder a day, then altogether at least 21,600 to 28,800 jin would be required. A portion could be provided by setting the oxen to graze on public grassland in the spring, summer, and autumn, but the greater part would have to come in the form of millet grass or "bought hay" (*fucao,* this was the term used in the Qiuling region of Shandong for wild grass cut, dried, and sold by poor peasants), and this would certainly be considered a difficult problem. Quite apart from the question of fodder, during the ploughing seasons each ox required 2 laborers to feed and handle it; the value of the surplus labor products produced under such conditions was minimal, at the same time large numbers of animals also required pens, fences, and stalls. Naturally, the managerial landlords would have had little incentive to make these extra investments. And there were other problems. For instance, moving the ploughs and ploughing teams was a cumbersome business and extremely time-consuming if the fields were far off. Consequently, oxen could only be used where the fields were close and compact.

Similar types of limitation acted upon sowing, inter-row tillage, and harvesting. If, for example, at the wheat sowing, 1,200 jin of fertilizer were used per mu (this is only an approximation, since the amount of fertilizer used for embedding the seeds and turning into the soil at sowing varied very greatly) and a double-tube seed drill (requiring 6 men and 1 draft animal) were used, they could sow between 10 and 12 mu per day. But the sowing season was short and, therefore, to sow large stretches of land would have required very large numbers of short-term laborers, to say nothing of sowing drills. Other examples could readily be multiplied. In 1 day 1 man could only weed ½ to 1 mu of shoots using the short-handled hoe. For later weedings with the long-handled hoe, it took a day for a single worker to cover 1 to 2 mu; at harvest time 1 man using the hand sickle could only cut between 2 and 4 mu per day. Such conditions presented very definite problems for managerial landlords using hired labor to farm large areas.

Transport was equally inhibiting. The typical vehicle in Shandong at that time was the small 2-handled pushcart which could carry up to 400 jin. Before the discovery of chemical fertilizer, it was the practice to bring large amounts of fresh earth to mix in with the night soil and other domestic waste to make fertilizer. The fertilizer had then to be shifted to the fields. In these operations, it was the small pushcart which was used. If the fields were 3 li away, then the return journey of 6 li could only be made about 10 times a day. At this level of labor efficiency, managerial landlords had to consider carefully the profit and loss involved in the use of relatively expensive short-term laborers at the busy seasons. From the exploiters' point of view, there came a point when it was simply more profitable to let out their lands rather than farm all of them directly. The survey data indicate that the amount of land that could profitably be directly farmed lay between 100 and 500 mu.

In the accumulation of land, the landlords were restricted by the freeholding peasants. The more land peasants lost, the more they tenaciously held on to what was left. Freeholding peasants generally owned about 10 to 30 mu of land. The reasons they fell on hard times were very different but, when that happened, the only way to survive was to sell a portion of the land they had inherited or the small amounts accumulated by the sweat of their brow. But there would come a point when they would sell no more and, when faced with another crisis, they would accept a lower standard of living, hire themselves out as laborers (usually short-term laborers), or borrow cash or grain, in short, hang on to what little land was left them with grim persistence. This meant that it was extremely difficult for a landlord in the same village to buy up more land, and his opportunities for further expansion grew ever smaller. Taihe tang, Shujing tang, and the others took all of 100 or even 200 years to gradually build up their lands, and Taihe tang, for example, had often to pay comparatively high prices in competition with middle or rich peasants for them. It took Taihe tang 145 years to accumulate 515 mu of land. (See Table 36.) In all, 104 separate purchases were involved, as detailed in Tables 3, 4, and 5. The Taihe tang land purchase account books show that they bought parcels of less that 4½ mu 67 times (64 percent of total purchases) and parcels of over 4½ mu 37 times (36 percent of total purchases). Taihe tang's experience shows just how lengthy the process of land accumulation was. It also shows that the purchases were made at the expense of the freeholding peasants.

A further problem in accumulating land was the practice of partible inheritance. It was the custom to divide family or clan property equally among all the sons. Sometimes the head of the

Table 36

Taihe Tang Land Purchases, 1761–1905

Amount of land purchased (in mu)	Less than 1	1-2.9	3-4.5	4.6-5.9	6-7.5	7.6-8.9	9-10	Over 10	Total
Number of purchases	7	21	39	7	14	4	6	6	104
TOTALS	67				37				104
PERCENTAGE	64				36				100

family in his old age would preside over such a division, in which case he and his wife, as well as the eldest grandson, would each receive a portion (daughters did not have the right of inheritance), the remainder being divided up among the sons. In this way, the lands so carefully brought together would be dispersed again. Thus Jinshu tang's predecessor, Qiangxue tang, had divided up an inheritance of 960 mu in 1854 into four portions of 240 mu, one each for Sanshu tang, Qishu tang, Rongshu tang, and Jinshu tang (the father having already died).[18] Thereafter, some of the lands were even further subdivided, and some of the families in this group became owner-peasants. The same had also taken place with the direct forerunner of Taihe tang. In 1792 the family lands of 351.4 mu were divided into two inheritance portions of 175.7 mu each for Li Ke-shi and Li Ke-fa. Later, when Taihe tang itself divided up (in 1907), their total of 515.7 mu went to the eldest grandson (66 mu) and the two sons (224.8 mu each).[19]

Both the difficulties of getting land from the peasants, which slowed down the process of accumulation, as well as the constant division and subdivision of the landlord's family into medium and small landlords and even back into the class of freeholding peasantry, were obstacles in the way of managerial landlords further developing the size and scope of their operations.

7.4 Feudal Remnants in the Economy
of the Managerial Landlords

Although the social nature of the managerial landlords contained the capitalist characteristics discussed above, it also retained many feudal characteristics. There was, therefore, a duality in their social status. As owners of the means of production, the managerial landlords had the following feudal characteristics:

1) Their aim in production was still, in part, self-sufficiency. In our opinion, their agricultural production can be divided into two parts—that intended for the landlord's family consumption and that intended for sale at the market. Managerial landlords were able to retain a portion of their total crop production for their own consumption. For this reason, the organization of their production included in its aims the provision for their own consumption needs. These needs included the food and cotton for all members of the landlord's household. They also included the outlays for wages for the laborers (that is, all the direct producers both male and female) both in cash and in kind as well as all the outlays for production materials (domestic animals, tools, seeds, fertilizer, and so on). In our opinion, only what was left after all these items of expenditure had been met can be considered under the heading of "production for the market." The ratio of consumption production to production for the market largely depended upon the size of the landlord's family. Generally, in order to reap the advantages of large-scale production, the landlords held up "five generations in one hall" as the ideal, and many of them were indeed very large families led by a patriarch. Thus Shujing tang, in the last quarter of the nineteenth century, had the reputation of being a family of "more than 100 members all living together."[20] Taihe tang at about the same time had about 30 family members living together.[21] Other examples were Han Shi-su's family in Maiqiu village, Jiaoxian district, which in 1894 numbered over 60 members; Zhang Cheng-han's family in Xuanjia village, Binxian district, which at the end of the nineteenth century also numbered over 60 members; and a landlord of Lingnantou village, Laiyang district, whose family numbered 34 members.[22] Of course, not every managerial landlord had such a large family. Nor were large families only found among the managerial landlords, since they were also found among rentier landlords. We have emphasized the size of landlord families because, where there were so many family consumers, the percentage of agricultural product put on the open market was lessened and the landlord's

self-sufficiency was correspondingly increased. The self-sufficient nature of the managerial landlord economy is also seen in the practice of setting up each married son's family as a small sub-unit. Cotton was handed out to the wives in these "sub-units" who set about providing the clothes for the family, using their own spinning wheels, looms, and so forth. Both Shujing tang and Taihe tang provide examples of this practice.

Although part of the expenditure for labor and means of production took the form of commodity exchange (since the laborers were not members of the landlord's family), the aim remained the basic one of production for the landlord's family. To put it another way, the landlords hired the labor and amassed the means of production not in order to produce for the market but rather in order to provide the daily necessities of their families. Seen from this point of view, it does not seem unreasonable to include expenditure for labor and means of production within the rubric of landlord self-sufficiency. We have dwelt on the natural economy of self-sufficiency, since it forms one of the basic characteristics of feudal society and hence serves to underline the feudal element of the managerial-landlord economy.

2) The management of the farming operation still retained the influence of control by the head of the family, as would be expected in an operation whose main purpose was the combination of production for family consumption and production of grain for the market. We did not find a single managerial landlord in Shandong who had left his family to set up a farm run like a modern enterprise. The heads of managerial landlord families were like local emperors, controlling everything to do with the family and making no distinction between agricultural production and family matters affecting livelihood. In his analysis of the necessary conditions of capitalist production, Lenin pointed out that "agriculture had to be organized on the same lines as any other commercial or industrial enterprise and not as the business of the lord."[23] In this respect, the managerial landlords clearly belonged to the latter category.

3) Managerial landlords were frequently rentier landlords at

the same time. This is easy to understand. As a landlord accumulated more and more land, much of it was outside his own village. This he would rent out. Even in his own village, as more and more land came in, it was convenient to let out sections of it. For example, Bi Dian-kui of Xinji village, Linyi district, owned 460 mu in 1900, of which he rented out 60; Lu Zun-shu of Baibu village, Pingdu district, owned 750 mu in 1897, of which he farmed 200 directly and let out 550; Ding Shao-chen of Chenjia village, Zhucheng district, owned 2,350 mu in 1896, of which he farmed 75 directly and let out 2,275; Yu Qing-liang of Zhangdai village, Yishui district, owned 500 mu in 1894, of which he farmed 50 directly and let out 450.[24]

In Chinese feudal society, the dominant relations of production were tenurial relations whereby middle and poor peasants and tenants were personally subjected to the landlords—a strongly feudal relationship. Consequently, the larger the amount of land let out by the managerial landlords, the more they retained feudal characteristics.

4) Although usury capital does not in itself represent any form of relations of production, it does have a very definite role in society. In our survey of 131 landlords from 46 districts, we found that 89 (68 percent of total) engaged in some form of usury or another (whether lending grain or cash, or opening cash shops and pawn shops, see Appendix B). Interest was usually between 30 percent and 50 percent a year, and it was often compound. Grain loans were usually at an annual rate of between 50 percent and 100 percent. In general, the landlords' debtors were neither rich landlords nor poor wage laborers but rather peasants with a certain amount of land, which the landlords were anxious to get into their own hands. Such peasants imagined that, by borrowing money or grain, they could avert ruin, but, once a peasant had entered into debt, it was extremely difficult for him to get out without giving up his land. Once the landlord had gained possession of the land, whether he chose to farm it directly or let it out depended upon how much land he owned at the time. The original peasant owner became either a tenant or a wage laborer, depending upon the land-

lord's decision. Usury had a definite role in the landlord economy of that time, a role which emerges only from a study of the actual conditions in which it operated. One thing is certainly very clear and that is that the landlords did not make loans to aid agriculture or handicrafts; most peasants were forced to borrow grain because of hardship and, as a result, they fell into the landlord's clutches; there are only a very few examples of peasants' using a landlord loan to finance a fairly large side occupation. For these reasons, it is our opinion that the managerial landlords' usury activities were still characteristically feudal.

5) In politics, the landlords exercised gentry prerogatives. The despotic government was particularly solicitous toward the class it represented and granted many special privileges to the local gentry. Apart from the licentiates' (*shengyuan*) being excused land taxes, the landlord class had the right to concern themselves with local affairs. They were frequently the organizers of calamity relief, the repair of temples and ancestral halls, and other such matters. They were also the arbiters of all forms of dispute, whether within the lineage or within the village. Their word could often carry the force of law. Whether it was a question of brothers' founding separate families, the adoption of children, the suicide of women, burial of relatives, dealing with robberies, or taking a case before the magistrate, they were the obvious activists. They could see to it that someone came off well, or, conversely, they could ruin someone. These broad powers deeply influenced the lives of the owner-peasants and poor peasants in the village. Those peasants, including the long- and short-term laborers who depended for their livelihood in whole or in part on working for the landlords had no option but to tremble before their power and do exactly as they were told.

Not only the managerial landlords but also the laborers who worked for them had numerous feudal characteristics.

The hired laborers still retained certain serf-like characteristics, especially the long-term laborers. The survey showed that, apart from the foreman, all the other long-term laborers could, besides doing their particular work, also be ordered at will by the landlord to go on errands, carry letters, look after his children, do sewing or needlework, guard the orchard, gather up the leftovers from the harvest, sweep the courtyard, accompany the landlord's relatives, and other such household tasks. Day or night, rain or shine, they had to do exactly as they were told. If they were slow or did something wrong, it was usually considered perfectly "legal" to shout at them and beat them, as reflected in the saying "You serve the family that supplies your rice." Landlords were supported in this type of behavior by the law (see Chapter 3). The *Prefectural Gazetteer of Qingzhou* records that the district magistrate of Zhucheng in 1743, Wang Zhi-zeng, "went out into the fields and found eight or nine peasants resting their heads on their hoes taking a noontime nap. He questioned them and found that they were hired laborers loafing. Zhi-zeng then told them that they were not farming on their own account, they were taking another person's money and food and were idling on the job. He gave them the punishment of 20 strokes of the heavy bamboo each. After this, the laborers worked twice as hard."[25] This can be taken as a small example of the way the feudal officials sided with the landlords in their exploitative treatment of the wage laborers.

Because of the harsh exploitation through feudal rents and because of the low productivity of the time, wages of the laborers were extremely low, and they were generally unable to support anyone apart from themselves. As a result, many were unable to marry or married late. These pressures led frequently to wage laborers' trying to become owner-peasants or tenants, especially as they approached middle age. Since agricultural production was not as complex as industrial production, on leaving the managerial landlord's employment, they were able to use the help of their wives and children to scratch a living on their own or rented land, putting up with the exploitation of the feudal state and landlords in order to live with their wives and children. Cheng Si-he's life followed just this pattern. At the time when we interviewed him in Jiujun market town, Zhangqiu district, he was seventy-one. At the age of fifteen, he had begun working for a managerial landlord family by the name of Shize tang. He had had to grind grain, put up fences, fetch water, take food out to the laborers, feed the oxen and pigs, and so on. His annual wage was 14 strings of cash. He continued working in this way until 1927, at which time his wage had risen to 30 dollars. In that year he borrowed a little money and, with that and the 2 mu he had managed to accumulate, he was able to leave Shize tang and marry and set up as an owner-peasant household. Other similar examples from the survey could also be cited. The fundamental reason that led wage laborers to turn into peasants or tenants was the lowness of their wages. As Marx put it: "The value of labor-power is determined, as in the case of every other commodity, by the labor-time necessary for the production, and consequently also the reproduction, of the special article ... Hence the sum of the means of subsistence necessary for the production of labor-power must include the means necessary for the laborer's substitutes, i.e., his children."[26]

The difference between the wage paid to the laborers by the Shandong managerial landlords and the value of the laborers' actual produce was very large. Thus, both former laborers and those who still worked for a pittance as laborers suffered in their different ways from feudal exploitation, and their spontaneous tendency was toward becoming owner-peasants and tenants.

Although there were occasions, perhaps, when the short-term laborers did not use their own tools when working for the land-lords or only used them to a limited extent and although their tools were smaller than those of the landlords, nevertheless there is no doubt that it was the usual practice for short-term laborers to bring their own small tools to the laborers' market and to take them and use them when working for the landlords. Thus it was common for the more than a thousand laborers who gathered at the short-term laborers' market in Jiujun market town towards the end of the Qing dynasty to bring their own tools with them as did the 700 or 800 laborers who gathered at the Wangcun market town short-term laborers' market. In our opinion, this practice is similar to the labor-service system found in Russia, whereby neighboring peasants brought their own tools to cultivate the landlord's fields. In his discussion of this system, Lenin pointed out: "The labor-service system and the patriarchal peasant economy inseparably connected with it are by their very nature based on routine technique and on the preservation of antiquated methods of production. There is nothing in the internal structure of that economic regime to stimulate the transformation of technique; on the contrary the secluded and isolated character of that economic system and the poverty and downtrodden condition of the dependent peasant preclude the possibility of improvements."[27]

The labor-service system is a remnant of the feudal economy. In his discussion of the different methods of obtaining surplus product under a labor-service economy and under a capitalist economy, Lenin observed that the latter type of economy was "based . . . on the producer being dispossessed of the land."[28]

The hiring of short-term laborers in China had the effect of slowing down differentiation among the peasantry. Thus, from a certain point of view, they represented a feudal element of the economy. But, at the same time, it should be pointed out that Lenin distinguished between two types of labor-service system. One was "labor-service that can only be performed by a peasant farmer who owns draft animals and implements," and the other was one that "can be performed by a rural proletarian who has no implements," and this latter type "constitutes a direct transition to capitalism."[29]

The short-term labor system in Qing Shandong did not belong to the first type because the majority of those hiring themselves out as short-term laborers did not own draft animals or heavy agricultural implements. The first type of labor-service system was practiced only by rich peasants and small managerial landlords who had emerged from the peasantry.

In both the long-term and short-term labor systems, there was still a marked use of payment in kind, even to the extent that, in certain cases, the entire wage was paid in kind. All the managerial landlords provided the laborers (both long- and short-term) with food in addition to cash. In the survey, we gathered details on the proportion of the wage paid in kind and in money, which show that the proportion paid in kind was considerable. For example, Taihe tang's foreman (long-term laborer), Feng Ba-zi, received an annual wage of 29.7 strings of cash (the equivalent of 454 jin of kaoliang at the contemporary price of 3,600 cash per dou). His wage in kind (food) (at two jin of kaoliang per day) amounted annually to 720 jin or 266 jin more than his money wage, that is to say 158.6 percent of his money wage. Taihe tang's short-term laborers received an average daily wage of 124 cash, which was the equivalent of 1.7 jin of kaoliang. Their wage in kind was 2 jin of kaoliang per day or 117.7 percent of their money wage. Nor was the money wage always paid entirely in money. For example, the Taihe tang wage labor accounts record that, in 1907, Qiu Si-zhang (long-term laborer) "took 1 sheng of maize valued at 400 cash"; in 1908, Feng Ba-zi (long-term) "took 2 sheng of wheat valued at 1,120 cash and 1 dou of kaoliang valued at 3,600 cash"; in 1908, Feng Peng-lin (short-term) "took 5 sheng of millet valued at 1,900 cash." These entries show that even the monetary part of the laborers' wages was on occasion paid in kind. Furthermore, the survey data show that it was a common practice in various places in Shandong at this time to pay the shepherd's wages, apart from his food, in wool, while the herdsman in some cases was paid entirely in grain. Payment in kind belongs to the natural economy, and its widespread use by the managerial landlords is another important piece of evidence that their economy retained certain characteristic feudal features.

Chapter 8

PRELIMINARY CONCLUSIONS

In the preceding chapter, we explained the comparatively progressive nature of the production process of the managerial landlord economy, as well as pointing out those features that hindered its further development and those of its characteristics that were feudal remnants and those that were capitalist in nature. These findings suggest that, in certain basic matters, there was a distinction between the economy of the managerial landlords and that of the rentier landlords.

In a discussion of the basic relations of production in feudal society, the *History of the Communist Party of the Soviet Union (Bolsheviks), Short Course,* states that "the basis of the relations of production under the feudal system is that the feudal lord owns the means of production and does not fully own the worker in production—the serf whom the feudal lord can no longer kill, but whom he can buy and sell."[1]

Lenin has given us the classic description of the characteristics of the structure of feudal economy derived from these basic relations of production: "Such an economy required that the direct producer be allotted the means of production in general, and land in particular; moreover that he be tied to the land, since otherwise the landlord was not assured of lands." And he goes on to say that "a condition for such a system of economy was the personal dependence of the peasant on the landlord. If the landlord had not possessed direct power over the person of the peasant, he could not have compelled a man who had a plot of land and ran his own farm to work for him. Hence, other than economic pressure, as Marx says in describing this economic regime, was necessary."[2]

The feudal landlords relied upon their *ownership* of land. Their use of extra-economic types of coercion to exact very high *rents* from the serfs (in China those "who were allotted the means of production in general, and land in particular," that is, the tenants) is the general characteristic of feudal ownership.

215

The various *novel* aspects of the economy of the managerial landlords clearly do not completely fit such a definition.

In our opinion the structure of the economy of the managerial landlords when compared with that of the rentier landlords shows the following important differences.

In the first place, the managerial landlords did not operate a system (as did the rentier landlords) in which the land was scattered, leading to an inadequacy on any given holding, of implements, transport, fertilizer, labor, animals, and specialization and resultant low yields. On the contrary, the managerial landlords brought the lands together into one operation and were able to provide sufficient implements, transport, fertilizer, labor, and animal power, as well as coordination of labor to be able to produce comparatively high yields.

Second, unlike the rentier landlord—the owner of the means of production—who no longer needed to have the direct producer tied to the land, but relied (and relied exclusively) on his owner-ship of the land and on the rent system to exploit the direct pro-ducer, the managerial landlord relied primarily upon money and the hiring of labor to exploit the surplus labor of the direct pro-ducers—the long- and short-term laborers.

To consider another aspect of the relations of production, in the managerial landlords' economy, the direct producer was no longer the tenant peasant who had to be allotted the means of production in general, and land in particular, and to be subjected to extra-economic exploitation, but, instead, the long-term laborer —basically no longer tied to the means of production, particularly to the land, and free from feudal constraints against selling his labor power—and the rural semiproletarian (the short-term laborer) who had still not entirely broken his ties with the land.

At the same time, the relationship set up by both types of laborers with their employers in the course of production was no longer the semi-bonded landlord-tenant relationship but a com-paratively free *monetary hiring relationship.*

In the third place, while the rentier landlords did everything in their power to turn peasants who had fallen on to hard times into tenants and thus once more to tie them to the land, the managerial landlords turned such ruined peasants into hired laborers, giving them proletarian or semiproletarian status. Thus, the differentiation of the peasantry was given a new content and, as a result, the internal relations of the agricultural labor market were strengthened, giving rise to an area advantageous to the growth of "a class accustomed to undertaking hired labor."

Furthermore, since the managerial landlords aimed to produce a comparatively large percentage of their grain for the market, they sold far more in the surrounding markets than did the rentier landlords. In seeking to expand their farming activities, the managerial landlords also produced a demand for land, implements, animals, and articles of consumption from the surrounding markets, and as a result somewhat spurred on the integration of the local markets of Shandong with the national market.

For the reasons summarized above, we conclude that the structure of the economy of the managerial landlords of Qing Shandong was a *transitional one already on the way toward a capitalist system.*

But, on the other hand, the production aims of the managerial landlords were still to a very considerable extent concerned with self-sufficiency. The control of their operation was still in the hands of the head of the family; they rented out portions of their land; they ran feudalistic moneylending activities; and in society they still exercised gentry prerogatives. The direct producers on their land, the long-term laborers, still retained characteristics of household serfs and their usual progression was to become tenants or small self-owner peasants. Their short-term laborers still brought their own tools to work with them, and payment in kind still accounted for a large portion of the wages of both long-term and short-term laborers. In view of these factors, we should not overlook the important feudal elements still present in the transitional economy of the managerial landlords.

In our opinion, it is necessary to recognize that the characteristics of the production relations of a particular economy can be different from the nature of the entire society of which they form a part; a single concept cannot necessarily encompass them both. In the matter of changes in production relations themselves, those that have just begun to change and those that have completely effected the change are not the same. For example, feudal production relations and fully developed capitalist relations both belong in the category of capitalist relations of production. But for one to grow into the other requires a period of development which in China was the period of the growth of the "embryo of capitalism." In the changing of a whole society, one beginning to take shape is different from one which is well developed. For example, a society which has only a certain number of developed capitalist production relations is different from one in which capitalist relations of production are widespread and dominant. A period of development is required to lead from the emergence of capitalism to the establishment of capitalism. The period in which more and more single elements of capitalist economy are emerging is the period of the formation of capitalism. Naturally, individual relations of production cannot be sharply separated out and treated separately from those found throughout a given society.

In our opinion, the economy of the managerial landlords in Qing Shandong was a structure which had just begun to change its nature; it had not yet become a fully capitalist phenomenon. For this reason, it belongs to the period of the early development of capitalism in China. If no new elements had emerged even though the managerial landlord economy had been widespread, it would have been insufficient to alter the nature of society. Granted a time when many elements of capitalism were appearing, the managerial landlord economy would have to be seen as an economic phenomenon during the period of the formation of capitalism. Thus, to affirm the capitalist nature of the managerial landlords in Qing Shandong is not to suggest that China had, at that time, already entered the period of the formation of capitalism. What can be affirmed is the point made by Comrade Mao Ze-dong: "As China's feudal society developed its commodity economy and so carried within itself the embryo of capitalism, China would of herself have developed slowly into a capitalist society, even if there had been no influence of foreign imperialism."[3]

APPENDIXES

The three appendixes which follow are based on the materials gathered for us by cadres and primary school teachers in each locality.

Since the conditions we were interested in in the questionnaires were the conditions of sixty years ago, we had to rely on the memories of old men. Memories can be mistaken and facts distorted and, furthermore, we were not able to administer the questionnaire directly. For these reasons, it is very likely that some of the figures in the appendixes are incorrect. Nevertheless, we believe that, for the most part, the material in the appendixes reflects actual conditions in Shandong at the end of the Qing dynasty. Our main arguments in this little study have been based on these materials and we therefore felt obliged to publish them so that readers could refer to them at their convenience.

We should also warn readers that the categories of differentiation for the classes in the villages in Appendix A are not the same as those used today. The categories we used were those most familiar to our informants, and they correspond to our understanding of the conditions of sixty years ago. For example, under "tenants" we have not distinguished between rich and poor tenants, and the present-day categories of poor and middle peasant would both be included in our "owner-peasant" category.

The authors
December 16, 1957

Appendix A

CLASS STRUCTURE OF 197 VILLAGES IN 42 DISTRICTS OF SHANDONG, c. 1900

Region 1 – Villages With Both Managerial Landlords and Rentier Landlords:

District/Village	Total number of households in village	Peasants			Rich Peasants	Landlords			Others
		Wage laborer households	Tenant households	Owner-peasant households	Hiring 1–3 long-term laborers	Hiring 4–8 long-term laborers	Hiring 9 or more long-term laborers	Renting out more than 50 mu	
Licheng/Yaojiacun	240	—	30	60	12	1	—	3	134
Zhangqiu/Qilangyuan	266	12	88	160	3	2	—	1	—
Zhangqiu/Qilangyuan-zhaizi	75	10	16	46	2	—	—	1	—
Zhangqiu/Lijiating	68	2	25	37	3	—	—	1	—
Zhangqiu/Zhaojiazhuang	38	1	16	20	1	—	—	—	—
Zhangqiu/Xiyingcun	174	8	25	135	4	—	—	2	—
Zhangqiu/Beiguancun	90	30	30	16	5	1	—	8	—
Zhangqiu/Xiguancun	320	50	50	100	40	10	10	60	—
Zhangqiu/Xibeiyucun	207	22	11	160	7	—	—	7	—
Zhangqiu/Qiaozhuang	143	2	15	120	3	—	—	3	—
Zhangqiu/Qiaozicun	60	6	30	24	—	—	—	—	—
Zhangqiu/Dong-gucun	62	8	18	34	2	—	—	—	—
Zhangqiu/Beiduozhuang	105	10	5	85	5	—	—	—	—
Zhangqiu/Dakangzhuang	253	150	15	75	11	1	—	1	—
Changshan/Qiujiazhuang	70	3	3	12	4	—	—	—	48
Changshan/Meijiazhuang	30	7	8	15	3	—	—	—	7
Zouping/Guanzhuang	70	6	5	35	3	1	—	3	17
Zouping/Shaojiacun	30	—	—	27	2	—	—	1	—

Village								
Tai-an/Shankoucun	371	40	30	250	17	15	—	19	—
Tai-an/Jiaogucun	343	35	14	250	14	1	—	3	26
Tai-an/Mazhuang Lijiacun	34	11	12	10	—	—	—	1	—
Tai-an/Mazhuang Donghaizi	50	14	11	22	1	1	—	1	—
Tai-an/Mazhuang Xihaizi	50	15	12	20	1	1	—	1	—
Tai-an/Mazhuang Wujiaxinzhuang	63	20	30	8	5	—	—	—	—
Tai-an/Bamudicun	75	10	3	52	7	3	—	3	64
Tai-an/Xiyangloucun	600	30	5	490	5	1	—	3	49
Tai-an/Kaijiacun	130	40	20	19	—	1	—	1	6
Tai-an/Anzhuang	600	150	130	300	12	1	—	1	3
Tai-an/Nankougou	190	30	45	111	1	—	—	—	1
Tai-an/Xijiangzhuang	180	34	40	104	1	—	—	—	1
Xintai/Beishidian	45	6	11	18	4	1	—	4	10
Feicheng/Dongxiangcun	628	120	180	300	4	3	2	9	—
Feicheng/Jinzhen	65	16	—	46	2	—	—	1	—
Pingying/Liboshicun	180	50	50	50	5	10	1	15	8
Pingying/Liusuocun	120	—	57	53	—	—	1	1	—
Pingying/Erhumiao	143	—	21	120	—	—	—	1	—
Yidu/Songjiazhuang	90	15	10	58	2	2	—	3	—
Yidu/Shenwangzhuang	100	20	15	55	4	2	—	4	—
Yidu/Nanxindian	80	10	8	56	3	1	—	2	—
Yidu/Shanjiazhuangzi	80	12	5	56	5	1	—	1	—
Yidu/Yuhuangmiao	100	10	5	79	5	1	—	—	—
Yidu/Hetaoyuan	200	30	10	146	10	2	—	2	—
Yidu/Putongzhuang	220	25	12	159	15	5	—	4	—
Yidu/Zihejie	200	20	18	135	10	7	—	10	—
Yidu/Hedongzhuang	100	10	15	67	5	2	—	1	—

Region 1 – Villages With No Rentier Landlords:

Village								
Licheng/Lijiacun	180	100	—	—	3	—	1	—	6
Licheng/Lijiazhai	197	30	—	157	10	—	—	—	—

Appendix A (cont.)

District/Village	Total number of households in village	Peasants			Rich Peasants	Landlords			Others
		Wage laborer households	Tenant households	Owner-peasant households	Hiring 1-3 long-term laborers	Hiring 4-8 long-term laborers	Hiring 9 or more long-term laborers	Renting out more than 50 mu	
Zhangqiu/Xiyaocun	70	—	—	67	1	2	—	—	—
Zhangqiu/Jiegouhe	78	20	—	50	7	—	1	—	—
Zhangqiu/Cuitianzhuang	27	2	—	23	1	1	—	—	—
Zhangqiu/Huangtianzhuang	21	2	—	18	1	1	—	—	—
Zhangqiu/Hantianzhuang	19	2	—	16	1	—	—	—	—
Zhangqiu/Ganqiaocun	51	3	—	47	1	—	—	—	—
Zhangqiu/Maliucun	72	3	—	67	2	—	—	—	—
Zhangqiu/Wencaocun	57	15	—	40	2	—	—	—	—
Zhangqiu/Dayecun	250	40	—	205	4	—	—	—	—
Zhangqiu/Zhaijiazhuang	320	20	—	150	8	5	1	—	137
Zhangqiu/Bucunnancun	102	2	—	98	1	1	1	—	—
Zhangqiu/Zhaijiazhaozhuang	44	—	—	43	—	1	—	—	—
Zhangqiu/Wangjiazhaozhuang	62	—	—	60	2	—	—	—	—
Zhangqiu/Liujiazhaozhuang	70	—	—	69	1	—	—	—	—
Zhangqiu/Guanzhuang	500	15	12.5	497	1	2	—	—	—
Zhangqiu/Beibijiazhuang	120	15	—	40	3	—	1	—	61
Zhangqiu/Biyangzhuang	75	12	—	30	5	—	1	—	27
Zhangqiu/Lifuzhuang	100	2	—	90	7	1	—	—	—
Zhangqiu/Xianggongzhuang	800	40	—	588	50	—	1	—	120
Zichuan/Sulizhuang	87	20	—	60	3	3	2	—	—
Zichuan/Wangdongcun	90	15	—	75	8	—	1	—	—
Zichuan/Dashangzhuang	140	—	—	137	3	—	—	—	—

Village									
Zichuan/Shengucun	76	55	—	10	—	—	1	—	10
Tai-an/Hexicun	104	12	—	81	8	—	—	—	3
Tai-an/Quanbocun	153	8	—	130	11	—	—	—	4
Tai-an/Yüejiatun	117	8	—	100	7	—	—	—	2
Feicheng/Sanhuangdian	13	4	—	8	1	—	—	—	—
Feicheng/Wangdian	45	14	—	29	2	—	—	—	—
Feicheng/Dongwangdian	27	5	—	21	1	—	1	—	—
Pingying/Guogoucun	100	2	—	96	1	—	—	—	—
Pingying/Qianyanghe	50	1	—	48	1	—	—	—	—
Pingying/Houyanghe	45	—	—	44	1	—	—	—	—
Pingying/Guquan	160	1	—	157	2	—	—	—	—

Region 2 – Villages With Both Managerial Landlords and Rentier Landlords:

Village									
Xiajin/Zhengbaotun	389	12	46	257	43	—	—	31	—
Xiajin/Zhangquantun	503	158	80	159	1	2	—	3	100
Xiajin/Wangtailaizhuang	202	11	3	155	12	1	—	—	—
Xiajin/Wangjing	240	21	6	207	6	—	—	—	—
Xiajin/Mozhuang	200	20	12	155	13	2	—	4	—
Tangyi/Dingliubazhai	90	21	23	35	5	—	—	1	—
Liaocheng/Diaozhuang	15	—	9	4	1	—	—	—	—
Liaocheng/Qiaohuangzhuang	10	—	6	—	4	—	—	4	—
Liaocheng/Zhoutangcun	35	7	10	11	3	—	—	8	—
Liaocheng/Xisilicun	92	4	8	70	2	—	—	2	—
Liaocheng/Dongsilicun	95	—	7	85	1	—	—	—	—
Liaocheng/Renmiao	63	5	7	47	4	—	—	2	—
Wenshang/Dongliloucun	224	75	22	119	4	2	—	3	—
Dongping/Wanggaizicun	29	15	2	5	1	2	1	—	—
Dongping/Dayangzhuang	124	—	6	107	11	—	—	1	—
Dongping/Houkoucun	31	2	11	12	5	—	—	—	1
Dongping/Qianhe-ai	72	15	37	3	7	—	—	—	10
Dongping/Zhangkoucun	73	7	3	62	1	—	—	—	—

Appendix A (cont.)

District/Village	Total number of households in village	Peasants			Rich Peasants	Landlords			Others
		Wage laborer households	Tenant households	Owner-peasant households	Hiring 1-3 long-term laborers	Hiring 4-8 long-term laborers	Hiring 9 or more long-term laborers	Renting out more than 50 mu	
Dongping/Yüloucun	71	15	35	18	2	—	—	1	—
Dongping/Dongliangcun	42	8	18	14	—	2	—	—	—
Dongping/Daliuzhuang	71	30	20	15	2	1	2	1	—
Dongping/Zhifang	50	20	10	16	—	1	1	2	—
Region 2—Villages With No Rentier Landlords									
Xiajin/Qiaoguantun	343	50	—	272	20	1	—	—	—
Xiajin/Yinziwangzhuang	161	10	—	140	11	—	—	—	—
Dexian/Fenghuangdian	210	?	—	?	4	?	?	—	—
Region 3—Villages with Both Managerial and Rentier Landlords									
Lijin/Beimacun	28	3	3	20	1	—	—	—	—
Boxing/Longhecun	656	250	130	170	8	5	2	1	—
Boxing/Tuntiancun	366	120	152	88	3	2	1	—	—
Linyi/Weizhuang	30	14	4	2	10	—	—	—	—
Linyi/Xinji	124	24	3	92	3	—	1	1	—
Linyi/Wanghuazhuang	50	25	10	14	1	—	—	—	—
Linyi/Dongzhaizhuang	40	25	8	5	2	—	—	—	—
Linyi/Yangguanying	83	40	17	19	5	—	—	—	—
Linzi/Nanfengkecun	30	5	18	5	—	—	1	1	2
Linzi/Xiguchengcun	70	3	3	40	10	1	—	1	12

Binxian/Shanliuducun	71	30	1	28	11	—	—	—	—	1	—
Binxian/Yinjicun	118	20	25	60	5	1	—	—	—	—	7
Binxian/Qianyincun	40	12	3	18	4	—	—	—	—	—	3
Binxian/Bakunzhangcun	23	5	6	12	—	1	—	—	1	—	—
Binxian/Xuanjiacun	58	15	10	31	10	—	—	—	—	—	—
Putai/Xiehecun	150	30	5	105	10	—	—	—	—	—	—

Region 3– Villages With No Rentier Landlords

Lijin/Yangdongcun	80	8	—	69	3	—	—	—	—	—	—
Lijin/Qianwangcun	59	2	—	54	3	—	—	—	—	—	—
Lijin/Daniucun	60	5	—	49	6	—	2	2	—	—	—
Binxian/Lizezhen	500	10	—	473	13	2	—	—	—	—	—
Binxian/Xiaowujiacun	80	6	—	74	—	—	—	—	—	—	—
Binxian/Guanjiacun	100	95	—	5	—	—	—	—	—	—	—
Binxian/Sunjiacun	53	39	—	11	3	1	—	—	—	—	—
Binxian/Zhengjiacun	130	99	—	22	8	—	—	—	—	—	—
Binxian/Bijiacun	110	73	—	30	7	—	—	—	—	—	—
Binxian/Diaoshilicun	118	60	—	55	—	3	—	—	—	—	—
Binxian/Dongliucun	31	22	—	8	1	—	—	—	—	—	—
Binxian/Liujiakoucun	38	30	—	8	—	—	—	—	—	—	—
Binxian/Tishanghucun	86	22	—	60	4	—	—	—	—	—	—
Binxian/Liujia-aicun	67	30	—	33	4	—	—	—	—	—	—
Huimin/Weijicun	350	150	—	170	22	4	4	4	—	—	—
Putai/Xiaomalicun	146	10	—	132	4	—	—	—	—	—	—
Boxing/Changjiacun	80	—	—	69	11	—	—	—	—	—	—
Boxing/Jiaojiacun	75	—	—	72	3	—	—	—	—	—	—
Boxing/Liushanrencun	70	—	—	68	2	—	—	—	—	—	—
Boxing/Beixiangchengcun	80	—	—	77	3	—	—	—	—	—	—
Boxing/Xiangchengli	85	—	—	83	2	—	—	—	—	—	—
Boxing/Longhecun	565	250	130	170	8	5	2	2	—	—	—

Appendix A (cont.)

| District/Village | Total number of households in village | Peasants | | | Rich Peasants | | Landlords | | Others |
		Wage laborer house-holds	Tenant house-holds	Owner-peasant house-holds	Hiring 1-3 long-term laborers	Hiring 4-8 long-term laborers	Hiring 9 or more long-term laborers	Renting out more than 50 mu	
Region 4 – Villages With Managerial and Rentier Landlords									
Changyi/Xishiqiaocun	19	—	—	13	1	2	1	2	—
Changyi/Beixingfucun	374	15	210	135	6	—	—	8	—
Yexian/Shilibaocun	60	1	53	2	2	—	1	1	—
Yexian/Xizhangjiacun	79	1	10	64	2	—	1	1	—
Penglai/Shangkougaojiacun	129	7	60	53	6	2	—	1	—
Penglai/Taizicun	20	—	10	8	—	—	—	—	2
Penglai/Dacaijiacun	92	6	31	50	1	—	—	1	3
Penglai/Erliujiacun	161	5	30	107	2	1	—	2	14
Penglai/Beilinyuan	155	?	?	?	21	?	?	1	—
Fushan/Dong-guancun	294	30	120	120	23	—	—	1	—
Fushan/Wangcun	86	56	8	18	3	—	—	1	—
Qixia/Zhongqiaocun	285	20	60	170	30	1	—	4	—
Qixia/Malingzhong	46	14	5	11	6	2	—	8	—
Zhaoyuan/Houkuangcun	40	2	5	24	3	3	1	2	—
Laiyang/Nanzuojiakuangcun	52	12	10	11	15	4	—	—	—
Laiyang/Zhongbupucun	10	6	2	—	1	—	—	—	—
Laiyang/Liangpocun	30	18	3	7	2	—	—	1	—
Laiyang/Lingnantoucun	80	12	?	?	?	1	—	—	—
Jiaoxian/Tanjiacun	99	30	4	60	5	1	—	1	—
Jiaoxian/Qianxiaozhuang	78	10	3	60	5	—	—	—	—
Jiaoxian/Nanloucun	98	10	2	80	6	—	—	—	—

Village									
Jiaoxian/Wangjiazhuang	43	6	24	10	2	1	—	—	—
Jiaoxian/Lingshenmiao	57	27	27	3	—	—	—	—	—
Jiaoxian/Guojiazhuang	91	30	40	20	1	2	—	—	—
Jiaoxian/Xiaozhuang	41	8	5	17	6	2	2	3	—
Pingdu/Qianjiazhuang	84	10	50	20	—	7	—	2	—
Pingdu/Gushancun	1,400	180	57	1,120	30	18	25	6	—
Pingdu/Baibucun	1,050	80	250	250	7	—	—	8	?

Region 4—Villages With No Landlords

Village									
Changyi/Lijiazhuang	63	2	—	58	3	—	—	—	—
Changyi/Yuejiazhuang	52	3	—	47	2	—	—	—	—

Region 5—Villages With Both Managerial and Rentier Landlords

Village									
Guanxian/Wangliukouzhai	115	10	5	87	6	7	—	—	—
Fanxian/Nanyangzhuang	20	—	14	5	—	—	—	1	—
Fanxian/Houlilou	24	—	11	10	—	1	—	1	1
Puxian/Guyunji	?	?	?	?	10	5	?	10	—
Puxian/Weiji	49	—	30	—	—	1	—	19	—
Puxian/Lizhuang	54	15	5	30	3	1	—	—	—
Puxian/Zhengzhuang	17	3	2	10	2	—	—	2	—
Heze/Tong-guji	304	20	30	250	2	—	—	2	—
Heze/Cuiliuzhuang	64	4	6	50	2	1	—	—	—
Tancheng/Guozhuang	110	50	3	54	2	1	—	—	—
Tancheng/Mazhuang	70	35	1	32	1	1	—	—	—
Feixian/Sunjiazhai	8	—	7	—	1	—	—	—	—
Feixian/Wangjialou	8	5	2	—	—	1	—	—	—
Feixian/Nanshilipu	10	—	8	—	2	—	—	—	—
Yishui/Xiaweicun	160	32	55	63	5	—	—	5	—
Yishui/Zhangdaicun	70	6	15	19	14	1	—	15	—
Zhucheng/Xiangzhoucun	1,086	40	500	250	124	32	20	120	—

228

Appendix A (cont.)

District/Village	Total number of households in village	Peasants			Rich Peasants	Landlords			Others
		Wage laborer households	Tenant households	Owner-peasant households	Hiring 1-3 long-term laborers	Hiring 4-8 long-term laborers	Hiring 9 or more long-term laborers	Renting out more than 50 mu	
Zhucheng/Futaicun	12	6	3	2	—	—	—	1	—
Zhucheng/Chenjiacun	88	10	70	2	2	1	—	3	—
Anqiu/Laihetao	81	50	25	—	2	—	—	4	—
Anqiu/Huawu	20	5	10	5	—	—	—	—	—
Zouxian/Dahuangzhuang	59	4	26	15	2	3	2	7	—
Region 5 – Villages With No Rentier Landlords									
Zouxian/Liangxiadian	257	21	—	225	6	3	2	—	—
Zouxian/Daniuchang	80	5	—	71	2	—	2	—	—

Source: Materials collected in March 1957.

Appendix B

ECONOMIC ACTIVITIES OF 131 MANAGERIAL LANDLORDS FROM 46 DISTRICTS OF SHANDONG, c. 1900

(Unit = shimu)

Finding number	District/Village	Name of landlord	Origin of wealth	Total land owned	Amount farmed with hired labor	Amount rented out	Business and handicraft activities	Extent of usury operations
Region 1								
1	Licheng/Lijiacun	Li Shulian	Official	1,000	1,000	—	Pharmacy/hostel	Neighboring villages
2	Licheng/ Laocengkou	Lou Xixian	Trade	500	300	200	Pharmacy/wine/ old clothes/ embroidery shops	Neighboring villages
3	Zhangqiu/ Guanzhuangcun	Li Yuangui	Farming	360	360	—	Flour mill	Neighboring villages
4	Zhangqiu/ Nanguancun	Wang Zibai	Trade	600	200	400	Wine/pharmacy and miscella- neous goods shops/oil press	Same village
5	Zhangqiu/Bucun	Zhang Lüeshi	Farming	360	240	120		Neighboring villages
6	Zhangqiu/Yujiacun	Yonghe tang	Trade	750	750	—	Cotton cloth store in Qing- jiang	
7	Zhangqiu/ Zhangyilangcun	Li Yulan	Trade	300	300	—	Silk and cotton shops	One cash shop and loans in neigh- boring villages

Appendix B (cont.)

Finding number	District/Village	Name of landlord	Origin of wealth	Total land owned	Amount farmed with hired labor	Amount rented out	Business and handicraft activities	Extent of usury operations
8	Zhangqiu/Shantoudian	Han Xiansheng	Trade	213	213	—	Cotton cloth shop	Cash shop
9	Zhangqiu/Xianggongzhuang	Yiyi tang	Trade	300	300	—	Three pharmacies/wine shop/cotton firm	Pawn shop/loans in neighboring villages
10	Zhangqiu/Bucunnancun	Li Jiashu	Coal mine	360	360	—	Old clothes/wine and cooking pot shops	Neighboring villages
11	Zhangqiu/Xiguancun	Gao Xiting	Trade	250	120	130	Wine shop	Pawn shop
12	Zhangqiu/Cuitianzhuang	Cui Chengfu	Trade	300	100	200	Carpenters/tea shop	Neighboring villages
13	Zhangqiu/Mingshui	Li Kunshan	Trade	600	600	—	Weaving works in Mingshui	Pawn shop in Jinan
14	Zhangqiu/Beiguancun	Zhang Jinghuan	Trade	250	100	150	Wine shop	Pawn shop/cash shop
15	Zhangqiu/Qilangyuan	Li Wenjiang	Trade	390	120	270	Cotton cloth store in Jinan	Neighboring villages
16	Zhangqiu/Dakangzhuang	Liu Qingxin	Trade	180	180	—	Condiment works/miscellaneous goods shop/salt shop/flour mill	Silver shop/loans in same village
17	Zhangqiu/Lifuzhuang	Song Kefa	Trade	180	180	—		Loans within a three mile radius

18	Zhangqiu/Xiyaocun	Wang Cunren	Farming	360	360	—	Oil store	Neighboring villages
19	Zhangqiu/Jiegouhe	Liu Dianyuan	Trade	400	400	—		Neighboring villages
20	Zhangqiu/Dongbucun	Nong jia	Trade	200	200	—	Pharmacy in Jinan, Zhoucun, and Zichuan	
21	Zhangqiu/Zhaizhaozhuang	Zhai Rong	Farming	180	180	—	Pharmacy in Yucheng	Neighboring villages
22	Zhangqiu/Nanduozhuang	Li Zhi zhong	Farming	150	150	—	Wine shop/miscellaneous goods shop/pharmacy	Neighboring villages
23	Zhangqiu/Wenzuzhen	Ma Xitian	Trade	150	150	—	Wine shop/cotton cloth firm/pharmacy	Neighboring villages
24	Zhangqiu/Wenzuzhen	Li Zhenru	Farming	120	120	—	Wine shop/pharmacy	
25	Zhangqiu/Wenzuzhen	Sun Maochun	Farming	120	120	—	Miscellaneous goods shop	
26	Zhangqiu/Wenzuzhen	Sun Hengce	Farming	150	150	—		
27	Zhangqiu/Wenzuzhen	Zhou Bingyong	Farming	150	150	—		
28	Zhangqiu/Wenzuzhen	Sun Yuanzhong	Farming	120	120	—		
29	Zhangqiu/Zhangjiacun	Zhang Chongluan	Trade	170	170	—		
30	Zichuan/Sulizhuang	Wang Subo	Farming	343	343	—	Felt cap works/flour mill	
31	Zichuan/Wangcun	Yi Shengjia	Trade	300	300	—	Yisheng wine shop	
32	Zichuan/Wangdongcun	Wang Jia	Trade	502	502	—	Tobacco shop/wine shop	Loans in same village

Appendix B (cont.)

Finding number	District/Village	Name of landlord	Origin of wealth	Total land owned	Amount farmed with hired labor	Amount rented out	Business and handicraft activities	Extent of usury operations
33	Zichuan/Wangcun	Yang jia	Trade	200	200	—	Wine shop/miscellaneous goods	Cash shop/loans in several villages
34	Zichuan/Linchicun	Xue Benhong	Trade	480	480	—	Wine and miscellaneous goods shops, two each	Neighboring villages
35	Zichuan/Shengucun	Shen jia	Trade	240	240	—	Condiment works	Neighboring villages
36	Zichuan/Dashicun	Bi jia	Trade	300	300	—		
37	Zichuan/Dashangzhuang	Niu Duanshu	Farming	140	140	—		
38	Zichuan/Zhangfangcun	Wang Jilang	Official	300	300	—	Iron implement shop	
39	Huantai/Qianchencun	Cheng Fangjun	Official	900	900	—	Wine store/oil press	Neighboring villages
40	Yidu/Yuhuangmiao	Cui Qingbu	Farming	240	180	60	Miscellaneous goods store	Neighboring villages
41	Yidu/Beiputongcun	Lu Guo	Official	300	200	100	Oil store/wine shop/miscellaneous goods store	Neighboring villages
42	Tai-an/Xiyangloucun	Wang Jinhan	Trade	400	400	—	Pharmacy	Neighboring villages
43	Tai-an/Mazhuang	Li Yugui	Farming	2,100	1,000	1,100	Three oil presses	Neighboring villages
44	Tai-an/Shankoucun	Wang Junping	Trade	800	240	560	One oil press	Neighboring villages

233

45	Tai-an/Jiaogucun	Ma Shengfan	Farming	300	180	120		Neighboring villages
46	Tai-an/Beishigou	Wu Xixian	Trade	1,000	30	970		Neighboring villages
47	Tai-an/Bamiaodi	Li Wan chun	Farming	160	120	40		Neighboring villages
48	Feicheng/Liuhejuan	Guo Ganjin	Farming	300	120	180		Neighborhood
49	Pingying/Guogoucun	Guo Yuwen	Farming	400	400	—	One distillery	
50	Pingying/Guzhuang	Zhu Qingxiao	Farming	205	145	60	Flour mill	
51	Pingying/Liboshicun	Yin Xukun	Farming	1,000	300	700	Silk goods store/pharmacy	Cash shop but very few loans
52	Pingying/Liusuocun	Ying Peiyuan	Farming	3,000	80	2,920		Neighboring villages
Region 2								
53	Dexian/Fenghuangdian	Cao Si	Farming	200	50	150	Wine shop	Neighboring villages
54	Xiajin/Zhengbaotun	Huang Hezu	Farming	650	650	—		Neighboring villages
55	Xiajin/Wangjingcun	Wang Zhonglang	Usury and farming	380	230	150		Neighboring villages
56	Xiajin/Mozhuangcun	Zhang Weishan	Farming	260	260	—		Neighboring villages
57	Liaocheng/Xisilicun	Li Mengyue	Official	300	200	100		Neighboring villages
58	Liaocheng/Zhoutangcun	Li Lingzhou	Farming	200	140	60	Oil press	Neighboring villages
59	Dongping/Huizihecun	Zhao Hengren	Trade	13,000	1,000	12,000	Oil press	Neighboring villages
60	Dongping/Shahezhan	Feng Zhaoyuan	Trade	190	80	110	Wine shop/dye works	
61	Dongping/Xiaoyangcun	Zhang Zhaobiao	Farming	3,800	350	3,450		
62	Wenshang/Ponansanliloucun	Li Xiaojie	Farming	200	120	80		Neighboring villages
63	Tengxian/Dayancun	Sun Dengrang	Farming	10,000	350	9,650	Cash shop	Neighboring villages

Appendix B (cont.)

Finding number	District/Village	Name of landlord	Origin of wealth	Total land owned	Amount farmed with hired labor	Amount rented out	Business and handicraft activities	Extent of usury operations
Region 3								
64	Huimin/Xinji	Wei Zhaoqing	Trade	550	550	—	Miscellaneous goods store	Three pawn shops
65	Binxian/Xuanjiacun	Zhang Chenghan	Farming	1,800	1,000	800	Oil press/cotton cloth store	Neighboring villages
66	Binxian/Zhengjiacun	Zheng Tian	Trade	480	480	—	Flour mill/ink stone shop/cotton cloth firm	
67	Binxian/Lizezhen	Wu Jiwu	Trade	2,000	1,850	150	Wine shop/oil press/cotton cloth shop/pharmacy/miscellaneous goods store	Cash shop and loans in neighboring villages
68	Binxian/Shanliuducun	Du Jietang	Farming	320	120	200		Loans in same village
69	Lijin/Daniucun	Niu Xuemeng	Farming	284	284	—	Old clothes store	Loans in same village
70	Lijin/Beimatoucun	Yang Huatian	Trade	280	150	130	Oil press/miscellaneous goods store	
71	Lijin/Bojiazhuang	Leshan tang Bo	Farming	144	144	—		

	Location	Name	Occupation				Business	Credit/Loans
72	Zhanhua/Wanjiacun	Han Zhaoli	Trade	480	260	220	Oil press	Neighboring villages
73	Putai/Mawancun	Liu Zeng	Trade	300	300	--	Oil press/miscellaneous goods store	
74	Boxing/Longhecun	Zhou Shusheng	Trade	777	777	--		Silver shop and loans in same villages
75	Boxing/Chang jiacun	Chang Huanxiu	Farming	400	400	--		Neighboring villages
76	Guangrao/Lüjiacun	Lü Anbin	Farming	500	500	--	Wine shop/oil press	Pawn shop
77	Linzi/Beigaoyangcun	Liu He	Trade	650	325	325	Wine shop/oil press/pharmacy	Neighboring villages
78	Linzi/Nanfengkecun	Wang Liji	Trade	420	240	180	Oil press	Neighboring villages
79	Linzi/Sunloucun	Wang Xuzeng	Official	1,380	180	1,200		Neighboring villages
80	Linzi/Zhutaicun	Kui Xing	Trade	900	900	--	Two wine shops	Neighboring villages
81	Linzi/Wulukou	Yu Binghui	Farming	420	360	60		
82	Linzi/Dongzhaocun	Bian Zhitun	Farming	350	350	--	Wine shop/water-powered mill for grinding scent for perfume-sachets	
83	Linzi/Dongwangcun	Zhang Xiangzou	Farming	660	660	--		
84	Linzi/Xiguchengcun	Cui Lishen	Farming	360	360	--		
85	Linyi/Xinji	Bi Dian-kui	Farming	460	400	60		Cash shop and loans in 19 neighboring villages
Region 4								
86	Penglai/Shangkougaojia	Gao Dajue	Farming	1,000	500	500		Neighboring villages
87	Penglai/	Li Peng	Trade	180	120	60	Cooking pot smithy/miscellaneous goods store	Pawn shop

Appendix B (cont.)

Finding number	District/Village	Name of landlord	Origin of wealth	Total land owned	Amount farmed with hired labor	Amount rented out	Business and handicraft activities	Extent of usury operations
88	Penglai/Anxiangyujia	Zou Huanzhang	Trade	720	100	620	Oil press/miscellaneous goods store/weaving works	Neighboring villages
89	Fushan/Dongguancun	Dacheng tang	Trade	3,000	700	2,300	Oil press/miscellaneous goods store/silk embroidery works	Cash shop and loans in neighboring villages
90	Qixia/Malingzhong	Li Xutian	Trade	3,000	80	2,920		Neighboring villages
91	Qixia/Zhongqiaocun	Gong Mingcheng	Farming	450	70	380	Restaurant in Peking	Neighboring villages
92	Zhaoyuan/Houkuangcun	Sun Yunzhang	Official	3,000	200	2,800	Two oil presses	
93	Zhaoyuan/Houkuangcun	Sun Yunshu	Official	1,000	100	900		
94	Laiyang/Qianpuhoucun	Sui Hanrong	Farming	600	300	300	Vineyard/oil press	Neighboring villages
95	Yexian/Beishilibao	Yue Zhaoxing	Trade	800	300	500	Grain store/rice wine works/noodle shop/fur coat shop	Neighboring villages

No.	Xian/Village	Name	Occupation				Business	Other
96	Yexian/Xizhangjiacun	Tong Qu	Trade	400	200	200	Straw hat and braid shop in same village, Jinan, Qingdao, Shanghai, and Yantai	
97	Changyi/Xishiqiaocun	Zhang Yunci	Trade	600	400	200	Silk store/flour mill	
98	Changyi/Beixingfucun	Lin Zhikui	Trade	360	160	200	Oil press	Pawn shop and loans in neighboring villages
99	Pingdu/Baibucun	Lu Zunshu	Trade	750	200	550	Oil press	Cash shop and loans in neighboring villages
100	Pingdu/Qianjiazhuang	Ma Zengshou	Farming	3,000	400	2,600	Inn/pharmacy	Neighboring villages
101	Jiaoxian/Maiqiucun	Han Shisu	Trade	20,000	600	19,400		Four cash shops
102	Jiaoxian/Beiliujiaxiaozhuang	Liu Qingzhen	Farming	600	100	500	Oil press	Neighboring villages
103	Jiaoxian/Wangjiacun	Wang Shaoxing	Trade	1,000	140	860	Oil press	Nine neighboring villages
104	Jiaoxian/Tanjiacun	Qing Sigan	Farming, and crop loans	800	150	650		Neighboring villages
Region 5								
105	Heze/Tong-guji	Jia Rang	Trade	300	300	—	Miscellaneous goods store	Neighboring villages
106	Heze/Tong-guji	Zhang Changli	Trade	1,060	960	100		Cash shop and loans in neighboring villages
107	Heze/Huangmiaocun	Liu Jinyu	Farming	200	182	18	Chicken snacks shop	Neighboring villages

238

Appendix B (cont.)

Finding number	District/Village	Name of landlord	Origin of wealth	Total land owned	Amount farmed with hired labor	Amount rented out	Business and handicraft activities	Extent of usury operations
108	Juye/Xieji	Xie Minghe	Trade	220	220	—	Wine store	
109	Juye/Beiganmiao-zhaozhuang	Zhao Fangyuan	Farming	520	300	220		
110	Jinxiang/Hujicun	Zhu Zhenbang	Trade	8,000	2,000	6,000		Same village
111	Puxian/Weizhuang	Wei Guangyuan	Farming	400	400	—		Silver shop and several dozen villages
112	Puxian/Guyunji	Chen Maode	Trade	1,800	600	1,200		Silver shop and neighboring villages
113	Puxian/Lizhuang	Li Dongzhou	Trade	500	350	150		
114	Fanxian/Nanyangzhuang	Yang Yuping	Farming	70,000	700	69,300		Loans to people in over 100 villages
115	Guanxian/Wangliukouzhai	Wang Jichun	Farming	350	350	—	Grain store/flower stall	Cash shop making loans within six-mile radius
116	Zouxian/Dahuangcun	Xu Yingxi	Farming	2,600	320	2,280		Loans to people in over 100 villages
117	Zouxian/Daniuchang	Guo Yongxin	Farming	800	600	200	Wine store/oil press	
118	Zouxian/Liangxiadian	Chen Yukui	Farming	1,056	1,056	—	Oil press	Neighboring villages
119	Tanxian/Caozhuang	Wu Qingrang	Trade	2,400	2,000	400	Wine store/oil press/miscellaneous goods store	Neighboring villages

No.	Village	Name	Occupation				Economic activities	Notes
120	Feixian/Laizhuang	Chen Jiafu	Trade	6,000	400	5,600	Wine store/oil press	Neighboring villages
121	Feixian/Mazhuang	Wang Xianling	Trade	11,000	200	10,800	Wine store/coal mine	Loans of grain to tenants
122	Feixian/Nanshigoucun	Li Zhuo	Trade	2,800	300	2,500	Wine store/oil press	Neighboring villages
123	Linyi/Zhuxiacun	Liu Shuang	Trade	1,000	200	800	Wine store/oil press	Neighboring villages
124	Yishui/Xiaweicun	Wang Zijin	Farming	320	80	240	Wine store/oil press	Neighboring villages
125	Yishui/Zhangdaicun	Yu Qingliang	Farming	500	50	450		
126	Anqiu/Baifenzicun	Li Fenzao	Trade	5,440	1,200	4,240	Two oil presses	
127	Zhucheng/Xisongguzhuang	Yang Zhongqin	Trade	1,500	340	1,160	Wine shop	
128	Zhucheng/Chenjiazhuang	Ding Shaochen	Farming	2,350	75	2,275	Miscellaneous goods store/pharmacy	Neighboring villages
129	Zhucheng/Danancun	Huidi Tang	Farming	1,200	100	1,100		Neighboring villages
130	Zhucheng/Xiangzhoucun	Zong Jian	Trade	2,040	152	1,888	Oil press/snack shop/pharmacy	
131	Zhucheng/Xuejiucun	Hui Xuediao	Farming	450	90	360		Neighboring villages

Note: [In the original the authors gave the names of each village in which landlords made loans; I have replaced the names with the formula "neighboring villages." The authors also supplied the name of each interviewer and the name and age of each person interviewed. These have been omitted in the translation. Their surnames suggest that many of those interviewed were descendants of the landlords, the details of whose economic activities they supplied.]

Source: Materials collected in March 1957.

Appendix C

CONDITIONS OF STARTING AND STOPPING WORK AND SOURCES OF INCOME OF WAGE LABORERS
IN 141 VILLAGES IN 47 DISTRICTS OF SHANDONG, c. 1900

Finding number	District/Village	Long-term laborers		Short-term laborers		
		Conditions of starting and stopping work	Main source of family's income	Amount of land owned (shimu)	Main source of family's income	Side industries and other occupations in the off season
1	Licheng/Lijiacun	Direct contract with landlord; with some had to pay respects at New Year	Wages	5	Own land; short-term labor	Selling pots, dishes
2	Licheng/Laocengkou	Portion of wage paid on starting; invitation to meal on finishing	Wages	4	Own land; short-term labor	—
3	Zhangqiu/Guanzhuangcun	Introduction by old long-term laborer	Wages	2–4	Own land	Tile worker; ginger porter; hemp selling; piglet breeding
4	Zhangqiu/Nanguancun	Started after intermediary had fixed wage	Wages	2–4	Own land; short-term labor	Peddler
5	Zhangqiu/Bucun	Started on evening of the 15th day of the 8th month (lunar calendar)	Wages	5	Own land; short-term labor	Peddler; wheelbarrow, carrying-pole, etc., porter
6	Zhangqiu/Yujiacun	Could start having settled wage directly with landlord	Own land	3–5	Own land	—
7	Zhangqiu/Zhangyilangcun	Started having been introduced by intermediary	Wages; own land	6	Own land	Selling vegetables, beancurd, sweet potatoes, kindling
8	Zhangqiu/Shantoudian	Guaranteed by recommender	Wages	4–5	Own land	Selling firewood; stone breaking; coal hauling

	Village	Starting day arranged by intermediary	Wages	1–3	Side occupations; short-term labor	Carrying-pole porter
9	Zhangqiu/Xianggongzhuang	Starting day arranged by intermediary	Wages	1–3	Side occupations; short-term labor	Carrying-pole porter
10	Zhangqiu/Xiguancun	Could start following introduction by laborer friend	Wages; own land	2–3	Own land	Carrying-pole porter; selling peanuts and vegetables
11	Zhangqiu/Cuitianzhuang	Introduction by friend; guarantor also required	Wages	5	Own land	Peddler, handicrafts
12	Zhangqiu/Mingshui	Fixed wage and starting day directly with hirer	Wages	3–5	Own land	Lime kiln worker or paper manufactory worker
13	Zhangqiu/Beiguancun	Introduction by friend	Wages; own land	3	Own land; short-term labor	Selling vegetables; miscellaneous occupations
14	Zhangqiu/Qilangyuan	Starting and stopping arranged through intermediary	Wages	2	Own land; short-term labor	Coal hauling; cutting firewood
15	Zhangqiu/Dakangzhuang	Introduction by intermediary	Wages	4–5	Own land; short-term labor	Firewood cutting; collecting manure; wheelbarrow porter
16	Zhangqiu/Lifuzhuang	Could start following introduction by intermediary	Wages; stone breaking	—	Own land; short-term labor	Small business; selling vegetables
17	Zhangqiu/Xiyaocun	Portion of wages received in advance having settled wages and dates directly	Wages	3–4	Own land; short-term labor	Coal hauling; smithying
18	Zhangqiu/Jiegouhe	Starting time arranged by intermediary	Wages	4–5	Own land; short-term labor	—
19	Zhangqiu/Dongbucun	Starting day arranged by intermediary	Own land	3–5	Own land; short-term labor	—
20	Zhangqiu/Zhaizhaozhuang	Introduced by old laborer	Wages	2–3	Own land; short-term labor	Ginger porter; selling hemp; cutting firewood; carter
21	Zhangqiu/Beizaofan	Could start following introduction by intermediary	Wages	1	Short-term labor	Selling vegetables, boiled water for tea
22	Zhangqiu/Nanduozhuang	Having fixed wage could start	Wages	3	Own land	Peddling vegetables; bundling dike staves; opening waste land

Appendix C (cont.)

Finding number	District/Village	Long-term laborers		Amount of land owned (shimu)	Short-term laborers	
		Conditions of starting and stopping work	Main source of family's income		Main source of family's income	Side industries and other occupations in the off season
23	Zhangqiu/Zhaijiazhuang	Following introduction by laborer friend; needed guarantor	Wages	3	Short-term labor	Peddling vegetables, beancurd
24	Zhangqiu/Zhangjiacun	Introduced by old laborer	Wages	3–4	Own land; short-term labor	—
25	Zichuan/Sulizhuang	Starting day fixed by foreman	Wages	3–4	Own land; short-term labor	Long-distance porter
26	Zichuan/Dashicun	Started work on 8th day of intercallary month following introduction by intermediary	Wages	5	Own land; short-term labor	Cutting mill stones in the hills; coal hauling
27	Zichuan/Wangdongcun	Started work following introduction by intermediary	Wages	4	Own land; short-term labor	Pushing handcart; carrying-pole porter
28	Zichuan/Dashangcun	Started and stopped work on the 8th day of the 12th month	Wages	6	Own land; short-term labor	Coal hauling; selling coal
29	Zichuan/Linchi	Depending on who the landlord decided was "O.K."	Small business	1–2	Rented land	Hired by landlord for minor jobs
30	Zichuan/Shengucun		Wages	1	Short-term labor	Wheelbarrow porter
31	Zichuan/Wangcun	Could start work following introduction by intermediary	Wages	5	Own land; side occupations	Wheelbarrow porter; selling fruit

				6-10		Coal hauling
32	Changshan/Zhangfangcun	Needed introduction by intermediary	Own land	—	Own land	Coal hauling
33	Changshan/Guanzhuang	Started work on 8th day of intercallary month following introduction by intermediary; stopped at next intercallary month	Own land	—	—	—
34	Xintai/Beishidian	—	Wages	—	Own land; short-term labor	—
35	Tai-an/Bamiaodi	Started and stopped work on dates arranged through intermediary	Wages	4	Own land	Collecting and peddling firewood
36	Tai-an/Shankoucun	On starting work took wine with landlord and guarantor; same on finishing but without guarantor	Wages; small plot of own land	5	Own land	Long distance portering of fruit from Mt. Tai
37	Tai-an/Jiaogu	Wage either arranged by intermediary or directly fixed with landlord	Wages	1–3	Own land	Mat weaving; stone breaking
38	Tai-an/Xiyangloucun	Intermediary needed	Own land; wages	15	Own land	Portering fish, tea
39	Tai-an/Fangjiazhuang	Intermediary needed	Wages	6	Own land; short-term labor	Selling vegetables; grain peddler
40	Tai-an/Mazhuang	Before starting the hirer had to pay half the wage	Own land; wages	7	Own land	Collecting manure, firewood
41	Tai-an/Beishigoucun	—	Wages	10	Own land	Mat weaving; stone breaking
42	Huantai/Qianchencun	Intermediary needed	Wages	20	—	—
43	Huantai/Shiqiaocun	Had to pay respects to landlord at the New Year	Wages	4	Own land; rented land	Mat weaving; peddler
44	Yidu/Beiputongcun	Before starting had to have 3 trial days; stopped work on the 1st of the 10th month	Wages; own land	10	Own land; short-term labor	Cutting hay; handcart porter; spinning silk yarn; weaving cane lids

Appendix C (cont.)

Finding number	District/Village	Long-term laborers		Short-term laborers		
		Conditions of starting and stopping work	Main source of family's income	Amount of land owned (shimu)	Main source of family's income	Side industries and other occupations in the off season
45	Yidu/Songjiazhuang	Could start work following introduction by friend	Wages	3	Short-term labor	Wheelbarrow; carrying-pole porter; selling vegetables
46	Yidu/Yuhuangmiao	Before starting had to have 3 trial days; could leave a few days ahead of time	Own land; wages	10	Own land	Cutting hay; firewood; spinning cotton yarn; carter
47	Feicheng/Liuhejuan	—	Wages; other labor	1	Short-term labor; own land	Breaking stones; carpenter;
48	Feicheng/ Dongxiangcun	Needed a guarantor on starting	Wages	1–5	Short-term labor; own land	—
49	Pingying/Guzhuang	Intermediary needed	Wages; own small plot of land	4	Own land	Selling beancurd; collecting manure; cutting firewood
50	Pingying/ Liboshizhuang	Intermediary needed	Wages; own land	5–10	Own land; rented land	Selling beancurd, vegetables, peanuts, sweet-potatoes, hot soup
51	Pingying/Liusuocun	Intermediary fixed wages and work required	Wages	7	Rented land; landlord's land	Selling beancurd; small business
52	Pingying/Guogoucun	—	Wages; own land	5	Own land	Gathering firewood; collecting manure; small business

Region 2

						Peddler
53	Dexian/ Fenghuangdian	Received a portion of wages in advance before starting work	Wages	6	Own land	Making and selling sundried bricks; making beancurd; selling peanuts
54	Xiajin/Zhengbaotun	On starting work intermediary fixed wages	Wages	10	Own land	Collecting manure; cutting hay
55	Xiajin/Qiaoguantun	—	Trade; own land	5	Short-term labor	Selling vegetables; collecting manure; making beancurd
56	Xiajin/Wanjingcun	Following introduction and discussion of wages through intermediary could start	Wages	6–7	Own land	Selling vegetables
57	Xiajin/Mozhuangcun	Intermediary needed before starting	Weaving; short-term labor; own land	3	Short-term labor; small business	Selling vegetables; coal hauling
58	Liaocheng/Diaozhuang	—	Wages	10	Short-term labor; farming	Cutting firewood; coal hauling
59	Liaocheng/Qiaohuangcun	—	Wages	10	Short-term labor;	Peddling sweet potatoes, turnips; wheelbarrow porter
60	Liaocheng/Houying	—	Farming for landlord	8	Own land	Making grass paper; peddling manure
61	Liaocheng/Xisilicun	Foreman went to labor market and invited	Wages; short-term labor	6	Farming; short-term labor	—
62	Liaocheng/Zhoutang cun	Needed guarantor (acquaintance or old long term laborer)	Farming	20	Farming; short-term labor	Selling vegetables, beancurd; carpentering
63	Dongping/Huizihecun	Needed guarantor; started work at Qingming festival (about April); ended on 1st of 10th month	Wages	8	Own land	

Appendix C (cont.)

| Finding number | District/Village | Long-term laborers | | Amount of land owned (shimu) | Short-term laborers | |
		Conditions of starting and stopping work	Main source of family's income		Main source of family's income	Side industries and other occupations in the off season
64	Dongping/Hezhancun	Intermediary and landlord decided on wage before starting	Rented land or own land	5–10	Rented land; own land	Peddling local products
65	Dongping/Mucun	Intermediary and landlord decided on wage before starting	Rented landlord's land	6–7	Rented landlord's land	Peddling peanuts, beancurd, sugar balls
66	Dongping/Xiaoyangcun	Three trial days before landlord's decision to hire	Farming own small plot	1–5	Own land	Selling beancurd, peanuts
67	Wenshang/Bonaniloucun	Intermediary needed to start; all accounts cleared before stopping	Wages; begging	6–8	Farming; small business	Peddling vegetables; mat weaving; basket making
68	Tengxian/Dayancun	Intermediary needed before starting work	Wages	2	Short-term labor	Weaving cotton cloth; fishing
Region 3						
69	Huimin/Xinji	Started work after intermediary had fixed terms	Wages	7	Short-term labor; own land	Selling peanuts, beancurd
70	Binxian/Xuanjiacun	Started work after intermediary had fixed terms	Wages or own land	15	Own land	Selling steamed bread rolls, beancurd
71	Binxian/Zhengjiacun	—	Portering	8	Own land	Making storage bins; working a mill stone

	Place		Wages	No.	Own land	Other income
72	Binxian/Shanliuducun	Introduction by intermediary	Wages	16	Own land	—
73	Binxian/Diaoshilicun	Before starting paid surety money; on finishing satisfactorily the wages were paid up	Wages	4	Short-term labor; own land	Coal hauling; selling beancurd, malt-sugar sweets
74	Binxian/Tishanghucun	Intermediary had to act as guarantor	Wages	13	Short-term labor; own land	Selling steamed bread rolls, vegetable oil, beancurd
75	Binxian/Lizezhen	Started work after intermediary had fixed terms	Wages	5	Own land	Small business; making beancurd; selling vegetables
76	Lijin/Daniucun	Intermediary's introduction; could stop if both landlord and laborer agreed	Wages; other labor	8	Short-term labor; own land	Small business; collecting manure; gathering hay; spinning cotton yarn
77	Lijin/Beimatoucun	—	Wages; farming	7	Own land	Collecting manure, firewood
78	Lijin/Bojiazhuang	—	Brine salt worker; cutting reeds	3-6	Brine salt worker; cutting reeds	Before the change of course of the Yellow River in 1855 most worked in the salterns
79	Zhanhua/Wanjiacun	—	Wages	5	Short-term labor; own land	Peddling peanuts, sweet potatoes, beancurd
80	Putai/Mawancun	At New Year and other festivals laborers had to pay their respects to the foreman	Wages	10	Short-term labor; own land	Repairing roofs for the landlord
81	Boxing/Longhecun	Started work on the 6th day of the 1st month; given a special meal on first day of work	Wages	3	Short-term labor	Collecting manure, firewood
82	Linzi/Beigaoyangcun	Arrangements made by intermediary	Wages	5	Wages; own land	Collecting manure; small business
83	Linzi/Nanfengkecun	Contract required	Wages	9	Farming; short-term labor	—

Appendix C (cont.)

Finding number	District/Village	Long-term laborers			Short-term laborers	
		Conditions of starting and stopping work	Main source of family's income	Amount of land owned (shimu)	Main source of family's income	Side industries and other occupations in the off season
84	Linzi/Sunloucun	Direct agreement between landlord and laborer on dates and wages	Wages	5	Own land	Selling beancurd; cutting firewood
85	Linzi/Zhutaicun	Only needed introduction by intermediary	Wages; rented land	7	—	Selling beancurd; cutting firewood, etc.
86	Linzi/Dongzhaocun	—	—	—	—	—
87	Linzi/Anledian	Guarantor required	Wages	7	Short-term labor; farming	Porter; peddler
88	Linzi/Xiguchengcun	Guarantor required	Wages	3–5	Short-term labor; farming	—
89	Guangrao/Lüjiacun	—	Wages; small plots of own land	6	Farming	—
90	Linyi/Dizisongcun	Following introduction by intermediary	Wages; small plots of own land	7	Half working landlord's land; half working rented land	Mill worker; porter
91	Linyi/Xinji	Following introduction by intermediary	Wages; small plots of own land	—	When land was insufficient short-term labor	—

Region 4

92	Penglai/Anxiangyujia	Guarantor required before starting work	Wages	8	Own land	Gathering firewood, hay
93	Fushan/Wangyuangcun	—	Wages	3–4	Farming; selling fish	Catching fish and selling them
94	Qixia/Malingzhong	—	Wages; own land	6	Farming; short-term labor	—
95	Qixia/Zhongqiaocun	Wages decided in discussion between landlord and laborer	Wages	5	Own land	—
96	Zhaoyuan/Houkuangcun	Guarantor required before starting work	Wages; rented land	8	Own land; short-term labor	Cutting firewood
97	Laiyang/Qianbuhoucun	Guarantor required on starting work; everything to be shipshape and Bristol fashion (*diliao chang-guang*) the work finished and wages paid up (*gongman qianwan*)	Wages	6	Own land; short-term labor	Gathering manure, firewood
98	Laiyang/Lingnancun	Guarantor required before starting work	Wages	6	Short-term labor	—
99	Laiyang/Nanzuojiakuang	Guarantor required before starting work	Wages	10	Farming; short-term labor	Carrying-pole peddler; selling peanuts, etc.
100	Yexian/Beishilibao	—	Farming; wages	3	Farming; short-term labor	Porter, but usually out of work
101	Yexian/Xizhangjiacun	Following introduction by intermediary started on 2nd day of 2nd month; stopped on 1st day of 10th month	Farming;	8	Farming	Making straw hats and braids

Appendix C (cont.)

Finding number	District/Village	Long-term laborers		Short-term laborers		
		Conditions of starting and stopping work	Main source of family's income	Amount of land owned (shimu)	Main source of family's income	Side industries and other occupations in the off season
102	Changyi/ Xishiqiaocun	Guarantor required. Wages fixed once a year	Wages	4	Farming; short-term labor	Collecting manure; weaving pongee
103	Changyi/ Beixingfucun	If from far-away village, guarantor required; if from near village, wages decided after discussion with landlord	Wages; rented land	5–8	Own land	Cutting grass from swamps, selling it
104	Pingdu/Baibucun	Introduction by intermediary followed by discussion of wages	Farming	7	Own land	—
105	Pingdu/Guercun	Wages decided in discussion between landlord and laborer	Wages; other work	8	Own land	Short-term labor; collecting manure; cutting grass
106	Pingdu/Qianjiazhuang	—	Wages	10	Farming; short-term labor	Porter; selling beancurd
107	Jiaoxian/Maiqiucun	Agreement made through intermediary	Wages	4–5	Farming; short-term labor	Small business
108	Jiaoxian/ Beiliujiaxiaozhuang	Guarantor required	Wages; rented land	2	Tenant farming; short-term labor	Making local cotton cloth
109	Jiaoxian/Wangjiacun	Following introduction by intermediary started work on 2nd day of 2nd month; finished on 1st day of 10th month	Farming	2	Farming	No side occupation in this village

110	Jiaoxian/Tanjiacun	Landlord went to labor market; a verbal commitment was given	Wages; farming	10	Farming	—

Region 5

111	Heze/Tong-guji	Following introduction by intermediary, started work on the 1st day of 10th month; stopped on the same date of succeeding year (had to pay respects to landlord)	Wages	8–10	Farming; short-term labor	Small business; sunk salt wells, sold salt
112	Heze/Huangmiaocun	Started on the 1st day of 10th month; stopped same date of succeeding year	Wages	5–8	Farming; short-term labor	Small business; making bean-curd
113	Tanxian/Xuzhaicun	Intermediary fixed wage before starting	Wages	6	Farming; small business	Small business; peddling vegetable oil; joinery
114	Puxian/Weizhuang	Had to do 2 or 3 trial days before starting	Farming	10	Own land	—
115	Puxian/Guyunji	—	Wages	10	Own land	Peddler
116	Puxian/Lizhuang	Intermediary fixed wage before starting	Wages	10	Own land	—
117	Fanxian/Houliloucun	Intermediary acted as guarantor	Wages	12	Own land	Carrying-pole porter; peddling food grains
118	Fanxian/Nanyangzhuang	Intermediary arranged starting and stopping time	Farming; small business	3–4	Own land	Peddling radishes; collecting manure; weaving mats
119	Zouxian/Dahuangcun	Following introduction by intermediary	Wages	4	Own land	—

Appendix C (cont.)

Finding number	District/Village	Long-term laborers		Amount of land owned (shimu)	Short-term laborers	
		Conditions of starting and stopping work	Main source of family's income		Main source of family's income	Side industries and other occupations in the off season
120	Zouxian/Daniuchang	Direct approach to landlord; 3 trial days before starting	Wages;	5-10	Own land; wages	Small business; peddling firewood
121	Zouxian/Liangxiadian	Following introduction by intermediary and agreement by landlord	Wages; other work	3	Own land	Carrying-pole trading; porters (short-term laborers had to pay respects to landlords)
122	Jinxiang/Hujicun	Following introduction by intermediary	Rented land	12	Own land	Selling manure
123	Tancheng/Caozhuang	Intermediary's introduction required to start work; had to pay respects to landlord at New Year	Wages	5-10	Own land; wages	Peddling tobacco, etc.
124	Feixian/Mazhuang	Introduction by foreman required; work started and stopped on the 15th day of the 8th month	Farming	—	Short-term labor; tenant farmer	Wheelbarrow porter
125	Feixian/Laizhuangpu	Following introduction by intermediary	Business	4	Farming	Peddler
126	Feixian/Nanshigou	—	Wages	—	Rented land; short-term labor	Picking mountain fruit; peddling contraband salt; selling beancurd
127	Feixian/Zhaozhuang	Contract required, also guarantor; had to pay respects to landlord at New Year	Wages	—	—	Peddling peanuts, vegetables

No.	Location	Hiring condition	Payment		Main occupation	Side occupation
128	Yishui/Zhangdaicun	—	Wages	5–7	Own land	—
129	Yishui/Xiaweicun	—	Household work	10	Own land	Gathering firewood; small business
130	Zhucheng/Futaicun	Guarantor required before starting	Wages	—	—	—
131	Zhucheng/Xisonggucun	If the landlord liked you, you were hired	Rented land	—	Short-term labor	Weaving mats; making reed rain hats
132	Zhucheng/Chenjiacun	Introduction by intermediary required	Wages; farming	—	Rented land	Transport
133	Zhucheng/Danancun	Introduction by intermediary required	Wages; rented land	5	Short-term labor; rented land	Small business; selling beancurd
134	Zhucheng/Xiangzhoucun	—	Wages	8	Short-term labor; rented land	Selling kindling; peanuts, bean-curd
135	Zhucheng/Xuejiucun	Guarantor required before starting	Wages	9	Own land	Porter; peddler
136	Anqiu/Yijiacun	Intermediary required; had to pay respects to landlord at festivals	Wages; small plots of own land	6	Farming; short-term labor	Cutting grass; peddling kindling
137	Anqiu/Dongzhaocongcun	Had to finish stipulated number of days	Rented landlord's land	—	Farming landlord's land	Small business; gathering firewood; making straw
138	Anqiu/Baifenzicun	Following direct approach to steward could start	Wages; small plot of own land	5	Own land or rented land	—
139	Guanxian/Wangliukouzhai	After discussion of wages could start	Own land	8	Farming; short-term labor	Odd jobs for landlord
140	Juye/Liuyingcun	Wages fixed in discussion	Wages	13	Own land	Peddling vegetables; grain husking
141	Juye/Xiejicun	Started having directly decided wage; stopped on completed payment of wage	Wages	10	Own land	Milling flour

Source: Materials collected in March 1957.

NOTES

Introduction

1. The full title of Jing and Luo's study is *Qingdai Shandong jingying dizhu de shehui xingzhi* (The social nature of managerial landlords in Shandong during the Qing dynasty). They wrote it while graduate students at Shandong University, at which Professor Luo Lun now teaches modern Chinese history and Mr. Jing Su works in the administration. The questionnaire materials tabulated in the appendixes were gathered for them in the relatively relaxed cultural period of "blooming and contending" in the spring of 1957. The book was published in 1959 by the Jinan People's Publishing House, which printed 1,600 copies. It received a substantial review in one of the leading intellectual journals in 1961 (*Xueshu yuekan*, 1961.4). Luo answered some of the points raised in this review in the same journal two years later (ibid., 1963.9). Meanwhile the book was quoted in articles in the leading Chinese historical journal, *Lishi yanjiu*. The first foreign notices of the book were made in a Japanese historical journal in 1966, Fujita Keiichi, "Shindai Santōshō keiei jinushitei shakai seishitsu," *Atarashi rekishigaku no tame*, 111:11-22 (1966), and in a Russian work, O. E. Nepomnin, *Genezis kapitalizma y sel'skom khozvaistve Kitaya* (Moscow, 1966), Chapter 3. The first notice of the book in English was published by Ramon Myers in an interpretative essay entitled, "Commercialization, Agricultural Development, and Landlord Behaviour in Shantung Province in the Late Ch'ing Period," *Ch'ing-shih wen-t'i*, 8.2:31-54 (1972).

2. *Selected Works of Mao Tse-tung*, English language edition (Peking, 1965), III, 77.

3. For the first round of debate on this subject which took place in the 1930s, see Benjamin Schwartz, "A Marxist Controversy on China," *Far Eastern Quarterly*, 13.2:143-153 (1954); and for the second round in the 1950s, see Albert Feuerwerker, "From 'Feudalism' to 'Capitalism' in Recent Historical Writing from Mainland China," *Journal of Asian Studies*, 18:107-115 (1958-59); and Tanaka Masatoshi, *Chūgoku kindai keizaishi kenkyū josetsu* (Tokyo, Tokyo University Press, 1973), pp. 205-241. The main steps in Jing and Luo's argument are taken from Lenin's *The Development of Capitalism in Russia* and, in their most simplified form, from *History of the Communist Party of the Soviet Union (Bolshevik), Short Course*.

4.   Two recent studies in English can serve to introduce much of the
      Chinese and Japanese scholarship on economic and social change in the
      Ming and Qing: Mark Elvin, *The Pattern of the Chinese Past* (London,
      Eyre Methuen, 1973), especially Part 3, and Evelyn Sakakida Rawski,
      Agricultural Change and the Peasant Economy of South China (Cam-
      bridge, Harvard University Press, 1972).

5.   The authors' description of this condiment works is based on interviews
      conducted in 1957 with surviving workers and the firm's last accountant.
      (See Chapter 5, Section 2.) The details are corroborated in the account
      of a Scottish missionary who visited Jining in 1891 and noted, "The
      town exports . . . enormous quantities of pickles: there is one factory in
      the city which employs 500 men in this work"; Alexander Armstrong,
      Shantung (Shanghai, 1891), p. 72.

6.   I have listed twentieth-century population estimates for the four towns
      discussed by Jing and Luo:

Linqing	(1930s):	80,000	(*Shandong, fensheng dizhi*, Shanghai, 1935, p. 188)
Linqing	(1931):	36,000	(*Linqing xianzhi*, 1934, ce 2)
Jining	(1911):	67,000	(*Shina shōbetsu zenshi, Santōshō*, Tokyo, 1917, p. 310)
Jining	(1937):	100,000	*(Santōshō, Zainei kenjō o chūshin to seru, nōsanbutsu ryūtsū ni*
Jining	(1942):	104,000	*kansuru ichi kōsatsu*, Peking, 1942, p. 1)
Zhoucun	(1911):	25,000	(*Shina shōbetsu zenshi, Santōshō*, (Tokyo, 1917, p. 82)
Zhoucun	(1929):	61,000	(*Zhongguo shiyezhi, Shandong*, Shanghai, 1935, *ding*, p. 142)
Yanshen	(1911):	37,000	(*Zhongguo shiyezhi, Shandong*, Shanghai, 1935, *ding*, p. 163)

      Linqing was the only one of the four towns not linked to a railway
      in the early decades of this century. It had been declining ever since the
      junk traffic on the Grand Canal had begun to be replaced by coastal
      steamers in the late nineteenth century. In the early twentieth century,
      the river running through the town silted up. The construction of rail-
      ways in other parts of Shandong also drew trade away from Linqing.
      For these reasons, the lower of the above two estimates is probably the
      more accurate.

7. V. I. Lenin, *The Development of Capitalism in Russia,* English language edition (Moscow, 1967), pp. 15, 614.

8. Elvin, *Pattern of the Chinese Past,* p. 204.

9. Ibid, p. 176.

10. Kokuritsu Pekin daigaku fusetsu nōson keizai kenkyūjo, *Santōshō Zainei kenjō o chūshin to seru nōsanbutsu ryūtsū ni kansuru ichi kōsatsu* (Peking, 1942), p. 1. Most twentieth-century surveys of Shandong record that about 90% of the population was rural. (See, for example, Amano Motonosuke, *Santōshō keizai chōsa shiryō: Santō nōgyō keizairon,* Dairen, 1936, p. 16.)

11. See Yamane Yukio, "Min Shin jidai kahoku ni okeru tekishi," *Shiron* 8:493–504 (1960). South China had filled up with intermediate markets in the Song dynasty (968–1227) in a surge of population growth and economic expansion, in part characterized by urban growth and structural economic change, no doubt made possible by the much greater availability than in the north of cheap inland and coastal transport. On this Chinese "medieval economic revolution," see Elvin, *Pattern of the Chinese Past,* Part II.

12. See the 1596, 1691, 1833, and 1907 editions of the *District Gazetteer of Zhangqiu* (Zhangqiu xianzhi). The 1907 edition lists only 30 market centers, but Jing and Luo record that there was a periodic market in Dongfanliu village at the beginning of this century. (See Chapter 4, Section 1.)

13. This passage is quoted by Jing and Luo from the *Imperial Encyclopaedia.* For the full reference, see Chapter 1, Section 1, note 22.

14. The *nouveaux riches* were sometimes referred to in contemporary sources as *caizhu* or simply *fujia.* The pornographic novel *Jinpingmei* has as its hero a wealthy merchant of Qinghe district, Linqing prefecture. There is an English translation of the novel by Clement Egerton under the title *The Golden Lotus,* 4 vols. (London, Routledge, 1939). Another Shandong novel from a slightly later date called *A Marriage to Awaken Men* (Xingshi yinyuan zhuan) is also filled with the activities of the new urban rich as well as many other aspects of Shandong social life at this time. It has been much quoted by Jing and Luo. On the business practices and style of life of the richest of the merchants in the Grand Canal

region, see P. T. Ho's "The Salt Merchants of Yangchow," *Harvard Journal of Asiatic Studies* 17.1–2:130–168 (June 1954), and C. P. MacKerras, *The Rise of the Peking Opera* (Oxford, Clarendon Press, 1972), Chapter 3.

15.   See Dwight H. Perkins, *Agricultural Development in China, 1368–1968* (Chicago, Aldine, 1969) for estimates of the size of trade at different levels of the marketing system, including trade in crops.

16.   On the introduction of New World crops such as tobacco, the peanut, and the potato, see P. T. Ho, *Studies on the Population of China* (Cambridge, Harvard University Press, 1959), and Perkins, *Agricultural Development,* for estimates of the changing amounts of land sown to these crops. The most important studies of the spread of cotton cultivation and the development of the cotton market in China were made by Nishijima Sadao and are collected in his *Chūgoku keizaishi kenkyū* (Tokyo, Tokyo University Press, 1966). Kataoka Shibako has two important articles on the commercialization of agriculture in north China (including Shandong) at this time. In the first, she has gathered materials similar to those used in this chapter by Jing and Luo. In the second of the two articles, she stresses the effects on marketing of the late Ming tax reforms which made taxes payable in silver. This is a point Jing and Luo have not considered. See Kataoka Shibako, "Mimmatsu Shinshō no Kahoku ni okeru nōka keiei," *Shakai keizaishigaku* 25 2/3:77–100 (1959), and "Kahoku no tochi shoyū to ichijō benpō," in *Shimizu hakusei tsuitō kinen Mindaishi ronsō* (Tokyo, Daian, 1962), pp. 139–163.

17.   See Yamane Yukio, "Min shin jidai..."

18.   Fu Yi-ling was the first to formulate the notion of three relatively advanced regions, in his research on the Jiangnan and southeast coastal regions. See his *Ming Qing nongcun shehui jingji* (Peking, Sanlian, 1961), p. 72. For stimulating discussions on the history of the Jiangnan region, see Elvin, *Pattern of the Chinese Past;* and on the southeast coastal region, see Rawski, *Agricultural Change.* Jing and Luo's book is the first on the Grand Canal region. There were, of course, many differences of development within these regions, and there were other areas of China that were also relatively commercialized (e.g., the central Yangzi valley or the capital region).

19.   I have added footnotes to the text of Chapter 1 on the decline of the

Grand Canal and its effects on the towns in this region. As long as the imperial roads were not closed by heavy rains, large amounts of goods were carried on them by mule litter, cart, or wheelbarrow. Myers "Commercialization," has conveniently summarized the Royal Asiatic Society's report on Shandong transport contained in "Inland Communications of China," *Journal of the North China Branch of the Royal Asiatic Society* 28:(1893/94).

The railway came to Shandong at the end of the nineteenth and beginning of the twentieth centuries. The Jinan-Jiazhou line was completed in 1904, the Boshan branch line in the same year, the Tianjin-Pokou line (passing through Jinan) in 1912, and the Jining branch line in the same year. The first treaty ports in the province were established during this period which, therefore, marks a convenient dividing line between "traditional" and "modern" in Shandong. Jing and Luo's questionnaire data fall just within the "traditional" period. A recent study of the introduction of the "modern" sector into Shandong may be found in David C. Buck's *Urban Change in China: Politics and Development in Tsinan, 1890–1949* (Madison, University of Wisconsin Press, 1977).

20. Chinese historians have collected considerable evidence to show that there was an improvement in the legal and social position of wage laborers in the course of the Qing dynasty. This improvement went hand in hand with a general loosening of the status order which accompanied the commercialization of the economy. For a brilliant article summarizing the general trends, see Li Wen-zhi, "Lun Qingdai qianqi de tudi zhanyou guanxi," *Lishi yanjiu*, 5:75–108 (1963), and, on the changing legal status of wage laborers, see Jing Jun-jian, "Ming Qing liangdai nongye guyong laodongzhe falü shenfen diwei de jiefang," *Jingji yanjiu*, No. 6 (1961).

21. See Kanbe Teruo, "Shindai koki Santōshō ni okeru 'danki' to nōson mondai," *Shirin* 55.4:61–98 (1972). It is one of the more curious omissions of Jing and Luo's study that nothing is said of the land tax as a possible influence on the nature of production or in any other context. On changes in the tax system in the sixteenth and seventeenth centuries as a stimulus to the commercialization of agriculture, see Kataoka Shibako, "Kahoku no tochi shoyū to ichijō benpō," and as a cause of rural unrest in the nineteenth century, see Kanbe, "Shindai koki..." Ramon H. Myers, *The Chinese Peasant Economy*, pp. 263–265, sums up tax changes in Shandong in the Qing and Republican periods.

22. A memorialist in the 1720s, for example, reported that there were 61
     districts in Shandong (out of 107) in which land was owned by people
     resident in other districts. (See *Yongzheng Donghua lu, juan* 12, p. 17.)
     It is often claimed that there was a rise in absentee landlordism in the
     twentieth century, leading to the breakdown of traditional forms of
     village leadership and control, and a more volatile situation in the
     villages. Absentee landlordism, however, was already widespread by the
     twentieth century. What happened was that the nature of absentee land-
     lordism changed as big landlords moved their wealth from the old urban
     centers integrated into the agricultural economy to the new treaty port
     cities which were parasitic to that economy.

23. See Myers, *Chinese Peasant Economy,* pp. 220–227. The only survey of
     landholding conditions in Shandong conducted at the end of the
     nineteenth century broadly confirms the details given by Jing and Luo;
     see G. Jamieson, "Tenure of Land in China and the Condition of the
     Rural Population," *Journal of the North China Branch of the Royal
     Asiatic Society,* 23:59–174 (1888).

24. See Elvin, *Pattern of the Chinese Past,* p. 255.

25. On Chinese gentry and officialdom of the late imperial period, see
     Chang Chung-li, *The Chinese Gentry* (Seattle, University of Washington
     Press, 1955), and *The Income of the Chinese Gentry* (Seattle, University
     of Washington Press, 1962); Hsiao Kung-chuan, *Rural China: Imperial
     Control in the Nineteenth Century* (Seattle, University of Washington
     Press, 1960); P. T. Ho, *The Ladder of Success in Imperial China* (New
     York, Columbia University Press, 1962).

26. The authors' approach leads them to emphasize economic relations at
     the expense of kinship interrelations which were an essential part of the
     local political and economic fabric of traditional China. For general
     descriptions of family and kin interrelations in a Shandong village
     (Taitou on the Shandong promontory), see Martin C. Yang's *A Chinese
     Village* (New York, Columbia University Press, 1945). Although Yang's
     descriptions are of a village in the 1930s and 1940s, the basic social
     fabric had not changed since the turn of the century. See also Myers,
     Chinese Peasant Economy, passim.

27. Shujing was the "hall name" (*tangming*) of the Bi family. Such names
     were usually inscribed on one of the principal rooms of the house (or
     on the clan hall if there was one) and were used in deeds, on boundary

stones, and so forth, to indicate that the property was owned by the particular branch of the family in question. I have followed the authors in sometimes referring to a family by its hall name for short, e.g., the "Shujing tang" for the "Shujing tang Bi family."

28. F. H. King, *Farmers of Forty Centuries* (London, Cape, 1911), p. 231.

29. "The less well-to-do or small farmers own 2-5 *mow* and act as super-intendents for the larger farmers"; ibid, p. 233.

30. Jing and Luo show that the average annual cash wage of rural laborers in central Shandong in 1906-1910 was 21.2 strings. Twenty years previously it was apparently 20 strings. (See Jamieson, "Tenure of Land.")

31. P. G. M. Stenz, *Der Bauer in Schantung* (Tsingtau, 1910), p. 13.

32. Yang Xiu-yuan, *Nongyan zhuoshi*, n.d., reprinted in *Qin Jin nongyan* (Peking, 1957), pp. 85-102.

33. Although Taihe tang had more animals than Shujing tang it apparently collected far less manure for reasons the authors do not explain:

	Oxen	Mules & donkeys	Horses & mules	Sheep	Pigs	Annual amount of manure collected
Taihe tang	9	8		100	40	5,000 carts (400 jin per cart)
Shujing tang	10			100	20	7,000 carts (400 jin per cart)
Jinxiu tang			70			1,000 carts (2,000 jin per cart)

Source: Chapter 4, Sections 1, 2, and 3.

Size of household is another factor, since the landlords, in common with the peasants, used human excrement in the preparation of compost. Apparently the Shujing tang annually collected 200 cartloads (400 jin per cart) in addition to the 7,000 cartloads of animal manure, but I have not included this in the table of average amounts of fertilizer per mu because the authors give no estimates for the other two landlords.

34. King, p. 231.

35. Details of the Jining farm budget are given in Stenz, *Der Bauer*, pp. 13-14.

36. J. L. Buck, *Land Utilization in China: Statistics* (Chicago, University of Chicago Press, 1937), p. 231.

37. "Farms and Orchards at Chefoo, Shantung," *Chinese Economic Journal,* 3.1:612 (1928). Stenz emphasizes the fact that large Shandong land-holders rented out most of their lands; "Die Grossgrundbesitzer, worunter ich Leute mit 1,000 bis 10,000 Morgen land rechne (von reicheren habe ich in Schantung nicht gehört) verpachten ihr Land ganz oder zum Teil an andere" (*Der Bauer*, p. 12). Jing and Luo are interested precisely in that part which was *not* rented out to others.

38. The only point at which the authors discuss differences of development in different regions of the province is in their discussion of laborers' money wages. (See Chapter 6, Section 3.) Their data in the Appendixes remain virtually unworked in this respect.

39. Lenin, *Preface to Second Edition,* p. 33.

40. The best study of changes in Shandong villages from the late nineteenth century to 1949 is Myers, *Chinese Peasant Economy.* For changes in Shandong city life during the same period, especially in the provincial capital, see David C. Buck, *Urban Change in China.*

Translated Text

[Note: All notes or comments added by the translator are enclosed in square brackets.]

Preface

1. Karl Marx: *Capital,* I, 715. [All quotations from *Capital,* vol. I are taken from the English language edition published by Lawrence and Wishart, London, 1970.]

Chapter 1

1. [The section of the Grand Canal linking Hangzhou to Jining was actually completed in the twelfth century; it fell into disuse in the thirteenth century and was reopened, as the authors state, during the Yuan dynasty (in 1283). In the fourteenth century it once more fell into desuetude, and it was only reopened and enlarged again in the early Ming (in 1411), at which time the canal was extended from Jining to Linqing and thence to Peking.]

2. The description is by Wang Yu, President of the Board of Rites in the mid-fifteenth century, quoted from the *District Gazetteer of Linqing (Linqing xianzhi)*, 1934 edition, Vol. 11.

3. Preface to the 1561 edition of the *Gazetteer of the Sub-Prefecture of Linqing* as quoted in the *District Gazetteer of Linqing* (1934), Vol. 1.

4. Preface to the 1672 edition of the *Gazetteer of the Sub-Prefecture of Linqing* as quoted in the *District Gazetteer of Linqing* (1934), Vol. 1.

5. "On the Customs of Dongchang Prefecture," "Political Divisions" section of *Imperial Encyclopaedia (Gujin tushujicheng, Zhifangdian, Dongchangfu fengsukao)*.

6. From He Wang-chang's preface to the 1749 edition of the *Gazetteer of the Sub-Prefecture of Linqing* as quoted in the *District Gazetteer of Linqing* (1934), Vol. 1. ["Surpassing both Linzi and Jimo," i.e., "very large"—Linzi and Jimo were both famous towns in ancient China, the capitals of the states of Qi and Zhao.]

7. From the *Gazetteer of the Independent Sub-Prefecture of Linqing,* 1784 *juan* 9.

8. [A Scottish missionary who traveled extensively in Shandong in the 1890s wrote of Linqing as he found it in 1891: "The most noticeable feature inside the city is its emptiness. There are a few temples, three yamens, and, perhaps, four hundred houses; the rest is waste land, except such places as have been cleared of broken brick to admit of cultivation. The reason for all this goes back to ... 1855 when the T'ai-p'ing rebels attacked the city, undermined and blew up a part of the wall, entered and killed a large number of the inhabitants, and many thousands of refugees who had fled thither for safety ... There are some fifty large tumuli in which the dead were buried ... To account for the great and general decline in business, it is enough almost to mention the T'ai-p'ings. Another cause, however, is the less frequent coming up of the grain fleets ... the steamers have of course cut into this; and the growth of Tientsin and Chefoo represents, perhaps, a corresponding loss all along the Canal," Alexander Armstrong, *Shantung* (Shanghai, 1891), pp. 67-68. The replacement of the grain tribute junks on the Grand Canal by coastal shipping was a process that had already begun in the first half of the nineteenth century, but it was accelerated with the advent of the steamer from the 1870s onwards. (See Hoshi Ayao, *Min-Shin jidai kōtsushi no kenkyū*, Tokyo, 1971, pp. 334-375.) This

process was the main reason for the steady decline of such Grand Canal towns as Linqing and Jining and deserves more emphasis than the authors give it. The opening of the Jinan-Peking railway in 1904 also contributed to the decline of the Grand Canal towns.]

9.   "Altogether the walls of Linqing are five miles in circumference; within the town itself, there are close on one million gentry and merchants as well as goods from both north and south." *Ming Qing shiliao, jiabian*, p. 923.

10.   The basis for our estimate is as follows: *The Imperial Encyclopaedia* records that the population of the whole of Dongchang Prefecture in the mid-fifteenth century was "54,239 households and 424,494 individuals. From the sixteenth to the eighteenth century it remained more or less constant." ("Political Divisions" section, *Dongchangfu, huyi kao*); in the latter part of the seventeenth century, the population of Linqing sub-prefecture was 30,823 households, 66,745 individuals (*Imperial Encyclopaedia*, "Political Divisions" section); the *Gazetteer of the Independent Sub-Prefecture of Linqing* of 1784 records that "the old *ding* quota was 63,819 ... Allowing for excluded categories such as gentry with privileged exemptions, palace scholars, licentiates, those who had been transferred to other registers and runaway households and including increases, the quota now stands at 20,263 *ding*," (ibid, *juan* 3, section on population). According to the *District Gazetteer of Linqing* (1934), Vol. 2, "There are no reliable population figures for the district before the Ming. *Ding* figures have survived from 1640 onwards."

> 1640: 10,649
> 1673: 16,587
> 1792: 20,263
> 1893: 69,551
> 1903: 96,931

In 1931, Linqing's number 1 sub-district (covering the area of the four urban units of administration known as *zhen* within the brick walls and the forty-one *zhen* within the earth walls) contained 8,064 households numbering 36,348 individuals (men and women); ibid. We know that all the figures on Linqing sub-prefecture mentioned above included both the area within the walls and the surrounding country areas of the sub-prefecture. Thus, in order to estimate the urban population, it is necessary to subtract the rural population. Furthermore, the *ding* figures did not include women or children, nor did they include those who had privileged exemption or those who for one reason or another were not registered. These latter were particularly numerous as suggested in an interesting comment of Gu Yan-Wu:

"There are many big merchants in Linqing; part of their business lies in collecting house rents, but they themselves are officially resident in other areas and are therefore not entered into the population registers at Linqing" (*Tianxia junguo libing shu, juan* 21). Taking these various points into account and using the emended old *ding* quota of 66,000 and allowing three people to each *ding,* we get a total of no more than 150,000 people for the sixteenth century for the town of Linqing itself at its most flourishing. [The authors do not make clear how they arrived at this figure. They presumably added a couple of thousand to the "old *ding* quota" of 63,819 to make 66,000 in order to allow for unrecorded categories. This they multiplied by 3 to allow for women and children, giving a total for the whole sub-prefecture of 198,000. Next they appear to have subtracted 48,000, presumably to allow for rural population, giving a total of 150,000 for the town of Linqing itself. If this was indeed how they arrived at the figure of 150,000, the figure should be treated with the greatest caution. Apart from anything else, an urban/ rural population ratio of 3:1 at this time would appear highly unlikely. For a discussion of urban/rural population ratios and population trends, see the translator's Introduction. For the effects of the decline in grain tribute traffic up the Grand Canal on Linqing's population in the nineteenth century, see note 8. Once source puts the population of Linqing in the 1930s at 80,000 (*Zhongguo fensheng dizhi, Shandong,* Shanghai, 1935, p. 188).]

11.   *Imperial Encyclopaedia,* "Political Divisions" section.

12.   Section on "Markets," 1784 edition of the *Gazetteer of the Sub-Prefecture of Linqing, juan* 2.

13.   Ibid.

14.   From the novel *A Marriage to Awaken Men (Xingshi yinyuan zhuan).* Chapter 25. [On the author and date of this novel, see note 16, to Chapter 3.]

15.   *Veritable Records of the Ming (Shenzong xianhuangdi shilu), juan* 376.

16.   Lu Can, *Shuoting, juan* 1. [The original has the character "Chen" instead of "Lu," but this is clearly a misprint.]

17. *Imperial Encyclopaedia,* "Political Divisions" section, under "Customs of Dengzhou Prefecture." The full passage reads: "The wealthy merchants of Dengzhou took their goods to Suzhou, Hangzhou, and Nanjing ... poorer ones traveled all the way to sell their goods at Linqing."

18. Ibid, under "Customs of Xuanhua Prefecture."

19. *Gazetteer of the Sub-Prefecture of Linqing,* 1784 edition, section on "Products."

20. *District Gazetteer of Linqing* (1934), Vol. 4, "Monograph on Economics" gives the following details: "Most famous of Linqing's old handicraft industries were the fine silks guild or *hada* store; enterprises which bought or sold were called "silk shops" (*sidian*); weaving was done by "loom shops" (*jifang*), and the dyers were called "fullers" (*jiangfang*). During the Qing dynasty when this industry was at its height, there were more than 700 "loom shops" within the walls of Linqing, as well as 7 or 8 "fullers," 10 firms specializing in buying raw silk and about 5,000 weavers ... the finished products were retailed in Inner and Outer Mongolia and in Chahar and Suiyuan."

21. Preface to the 1672 edition of the *Gazetteer of the Sub-Prefecture of Linqing* as quoted in the 1934 edition of the *District Gazetteer of Linqing.*

22. "On the Customs of Dongchang Prefecture," in "Political Divisions" section of the *Imperial Encyclopaedia.*

23. *District Gazetteer of Linqing,* 1934, Vol. 1.

24. [The late Ming novel *Jinpingmei* is set in a district town just next to Linqing and contains a wealth of often amusing detail on the life of the *nouveaux riches* of the time. For an English translation, see Clemont Egerton, *Golden Lotus,* 4 vols. (London, Routledge, 1939).]

25. Preface to the 1784 edition of the *Gazetteer of the Independent Sub-Prefecture of Linqing.*

26. *Gazetteer of the Independent Sub-Prefecture of Linqing,* 1784, *juan* 9.

27. Ibid.

28. Ibid.

29. *District Gazetteer of Linqing,* 1934, Vol. 4. Earlier editions of the gazetteer give the official quotas as 76,271 taels in the last years of the Ming, 29,684 taels in 1686, and 34,252 taels in 1775. These official quotas are not as near the actual figures collected as those given in the 1934 edition, which appear more reliable.

30. [The first development of Jining as a transshipment center came somewhat earlier than the authors state. Already by the twelfth century the canal was extended to the Jining region and, following a period of disuse, was reopened in 1283. Sometime during the late thirteenth century, Marco Polo passed through Jining and he describes the town as much more than "mainly an administrative and military center" (Jing and Luo):

> When the traveller leaves Tandinfu (Yanzhou), he continues southwards for three days, passing many splendid cities and towns, centers of thriving commerce and industry ... at the end of this time he reaches the splendid city of Sinju Matu (Jining), a city of great size and wealth and great commercial and industrial activity ... They have a river which they turn to good account, as I shall tell you. The truth is that this river flows from the South as far as this city Sinju Matu; and the townsmen have made it into two, one half flowing eastwards and the other westwards, so the one leads to Manzi and the other through Cathay. And I assure you that this town has so much shipping that no one who has not seen it could believe it. You must not suppose that they are big ships; but they are such as best suit a large river. And I assure you that the amount of merchandise transported to Manzi and through Cathay by this multitude of craft is simply staggering. And then, when the boats come back, they carry return cargoes. So it is indeed a marvellous sight to see the traffic going up and down this river. (R. E. Latham, tr., *The Travels of Marco Polo*, London, Penguin Books, 1958, pp. 170-171.)

The river referred to by Marco Polo was in fact the Wen and Si rivers which join within the borders of Jining and whose courses were followed by the Grand Canal. The Wen River flows north (Marco Polo's eastwards) and the Si River flows south (Marco Polo's westwards).

Jining no doubt declined in the troubled times of the fourteenth century, and Jing and Luo are perfectly correct, therefore, in linking the rise of the town during the Ming and the Qing to the reopening of the Grand Canal (in 1411).]

31. The *Imperial Encyclopaedia,* section on the "Customs of Yanzhou Prefecture."

32. Yang Ding-guo's "Record of the repaving of Yijing passage" in *Gazetteer of the Independent Sub-Prefecture of Jining,* 1859 edition, *juan* 4.

33. Zheng Yu-qiao, "Record of the Defense" in ibid., *juan* 4, part 5.

34. Ibid., *juan* 3, part 1.

35. Ibid., *juan* 3, part 5, population total for internal division of the town.

36. See *Collection of Epigraphy from Jizhou (Jizhou jinshi zhi) juan* 4, p. 75.

37. Wu Sheng: "On the Miscellaneous Taxes" (Zashui Lun) in *Gazetteer of the Independent Sub-Prefecture of Jining,* 1840 edition, *juan* 3, part 4. Wu Sheng had this to say about the trade tax: "The original regulations for the trade tax (*kecheng*) were that it was only levied on goods coming into the prefecture from outside. It was called 'incoming goods tax' (*luodi shui*). Goods produced in Jining were not to be taxed. In the past, simple country bumpkins who should not have to pay this tax have in fact been paying it ... Wheelbarrow porters, muleteers, and peddlers carrying their wares over their shoulders, even if they come from outside the prefecture, since they have few goods and limited capital and rely in their own muscle power for an uncertain profit, should not be taxed under the old regulations." On the "brokerage tax" (*yaza shui*), Wu Sheng says: "The old regulations stipulate that all merchants and traders who are not registered in Jining are liable to this tax. It is levied after they have bought their goods according to the distance they intend to take them. No account is taken of the nature or value of the goods but it is reckoned by the number of carts or mules for goods moving out overland and by bundles and packages for those going out by boat." Ibid.

38. Ibid.

39. "Stele Recording the Dabei Pavilion," in *Collection of Epigraphy from Jizhou (Jizhou jinshi zhi) juan* 5, p. 27.

40. "Products of Yanzhou Prefecture," in "Political Divisions" section of the *Imperial Encyclopaedia.*

41. *Gazetteer of Yixian District.*

42. According to the sub-section on "Products of Yanzhou Prefecture" in

the *Imperial Encyclopaedia,* "Sixty to seventy per cent of the clothing materials, food, and implements used in Yanzhou are bought and shipped up from the Yangzi provinces." The *Gazetteer of the Independent Sub-prefecture of Linqing* (section on "Streets and Markets") notes that "the glutinous millet consumed in Linqing which comes up the Wen River is all from the area around Jining as is all the cotton cloth." In a communication of 1906 from the district magistrate to the provincial governor, we find the following description of Jining: "The town is a transshipment center, its local products are abundant, and many merchants gather here. Annual production of jujubes, persimmons, peanut cake oil, pickled vegetables, cotton cloth, food grains, leather, and so forth is not less than several million units. An equally large amount of goods, such as cottons, silks, satins, etc., are also shipped in every year," (*District Gazetteer of Jining,* 1927).

43.   [This paragraph was placed in a footnote in the original, but I found it sufficiently interesting to put it into the main text.]

44.   [One modern scholar cites evidence to show that, at the end of the Ming, between 10%–15% of the total capacity of the grain transport fleet was taken by private goods. See *The Ming Tribute Grain System* by Hoshi Ayao, translated by Mark Elvin (Michigan Center for Chinese Studies, Ann Arbor, 1969), pp. 45–46. By the end of the nineteenth century, the grain tribute junks on the canal had been largely replaced by coastal steamers. See note 8.]

45.   Bao Shi-chen: *An Wu sizhong, juan* 6, *Zhahe riji.*

46.   See the sections on "Streets and Markets," "Local Products Goods," etc. in the *Gazetteer of the Independent Sub-Prefecture of Jining* and various stelae recording tax exemptions and labor-service exemptions for different trades in *Collection of Epigraphy from Jizhou, juan* 5. [The Scottish missionary Alexander Armstrong visited Jining in 1891 and linked the rise of its handicraft industries with its decline as a transshipment center on the Grand Canal: "Formerly it (Jining) was a great mart on the Canal, but as the traffic has become less, Chi-ning has grown into a manufacturing center. Brass, iron and bamboo wares are produced and exported in large quantities. Making silk thread and silk, forms another great industry. Vermicelli, red wine and fine cut tobacco, are among some of the other productions. Chi-ning exports, too, enormous quantities of salt pickles: there is one factory in the city which employs 500 men in this work." *Shantung,* p. 7. The salt-pickling factory

mentioned by Armstrong is almost certainly the Yu tang condiment
works which is the subject of Chapter 5, Section 2.]

47.   [The authors examine the history and operation of one of Jining's largest
      condiment works in Chapter 5, Section 2.]

48.   [White brass (also called white copper) is an alloy of zinc, nickel, and
      copper and was used extensively throughout China.]

49.   Qiu Xin-ni: *Guang jian qi shuo* in *Qiewen zhai wenchao, juan* 5.

50.   *Jining zhili zhouzhi, juan* 5. [The meaning of "western" looms (*xiji*) in
      this passage is not clear; it is possible that *xi* is a printing mistake for *mu*
      (wood) which would make better sense—"wooden" looms being a
      recognized phrase.]

51.   See the 1801 edition of the *District Gazetteer of Changshan (Changshan
      xianzhi), juan* 8, section on "Heroes" under Zhou Shi-zhen.

52.   Li Hua-xi was born in Changshan district and had become a *jinshi* in
      1634; he was made expectant prefect of Huizhou before taking up
      appointment as Governor-General of the Northwest Border during the
      crisis at the end of the Ming period. After the Ming surrender, he was
      raised from Vice-Minister of War to Minister of Punishments, see ibid.,
      juan 7.

53.   Ibid., *juan* 7.

54.   Ibid., *juan* 13.

55.   Ibid., *juan* 10, Shi Chao-zuo.

56.   Pu Song-ling, *Strange Tales from Liaozhai (Liaozhai zhiyi), juan* 15.

57.   *District Gazetteer of Changshan,* 1801 edition, under "Markets"
      recording the 1734 text of the stele on Jiaojiaqiao private market.

58.   Ibid., *juan* 30.

59.   [These were the "four big market towns" of the empire, a phrase first
      used in the seventeenth century. None of them were administrative
      centers.]

60. *District Gazetteer of Changshan, juan* 13.

61. Bao Shi-chen: *An Wu sizhong, juan* 6, *Zhahe riji.* [There was a common saying in the nineteenth century that attests to the importance of Zhoucun: "One market in Henan; one fair in Zhili; and one village in Shandong" (*Henan yiji Zhili yizhen Shandong yicun*). The towns referred to were Zhuxian zhen, Hinji, and Zhoucun respectively.]

62. "Record of an Investigation of the Districts and Rural Sub-units of Shandong" (*Shandong ge xian xiang tu diaocha lu*).

63. *Summary of the Investigation Report for the Jiaozhou-Jinan Railway, (Jiao Ji tielu diaocha baogao zongbian), juan* 2, "Commerce."

64. See *Gazetteer of Changshan District; Investigation Report for the Jiaozhou-Jinan Railway;* separate publication, "Industrial and commercial conditions of Zhoucun" (*Changshan xian Zhoucun Gongshangye qingxing*); *Chinese Industrial Gazetteer, Shantung (Zhongguo Shiyezhi, Shandongsheng,* section on Zhoucun).

65. *Qingzhou fuzhi,* 1859 edition, *juan* 32.

66. *Zichuan xianzhi,* 1776 edition.

67. *Jinan fuzhi,* 1841 edition, "Fengsu bian, Changshan xian."

68. Yu Wei-lin in *Qidong xianzhi* 1880, *juan* 8.

69. *Qidong xianzhi,* Zhou Yi-xun: "Bushi ji."

70. *Chinese Industrial Gazetteer, Shantung,* p. 213.

71. *Xingjiao Shandong ji* in *Xiaohang wencun, juan* 1.

72. [*Liuli* is an opaque, glass-like substance which I have translated as "glass" throughout this section.]

73. [Compare the similar distinction made between "rice coal" and "iron coal" by Song Ying-xing, the author of the famous 1637 survey of industrial technology, *The Creations of Nature and Man* (T'ien-kung k'ai-wu) translated by E-tu Zen Sun and Shiou-chuan Sun (University Park and London, University of Pennsylvania Press, 1966), p. 205.]

74.   *Yanshan zaji*, 1666. Sun Ting-quan (1613–1674) became a *jinshi* just before the fall of the Ming. Under the first Qing Emperor he was head of the Board of Personnel and in the 1660s he became a Grand Secretary. [Alexander Williamson visited Boshan in 1869 and described the coal fields there as follows: . . . the hills behind the town "are perforated with coal-pits. Several varieties are extracted: some fine bituminous coal, some partly bituminous and partly anthracite, gas coal and other kinds difficult to class. This district is famous all over the country, and supplies the neighbouring towns and cities. Approaching this place I met a very unexpected product carried on wheelbarrows, often bound for distant places. This was coke; and, on reaching Boshan, I found it manufactured in immense quantities: I saw three different kinds of coke stored in large yards, and exported abundantly. It is used for smelting silver, and for purposes where great heat is required. This speaks volumes for the quality of the coal . . . The coal from this district is conveyed by carts and wheelbarrows, etc. to Lijin, on the Yellow River, about seventy-five miles distant, and there exported in all directions. This coal and coke are famous above all in Shantung; perhaps because they can work the pit better and get at the fine coal." *Journeys in North China* (London, 1870), I, 115–116.]

75.   *Boshan xianzhi* (1753). [Compare the much fuller description of iron making in Song Ying-xing, pp. 248–249.]

76.   *Qingzhou fuzhi*, "wuchan, Boshan xian."

77.   *Yanshan zaji*. [Three centuries later Williamson wrote: "Among the manufactures of Shantung, glass is entitled to special mention, as it proves to be a most important article of internal commerce . . . I found them making excellent window glass, blowing bottles of various sizes, moulding cups of every description, and making lanterns, beads, and ornaments in endless variety. They also run it into rods, about 30 inches long, which they tie up in bundles and export to all parts of the country. The rods of pig-glass cost 100 cash per catty at the manufactory. The glass is extremely pure; they colour it most beautifully, and have attained considerable dexterity in manipulation: many of the articles were finely finished." Williamson, I, 131–132.]

78.   [For a general description of the many different types of organization found in the mining industry in the Qing period, see E-tu Zen Sun, "Mining Labor in the Qing Period," in Albert Feuerwerker, Rhoads Murphy, and Mary C. Wright eds., *Approaches to Modern Chinese History* (Berkeley and Los Angeles, University of California Press, 1967), pp. 45–67.]

79. *Yanshen zhenzhi, juan* 2.

80. Ibid.

81. *Boshan xianzhi* (1753) and *Yanshan zaji.*

82. *Yanshen zhenzhi, juan* 2.

Chapter 2

1. *Yanshen zhenzhi, juan* 2, *fengsu.*

2. *Linqing zhili zhouzhi, juan* 2, *shigu.*

3. *Zhangqiu xianzhi, juan* 6, *lisu.*

4. Zhang Si-mian's memorial is printed in the literature section of *Ye xianzhi* 1893, *juan* 6. He was district magistrate of Yexian from 1750 to 1758.

5. *Yidu dingren ji, juan* 1.

6. *Nongzheng quanshu, juan* 35.

7. Quoted in the 1874 edition of *Linyi xianzhi, juan* 2.

8. *Laiqinguan ji, juan* 18. [The authors are mistaken in identifying the year *renxu* as 1622, because Xing Dong died in 1612. It presumably refers therefore to the year 1562.]

9. *Qidong xianzhi, juan* 1. [See Chapter 1, Section 3 for further quotations on the Qidong cotton-cloth market.]

10. *Zhaoyu zhi. ce* 32, quoted in the *Imperial Encyclopaedia;* see the following note.

11. *Gujin tushu jicheng, zhifangdian, Dongchangfu, wuchangkao.* [The 1798 edition of the *District Gazetteer of Qingping (Qingping xianzhi)* says: "The women work mainly at spinning and, when they have finished the spinning, they set up looms and weave cloth. Either they sell it or keep it at home. All the household's clothes and daily needs are met in this way."]

12. *Shandong tongzhi.* [The 1891 edition of the *District Gazetteer* of Fei-cheng (*Feicheng xianzhi*), under "Customs," notes that "The women work hard at spinning and weaving. The rich can do it to provide for their own needs, but the poor have to do it to support their families. For thirty miles around, the sound of weaving shuttles is heard continuously, and for several tens of years a special cotton market has been set up," ibid., *juan* 8.]

13. *Chongxiu Jiaqing yitong zhi, juan* 60, *Dongchang fu,* 2.

14. This passage is taken from a piece entitled "Exhortation to Contribute Charity Grain" in Xu Zong-gan's collected works *Siweixinzhai wenbian.*

15. *Tengxian zhi, juan* 9.

16. Sheng Bai-er: "Record of Mr. Zang Xian's maize cultivation" in *Jining zhili zhouzhi,* 1785 edition, *juan* 3 (2). Zang Xian was a provincial graduate of 1672.

17. Quoted in the 1937 edition of *Jining zhili zhouzhi, juan* 33.

18. *Gujin tushu jicheng, zhifangdian, Yanzhoufu, wuchan kao.*

19. *Yixian zhi, juan* 7.

20. V. I. Lenin, *The Development of Capitalism in Russia* (Moscow, 1967), p. 292.

21. Literature section of the 1846 edition of *Tengxian zhi.*

22. 1846 edition of *Tengxian zhi, juan* 8, *bing.*

23. 1846 edition of *Tengxian zhi, juan* 3, *Wuchan kao.*

24. *Gujin tushu jicheng, zhifangdian, Yanzhoufu wuchan kao.*

25. *Yixian zhi, wuchan.*

26. *Tengxian zhi, fangchan.*

27. *Gujin tushu jicheng, Zhifangdian, Yanzhoufu wuchan kao.*

28. 1859 edition of *Qingzhou fuzhi, juan* 32.

Chapter 3

1.   *Selected Works of Mao Tse-tung,* English language edition (Peking, 1965),
     II, 309.

2.   According to the *Qingchao wenxian tongkao,* section on "Land Tax," in
     1924 there were 24,427 qing of military settlement land, 418 qing 22 mu of
     school land, and 967,741 qing 16 mu of people's land.

3.   See, for example, *Zhucheng xianzhi,* 1892 edition, *juan* 34. "During the
     Ming period garrison troops were stationed in the district at the opening
     of a pass through the Nanshan and were given mountain land to cultivate
     as part of their pay. The rent on every 50 mu was 6 dan. Later though
     the number of troops was reduced, the rent remained the same and the
     people found it intolerable." The 1936 edition of the provincial gazetteer
     records that, in 1783, the government sought out along the banks of the
     Yellow River "over 100 qing of wasteland in the marshes behind the
     dikes which could be brought under cultivation. East of Liubao to Hewei
     there had once been 23 qing of government land, and in Cao xian dis-
     trict along the old course of the river there were over 20 qing of barren
     sandbank land. Officials called for tenants to come and rent these
     lands"; *Shandong tongzhi,* 1936, *juan* 74, p. 2398. Another source
     records that, in Jinxiang district, the Puji tang clan branch owned 1,186
     mu of charity land from which they received 1,431 dou of grain; they
     also owned 410 mu of charity land in Jiaxiang district from which they
     received a rent of 910 dou and 65 jin of firewood, *Jining zhili zhouzhi,*
     juan 4. [In effect most of the government-owned land in north China
     had passed into private hands by the early nineteenth century. The
     same had happened with school land. *See* Ramon H. Myers, *The Chinese
     Peasant Economy: Agricultural Development in Hopei and Shantung,
     1890–1949* (Cambridge, Mass., Harvard University Press, 1970), pp.
     217–220, for an outline of this process and references.]

4.   *Shandong tongzhi, juanshou.*

5.   *Donghua lu, juan* 16, edict of the seventh month of 1707; *juan* 18,
     edict of the fifth month of 1712.

6.   *DaQing lüli, juan* 20, section on *binglu guanjin,* entry on "Illicit emigra-
     tion and smuggling," *sichu waijing ji weijin xiahai.*

7.   *Shandong tongzhi, juanshou.*

8. V. I. Lenin, *The Development of Capitalism in Russia* (Moscow, 1967), p. 71.

9. *Gujin tushu jicheng, zhifang dian, Dengzhoufu, fengsukao.*

10. Ibid., Yanzhoufu, Ciyang district, Ningyang district, Zou district, Yi zhou sub-prefecture.

11. *Zhangqiu xianzhi, juan* 10.

12. *Yanshan zaji, juan* 3.

13. *Juyilu, juan* 33.

14. *Qingzhou fuzhi,* 1859.

15. *Qingping xianzhi,* 1936.

16. *Xingshi yinyuan zhuan, hui* 28. The author of this novel signed himself with the nom de plume Xi Zhou-sheng. The action of the novel purports to take place in the mid-fifteenth century. The novel's date is not known. An eighteenth-century scholar, Yang Fu-ji, in his *Menglan xiaobi,* suggested that the author was the famous writer Pu Song-ling of Zichuan district. According to the research of Lu Da-huang, published in *Guangming ribao,* Literary heritage, no. 70, this is an unfounded tradition. What is certain, however, is that the novel was completed between the late fifteenth and early seventeenth centuries and that it contains a great deal of interesting material on Shandong's changing society in this period.

17. *Da Qing lüli, juan* 28 and *juan* 27.

18. *Wenshizhe,* 1951, No. 15. The *Imperial Encyclopaedia* also contains an eighteenth-century reference to "base people and serf laborers" in Anqiu (*Gujin tushu jicheng zhifangdian Qingzhoufu fengsukao*).

19. *Tengxian zhi.*

Chapter 4

1. These data were gathered in interviews with the following old men: Li Heng-kui, Li Heng-qing, Gong Zi-zhen, Gong Chuan-jie and Li Heng-

tong, all of Dongfanliu village; Wang Shu-cai, and Chu Qing-xiu of Dongqingye village; Xi Jian-yun of Xifanliu village; and Zhang Xing-quan and others of Zhangjia village. Besides the interview materials, we also used the receipt stubs of the land deeds of Taihe tang covering the years 1761 to 1905; various wage labor account books, cash on hand accounts, and loan accounts of Taihe tang dating from 1875 to 1908. Finally we used the memorial stele of two of the key Taihe tang land-lords in the late nineteenth century, Li Fang-biao and Li Fang-cai.

2. [Taihe was the "hall name" (*tangming*) of the Li family. Such names were usually inscribed on one of the principal rooms of the house (or on the clan hall if there was one) and were used in deeds, on boundary stones, and so forth to indicate that the property was owned by the particular branch of the family in question. I have followed the authors in sometimes referring to the "Taihe tang Li family" as simply the "Taihe tang" for short.]

3. It was a local custom that neighbors had rights of first refusal when land was up for sale.

4. [In Chapter 7, Section 3, the authors explain that the direct forerunner of Taihe tang had split the family land of 351.4 mu into two equal inheritance portions of 175.7 mu each for Li Ke-shi and Li Ke-fa. Un-fortunately, they say nothing more to clarigy Taihe tang's early history.]

5. [These societies were popular all over north China. The operations of one are described in great detail in Sidney D. Gamble, *Ting Hsien, A North China Rural Community* (New York Institute of Pacific Relations, 1954), pp. 260-270.]

6. Calculated from Li Fang-Cai's memorial stelae.

7. The data in this section were gathered in interviews with Bi De-yin, the great grandson of the nineteenth-century manager of the silk work-shop, Bi Yuan-rong; Bi De-kuan, another of his descendants; Nie Xing-de, who had been a weaver in the workshop; and other old men of Lijia village. We also consulted the genealogy of the Bis of Zichuan, the memorial tablets in the Bis' ancestral hall, and local gazetteers of Zichuan district.

8. [Shujing tang was the "hall name" (*tangming*) of the Bi family. See note 2 above.]

9. To avoid repetition, we have cut out materials similar to those already presented on Taihe tang in Section 1.

10. [On the silk industry in the Qing period, see E-tu Zen Sun, "Sericulture and Silk Textile Production in Ch'ing China," in *Economic Organization in Chinese Society,* W. E. Willmott, ed. (1972) and Shih Min-hsiung, *The Silk Industry in Ch'ing China,* translated by E-tu Zen Sun (Ann Arbor, Center for Chinese Studies, University of Michigan, 1976).]

11. [For a similar story of an enterprising countryman making extra money by selling cloth in a Shandong local town (although this story takes place in the early twentieth century and has a very different ending), see the novel *The Travels of Lao Ts'an* by Liu T'ieh-yün (translated from the Chinese by Harold Shadick, Ithaca, Cornell University Press, 1952), pp. 57–59. The novel contains a considerable amount of incidental detail on Shandong life at the turn of the century.]

12. The data presented here are based on our interviews with the following old men of Jiujun market town in Zhangqiu district: Meng Guang-zhen (73 sui); Meng Guang-zhi (64); Meng Zhao-ying (64); Meng Zhao-kui (53); Li Jian-hou (60); Chen Shou-min (62); Zhao Lu-jin (56); Gao Qing-yu (76); Cheng Si-he (71); Zhao Guang-an (48); old Mrs. Zhang (63); and others. We also used the genealogy of the Meng clan, the memorial stelae in the Meng ancestral hall, and the local gazetteers of Zhangqiu district. In order to round out our presentation of the economic activities of this branch of the Mengs, we have at certain points used early Republican data.

Chapter 5

1. The data presented in this section are based on our interviews with the individuals listed in Ch.4 note 12. We also used the land account books of Jinshu tang, the genealogy of the Meng clan, memorial stelae in the Meng ancestral hall, and local gazetteers of Zhangqiu district, etc. In order to round out our presentation of the economic activities of this branch of the Meng clan, we have at certain points used early Republican data.

2. [Something has clearly gone awry in this table in the original. If the minimum amount of land in each category of landowners is multiplied by the number of households in each category and even if it is assumed that the 700 poor peasant/laborer households owned no more than 3

mu each, the total cultivated acreage of Jiujun comes to 18,990 mu
(450 + 60 X 99 + 100 X 45 + 400 X 15 + 700 X 3). Yet the authors
give the total as 11,400 mu.]

3.   The data presented here are based on our interviews with the following
old men who had been workers in the Sun's soy-bean products manufactory. We also used the genealogy of the Sun clan, the *Prefectural Gazetteer of Jining* and the *Provincial Gazetteer of Shandong*. Sun Shu-yu was
born in 1888 and had worked on the manufacturing side of the business.
Yang Qing-yun was born in 1895 and had worked in the pickling department. Dong Sheng-ren was also born in 1895 and had worked in the liquor
fermenting department. Sun Du-chen was born in 1897 and was the grandson on his father's mother's side of Grand Councillor Sun Yu-wen. Yuan
Feng-er was also born in 1897 and had been for several decades the chief
accountant of the shop attached to the manufactory. Since most of the
Sun descendants had left the area after 1944 and they no longer had any
contacts there, we were unable to collect complete records on the process
of the Suns' land accumulation. We have included here the little that we
were able to find on this subject.

4.   [Sun Kuo-tu (1717–1787) was in fact a provincial graduate and served
as a district magistrate in Jiangsu for a number of years; see A. W.
Hummel, *Eminent Chinese of the Ch'ing Period* (Washington, U. S.
Government Printing Office, 1943–1944), pp. 683–685.]

5.   These figures were obtained in an interview with the former accountant
Yuan Feng-er, the account books of the business having been destroyed
by fire in early 1946.

6.   [In 1891, Alexander Armstrong visited Jining and, in a comment which
is almost certainly about the Yu tang, noted 500 workers: "Chi-ning
exports, too, enormous quantities of salt pickles; there is one factory in
the city which employs 500 men in this work," *Shantung*, p. 72.]

Chapter 6

1.   [In the original at this point the authors list the names of the villages in
which they found both managerial and rentier landlord relations of production. Since they list these villages in Appendix A, I have cut this
information from the main text.]

2. [In the original the authors list the names of the villages in which the only landlords they found were managerial landlords. Since they also provide this information in Appendix A, there seemed no point in repeating it in the main text.]

3. For example, 69-year-old Shi Jin-you told us: "At the end of the nineteenth and the beginning of the twentieth centuries, there was a managerial landlord in Nanyang village, Fan District (Region 5) named Yang Yu-ping [Appendix B, landlord no. 114] who at the height of his wealth owned 70,000 mu of land. He was never an official either under the Empire or in the Republic, being only concerned with amassing wealth. He had originally lived at some distance north of the Yellow River. One year there had been a great flood, and people had fled from along the Yellow River. After the flood, there was a great deal of land left uncultivated. Yang Yu-ping seized the opportunity and began to cultivate it. He harvested a crop of wheat and, since there was no demand for land along the river, he was able to buy at the low price of 30 jin of wheat per mu. He bought huge quantities of land and, in this way, founded the fortunes of his family."

4. [In the original, the authors list the names of the landlords conducting nonfarming activities and their villages in the main text. Since this material is all provided in Appendix B, I have left it out of the main text.]

5. [In the original, the authors write out in the main text the information found in Table 31. This repetition has been omitted in the translation. In the original, cash amounts in Table 31 were given in fractions of a string, e.g., 0.03; I have transposed the entire column into actual cash, thus 0.03 becomes 30.]

6. [In the original, the authors write out in the main text the information found in Table 33. This repetition has been omitted in the translation.]

7. [In the original, the authors write out the names of each village in which short-term laborers were found to own (or rent) land. Since this information is given in tabulated form in Appendix C, it has been omitted from the main text in the translation.]

Chapter 7

1. There were many different types of plough. Ploughshare ploughs were ploughs in which the shovel and the ploughshare were joined together, whereas the shovel plough had no ploughshare and the shovel was either oval shaped or triangular.

2. See Xu Guang-qi, *Comprehensive Treatise on Agriculture (Nongzheng quanshu), juan* 21.

3. As of October 1957, it was the practice in the neighborhood of Fushan-hou village to use donkey teams for ploughing, while in the neighborhood of Dawa shoulder ploughs were still used. According to some of the old peasants, "Such ploughs had been in use since ancient times." In Fushan-hou (a village of 350 households), there had only been 3 or 4 seeding drills, and these had all been owned by landlords or rich peasants. Most of the middle and poor peasants "had little land (3 to 5 or 7 to 8 mu), and it wasn't worth getting more even if they could have afforded it."

4. [For a detailed description of the preparation of compost in Shandong villages at this time, see F. H. King, *Farmers of Forty Centuries* (London, Cape, 1911), pp. 250-252.]

5. [In the original, the authors supply the names of 87 villages in which they found that landlords' yields were higher than those on ordinary peasants' land, although they only give actual yield figures for the 41 villages listed in Table 35. The 87 villages were as follows:

District/Village	District/Village
Licheng/Laocengkou	Zhangqiu/Zhaijiazhaocun
Licheng/Yaojiacun	Zhangqiu/Beicaoyuan
Zhangqiu/Guanzhuangcun	Zhangqiu/Nanduozhuang
Zhangqiu/Bucun	Zhangqiu/Zhaijiazhaocun
Zhangqiu/Zhangyilancun	Zhangqiu/Zhangjiacun
Zhangqiu/Xianggongzhuang	Zichuan/Sulizhuang
Zhangqiu/Mingshui	Zichuan/Wangdongcun
Zhangqiu/Qilangyuan	Zichuan/Wangcun
Zhangqiu/Dakangzhuang	Zichuan/Linchicun
Zhangqiu/Xiyaocun	Zichuan/Shengucun
Zhangqiu/Jiegouhe	Huantai/Qianchencun
Zhangqiu/Dongbu	Yidu/Songjiazhuang

District/Village   District/Village

Yidu/Beiputongcun   Linzi/Zhutaicun
Yidu/Yuhuangmiao   Linzi/Dongzhaocun
Anqiu/Baifenzicun   Linzi/Nanfengkecun
Anqiu/Yijiezhuang   Laiyang/Qianbuhoucun
Zhucheng/Futaicun   Laiyang/Lingnancun
Zhucheng/Xisong-guzhuang   Laiyang/Nanzuojiakuangcun
Zhucheng/Chenjiacun   Linyi/Xinjicun
Zhucheng/Xiangzhoucun   Linyi/Dizisongcun
Zhucheng/Xuejiucun   Penglai/Shangkougaojia
Taian/Xi Yanglouzhuang   Penglai/Beilinyuan
Taian/Fangjiazhuang   Penglai/Anxiangyujia
Taian/Bamiaodi   Qixia/Zhongqiaocun
Taian/Beikoucun   Qixia/Malingzhong
Taian/Jiaogucun   Changyi/Xishiqiaocun
Taian/Beishigoucun   Changyi/Beixingfucun
Taian/Liusuocun   Changyi/Baibucun
Xiajin/Qiaoguantun   Pingdu/Guxiancun
Xiajin/Mozhuang   Pingdu/Qianjiazhuang
Dongping/Weizihecun   Jiaoxian/Maiqiucun
Dongping/Xiaoyangzhuang   Jiaoxian/Beiliujiaxiaozhuang
Wenshang/Bonanliloucun   Jiaoxian/Wangjiacun
Tengxian/Dayancun   Jiaoxian/Tanjiacun
Binxian/Goushilicun   Puxian/Weizhuang
Xintai/Beishidiancun   Puxian/Guyunji
Dexian/Fenghuangdian   Feixian/Mazhuang
Tangyi/Dingliubazhai   Feixian/Nanshigou
Lijin/Beimatoucun   Zhaoyuan/Houkuangcun
Lijin/Daniucun   Yexian/Xizhangjiacun
Putai/Mawancun   Fanxian/Nanyangzhuang
Zhanhua/Wanjiacun   Zouxian/Dahuangcun
Fuxing/Changjiacun   Yishui/Xiaweizhuang
                                      Huimin/Xinjicun]

6. [See Appendix B, landlord numbers 41, 42, 62, 57, 74, 72, 127, 112, 100, 95; see also Introduction, Table 10, Mu per Long-and Short-Term Laborer on 13 Managerial Landlords' Farms.]

7. Lenin: *The Development of Capitalism in Russia,* p. 197.

8. [At this point in the text, the authors give the names of a dozen or so

landlords in their survey conducting nonfarming activities. Since this information is given in full in Appendix B, I have cut it from the text.]

9. Computed on the basis that, if yield per mu is 300 jin and each mu requires 8 labor days, wage laborers require 15 jin and other subsidiary workers also require 15 jin, the total laborer requirement equals 30 jin or 1/10 total production.

10. Reckoned on the basis that rent equals half the crop.

11. We have not counted the land tax and other taxes payable by the landlords to the government in the above equation, nor have we counted the seed grain laid aside by the managerial landlords, which amounted to approximately 1% of total yield. [Land-tax payments on a 720 mu farm at this time amounted to less than 1% of total outgoings. See P. G. M. Stenz, *Der Bauer in Schantung* (Tsingtao, 1910), p. 14.]

12. Frederick Engels: *Anti-Dühring* (Moscow, 1954), p. 290.

13. Tenants and owner peasants also hired short-term labor in the busy seasons, but there was a fundamental difference between their hiring of short-term labor and the rich peasants' and managerial landlords' hiring of long- and short-term labor. The tenants and owner peasants hired short-term labor as a subsidiary labor force to help solve temporary production problems, while the rich peasants and managerial landlords hired labor in order to produce *commercial* crops.

14. *Capital,* I, 169.

15. *Selected Works of Mao Tse-tung,* English language edition (Peking, 1965), I, 139. Emphases added by J. S. and L. L.

16. *Karl Marx and Frederick Engels Selected Works* (London, Lawrence and Wishart, 1968), p. 420.

17. [Something clearly went awry in the original at this point. The authors stated that they would give the kaoliang equivalents of Chen's and Zhang's wages. In fact they give the wheat equivalents of 13.9 jin; ½ jin, and 4.5 jin, respectively. I have calculated the kaoliang equivalents and substituted these in the text. Although the original gives 52 jin per dou of kaoliang. I have calculated on the basis of 55 jin, which is the figure

they give everywhere else in the text, including for Dongfanliu at this time (Chapter 4, Section1). The kaoliang and wheat prices given by the authors for Dongfanliu in 1908 are approximately three times higher than all other grain quotations given by the authors. (See, for example, Tables 31 and 33 for wheat prices from all over Shandong.) E. W.]

18. According to Jinshu tang land account books and interviews.

19. According to Taihe tang land deeds.

20. As recorded on Bi Yuan-rong's memorial stele.

21. Calculated from Li Fang-cai's memorial stele.

22. Figures taken from survey data; see Appendix B, landlord numbers 101 and 65.

23. Lenin, *The Development of Capitalism in Russia,* pp. 195–196.

24. See Appendix B, landlord numbers 85, 99, 128, and 125.

25. *Qingzhou fuzhi,* 1859.

26. *Capital,* I, 170–172.

27. *The Development of Capitalism in Russia,* pp. 231–232.

28. Ibid., p. 194.

29. Ibid., pp. 207–208.

Chapter 8

1. *History of the Communist Party of the Soviet Union (Bolsheviks), Short Course* (New York, 1939), p. 124.

2. *The Development of Capitalism in Russia,* pp. 194–195.

3. *Selected Works of Mao Tse-tung,* III, 77.

BIBLIOGRAPHY

1. Manuscripts and Stelae
2. Printed Works
3. Works Cited in the Translator's Introduction and Notes

1. Manuscripts and Stelae

Jinshu tang Mengs of Jiujun market town, Zhangqiu district
(*Zhangqiu xian Jiujun zhen Jinshu tang Meng jia* 章丘县
旧军镇矜恕堂孟家).
　　Genealogy of the Meng clan (*Mengshi jiapu* 孟氏家譜).
　　Land accounts, 1718–1911 (*dimu zhang* 地苗賬).
　　Memorial stelae in the ancestral hall (*Citang beiwen* 祠堂
碑文).

Jinxiu tang Mengs of Jiujun market town, Zhangqiu district
(*Zhangqiu xian Jiujun zhen Jinxiu tang Meng jia* 章丘县
旧军镇进修堂孟家).
　　Genealogy of the Meng clan (*Mengshi jiapu* 孟氏家譜).
　　Memorial stelae in the ancestral hall (*Citang beiwen* 祠堂
碑文).

Shujing tang Bis of Lijia village, Zichuan district (*Zichuan xian
Lijia zhuang Shujing tang Bi jia* 淄川县栗家庄树
荆堂畢家).
　　Genealogy of the Bis of Zichuan (*Zichuan Bishi shipu* 淄
川畢氏世譜).
　　Memorial Stelae in the ancestral hall (*Citang beiwen* 祠堂
碑文).

Taihe tang Lis of Dongfanliu village, Zhangqiu district (*Zhangqiu
xian Dongfanliu cun Taihe tang Li jia* 章丘县東矾硫
村太和堂李家).
　　Cash on hand accounts (*Duijin zhang* 堆金賬).
　　External loan accounts, 1875–1908 (*Waijie zhang* 外借
賬).
　　Receipt stubs of land deeds, 1761–1905 (*Wenqi cungen*
文契存根).

Wage-labor accounts (*Gugong zhang* 雇工賬).
Memorial Stelae (*Beiwen* 碑文).
Yu tang Suns of Jining Prefecture (*Jining zhou Yu tang Sun jia* 济宁州玉堂孙家).
Family history of the Suns (*Sunshi jiazhuan* 孙氏家传).

2. Printed Works

[In the original, the authors usually cite the work of a particular writer by giving just the title of the work. Sometimes they also give the date of printing (for example they give the reign name in which a gazetteer was edited); but frequently they give no date at all. In the following list all works cited in the authors' text have been brought together and dated and identified insofar as this has been possible.]

Bao Shi-chen 包世臣 . *Zhahe riji* 閘河日記 (Grand Canal diary), 1829, in *Anwusizhong* 安吳四種. 1851, *juan* 6.
Boshan xianzhi 博山县志 (District gazetteer of Boshan), 1753.

Changshan xianzhi 長山县志 (District gazetteer of Changshan), 1801.
Changshanxian Zhoucun gongshangye qingxing 長山县周村工商業情形 (Industrial and commercial conditions of Zhoucun Changshan district) in separate publication of *Jiao Ji tielu jingji diaocha baogao* 胶济铁路經济調查报告 ·

Da Qing Lüli 大清律例 (Qing Code with sub-statutes). 1811 edition.
Donghua Lu 東華錄 (Records from the Eastern Gate), Wang Xianqian 王先謙 , ed. *Shiyi chao Donghua lu* 十一朝東華錄 . 1884.

Engels, Frederick. *Anti-Dühring*. Moscow, Foreign Languages Publishing House, 1954.

Ge Mao-chun 葛懋春. "Cong Changwei tugai gongzuo zhong kan fengjian boxue" 从昌濰土改工作中看封建剝削 (Feudal exploitation seen in the course of land reform at Changwei), *Wenshizhe* 15 (1951).

Gu Yan-wu 顧炎武. *Zhaoyu zhi* 肇域志(Historical gazetteer).

Gu Yan-wu 顧炎武. *Tianxia junguo libing shu* 天下郡国利病書 (The characteristics of each province in the empire). Preface dated 1662.

Gujin tushu jicheng 古今圖書集成 (The imperial encyclopaedia). 1725.

History of the Communist Party of the Soviet Union (Bolshevik) Short Course. New York, 1939.

Imperial Encyclopaedia. See *Gujin tushu jicheng.*

Jiaqing chongxiu yitongzhi 嘉慶重修一統志 (Jiaqing revision of the comprehensive gazetteer of the Qing). Completed 1820, printed 1842.

Jiao Ji tielu diaocha baogao zongbian 胶济鉄路調查報告总編 (Summary of the investigation report for the Jiaozhou-Jinan railway).

Jinan fuzhi 济南府志 (Gazetteer of Jinan prefecture), 1841.

Jining xianzhi 济宁县志 (District gazetteer of Jining), 1927.

Jining zhili zhouzhi 济宁直隶州志 (Gazetteer of the independent sub-prefecture of Jining), 1785, 1840, 1859, 1937.

Jizhou jinshi zhi. See Xu Zong-gan.

Lenin, V. I. *The Development of Capitalism in Russia.* Moscow, Foreign Languages Publishing House, 1967.

Linqing xianzhi 临清县志 (District gazetteer of Linqing), 1934.

Linqing zhili zhouzhi 临清直隶州志 (Gazetteer of the independent sub-prefecture of Linqing), 1784.

Linyi xianzhi 临邑县志 (District gazetteer of Linyi), 1874.

Lu Can 陸燦, 1494–1551. *Shuo ting* 説听 2 *juan,* in *Shuoku.*

Lu Da-huang 路大荒. "Liaozhai quanji zhong de *Xingshi yin-yuan zhuan* yu *Guci ji* de zuozhe wenti," 聊齋全集中的醒世姻緣传与鼓詞集的作者問題 (The problem of the authorship of *Xingshi yinyuan zhuan* and the *Guci ji* in the Liaozhai complete works), *Guangming ribao,* Literary heritage, No. 70 (Sept. 4, 1955).

Mao Tse-tung. *The Selected Works of Mao Tse-tung,* English language edition. 4 vols. Peking, Foreign Languages Press, 1965.

Marx, Karl. *Capital,* vol. 1. London, Lawrence and Wishart, 1970.

Marx, Karl and Frederick Engels. *Selected Works.* London, Lawrence and Wishart, 1968.

Ming Qing shiliao jiabian 明清史料甲編 (Historical materials of the Ming and Qing, first series). Shanghai, Commercial Press, 1930–1931.

Pu Song-ling 蒲松齡. *Liaozhai zhiyi* 聊齋志異 (Strange tales from Liaozhai). 1766.

Qidong xianzhi 齐東县志 (District gazetteer of Qidong), 1685, 1880.

Qingchao xuwenxian tongkao 清朝續文獻通考 (Encyclopaedic history of Qing institutions, continued). 1921.

Qingping xianzhi 清平县志 (District gazetteer of Qingping), 1936.

Qingzhou fuzhi 青州府志 (Gazetteer of Qing prefecture), 1859.

Qiu Xin-ni 丘心尼. *Guang jian qin shuo* 廣僉戚説 in *Qiewen zhai wenchao* 切問齋文鈔, 1775, *juan* 5.

Shandong ge xian xiang tu diaocha lu 山東各县乡土調查錄 (Record of an investigation of the districts and rural sub-districts of Shandong), Lin Xiu-zhu 林修竹 comp. Jinan, 1920.

Shangdong tongzhi 山東通志 (Gazetteer of Shandong), 1736, 1892, 1936.

Shenzong Xianhuangdi shilu 神宗顯皇帝實錄 (Veritable records of the Shenzong Emperor). 1630.

Sun Ting-quan 孫廷銓 *Yanshan zaji* 顏山雜記 (Miscellaneous records of Yanshan). 1666.

Tengxian zhi 滕縣志 (District gazetteer of Teng), 1846.

Wang Shi-zhen 王士禎. *Juyi lu* 居易錄. 1701.

Wang Zhao 王照. *Xingjiao Shandong ji* 行脚山東記 (Diary of an itinerant priest in Shandong), 1900, in *Xiaohang wencun* 小航文存 1930, *juan* 1.

Xi Zhou-sheng 西周生. *Xingshi yinyuan zhuan* 醒世姻緣傳 (A marriage to awaken men). 16th century (?).

Xing Dong 邢侗, 1555–1612, *Laiqinguan ji* 来禽館集.

Xu Zong-gan 徐宗干, comp. *Jizhou jinshi zhi* 濟州金石志 (Collection of epigraphy from Jizhou), 1845. [This is the same work as *Jining jinshi zhi* 濟寧金石志].

Xu Zong-gan 徐宗干. *Siweixinzhai wenbian* 斯未信齋文編. 1855.

Xu Guang-qi 徐光啟. *Nongzheng quanshu* 農政全書 (Comprehensive treatise on agriculture). 1639.

Yang Fu-ji 楊復吉. *Menglan xiaobi* 梦闌瑣笔, in *Zhaodai congshu*.

Yanshen zhenzhi 顏神鎮志 (Gazetteer of Yanshen market town), 1670.

Yexian zhi 掖縣志 (District gazetteer of Ye), 1893.

Yidu dingren ji 益都丁壬集

Yixian zhi 嶧縣志 (District gazetteer of Yixian), 1893.

Zhangqiu xianzhi 章丘縣志 (District gazetteer of Zhangqiu), 1907.

Zhongguo shiye zhi, Shandong sheng 中國實業志, 山東省

(Chinese industrial gazetteer, Shandong). Shanghai, Ministry of Industry, 1934.

Zhucheng xianzhi 諸成縣志 (District gazetteer of Zhucheng), 1892.

Zichuan xianzhi 淄川縣志 (District gazetteer of Zichuan), 1776.

3. Works Cited in the Translator's Introduction and Notes

Amano Motonosuke 天野元之助. *Santōshō keizai chōsa shiryō: Santō nōgyō keizairon* 山東省經濟調查資料山東農業經濟論 (Economic research materials relating to Shandong province: An essay on the Shandong agricultural economy). Dairen, South Manchurian Railway Company, 1936.

Armstrong, Alexander. *Shantung.* Shanghai, Shanghai Mercury Office, 1891.

Buck, David C. *Urban Change in China: Politics and Development in Tsinan, 1890–1949.* Madison, University of Wisconsin Press, 1977.

Buck, J. L. *Land Utilization In China: Statistics.* Chicago, University of Chicago Press, 1937.

Chang Chung-li. *The Chinese Gentry.* Seattle, University of Washington Press, 1955.

——— *The Income of the Chinese Gentry.* Seattle, University of Washington Press, 1962.

Egerton, Clement, trans. *The Golden Lotus.* 4 vols. London, Routledge, 1939.

Elvin, Mark. *The Pattern of the Chinese Past.* London, Eyre Methuen, 1973.

"Farms and Orchards at Chefoo, Shantung," *Chinese Economic Journal* 3.1:612–629 (1928).

Feicheng xianzhi 肥城縣志 (District Gazetteer of Feicheng), 1891.

Feuerwerker, Albert. "From Feudalism to Capitalism in Recent Historical Writing from Mainland China," *Journal of Asian Studies* 18:107–115 (1958–1959).

Fu Yi-ling 傅衣凌 . *Ming Qing nongcun shehui jingji* 明清农村社会经济 (Village society and economy in Ming and Qing). Peking, Sanlian shudian, 1961.

Fujita Keiichi 藤田敬一 . "Shindai Santōshō keiei jinushitei shakai seishitsu" 清代山东省经营地主底社會性質 (The social nature of managerial landlords in Shandong during the Qing dynasty), *Atarashi rekishigaku no tame* 111:11–22 (1966).

Gamble, Sydney D. *Ting Hsien, A North China Rural Community.* New York, Institute of Pacific Relations, 1954.

History of the Communist Party of the Soviet Union (Bolshevik), Short Course. New York, 1939.

Ho, P. T. "The Salt Merchants of Yangchow," *Harvard Journal of Asiatic Studies* 17.1–2:130–168 (June 1954).

——— *Studies on the Population of China, 1368–1953.* Cambridge, Harvard University Press, 1959.

——— *The Ladder of Success in Imperial China: Aspects of Social Mobility, 1368–1911.* New York, Columbia University Press, 1962.

Hoshi Ayao. *The Ming Tribute Grain System.* Mark Elvin trans. Ann Arbor, University of Michigan, Center for Chinese Studies, 1969.

Hoshi Ayao 星斌夫 *Min-Shin jidai kōtsūshi no kenkyū* 明清時代交通の研究 (Studies on the history of communications in the Ming and Qing). Tokyo, Yamakawa shuppansha, 1971.

Hsiao Kung-chuan. *Rural China: Imperial Control in the Nineteenth Century.* Seattle, University of Washington Press, 1960.

Hummel, Arthur W. (ed.). *Eminent Chinese of the Ch'ing Period (1644–1912).* 2 vols. Washington, Government Printing Office, 1943–1944.

"Inland Communications in China," T. W. Kingsmill, ed., *Journal of the Royal Asiatic Society, China Branch* 28:1–213 (1893–1894).

Jamieson, G. "Tenure of Land in China and the Condition of the Rural Population," *Journal of the North China Branch of the Royal Asiatic Society* 23:59–174 (1888).

Jing Jun-jian 經君健 . "Ming Qing liangdai nongye guyong laodongzhe falü shenfen diwei de jiefang" 明清兩代农业雇佣劳动者法律身分地位的解放 (The liberation of rural hired laborers during the Ming and Qing from legal status positions), *Jingji yanjiu* 6 (1961).

Jing Su and Luo Lun 景甦 罗崙 . *Qingdai Shandong jing-ying dizhu de shehui xingzhi* 清代山东经营地主底社會性質 (The social nature of managerial landlords in Shandong during the Qing dynasty). Jinan, People's Publishing House, 1959.

Jinpingmei 金瓶梅. See Egerton, Clement, trans.

Kanbe Teruo 神戶輝夫 . "Shindai kōki Santōshō ni okeru 'danki' to nōson mondai," 清代後期山東省におけ る団匪と農村問題 (The "rebel bands" in Shandong at the end of the Qing dynasty and rural problems), *Shirin* 55.4:61–98 (1972).

Kataoka Shibako 片岡芝子 . "Mimmatsu Shinsho no Kahoku ni okeru nōka keiei," 明末清初の華北における 農家經營 (The peasant economy of North China in the late Ming and early Qing), *Shakai keizai shigaku* 25 2/3: 77–100 (1959).

Kataoka Shibako 片田芝子 . "Kahoku no tochi shoyu to ichijō benpō," 北方の土地所有と一條鞭法 (Landholding in North China and the single-whip tax reform), *Shimizu hakase tsuitō kinen Mindaishi ronsō* 清水博士追悼記念明代史論叢 (Studies in Ming history in honor of the late Dr. Shimizu). Tokyo, Daian, 1962

King, F. H. *Farmers of Forty Centuries.* London, Cape, 1911.

Kokuritsu Pekin daigaku fusetsu nōson keizai kenkyūjo 國立北京大学附設農村經濟研究所　*Santōshō, Zainei kenjō o chūshin to seru nōsanbutsu ryūtsu ni kansuru ichi kōsatsu* 山東省濟寧縣城を中心とせる農業物流通に關する一考察 (A study of agricultural commodity circulation in the district of Jining centering on the district seat). Peking, 1942.

Latham, R. E., trans. *The Travels of Marco Polo.* London, Penguin Books, 1958.

Lenin, V. I. *The Development of Capitalism in Russia,* English language edition. Moscow, Foreign Languages Publishing House, 1967.

Li Wen-zhi 李文治. "Lun Qingdai qianqi de tudi zhanyou guanxi," 論清代前期的土地占有關係 (On the landholding relations in the early Qing), *Lishi yanjiu* 5:75–108 (1963).

Liu, T'ieh-yün. *The Travels of Lao Ts'an.* Harold Shadick, trans. Ithaca, Cornell University Press, 1952.

MacKerras, C. P. *The Rise of the Peking Opera.* Oxford, Clarendon Press, 1972.

Mao Tse-tung. *Selected Works of Mao Tse-tung,* English language edition. 4 vols. Peking, Foreign Languages Press, 1965.

Myers. Ramon H. *The Chinese Peasant Economy, Agricultural Development in Hopei and Shantung, 1890–1949.* Cambridge, Harvard University Press, 1970.

——— "Commercialization, Agricultural Development, and Land-lord Behaviour in Shantung Province in the Late Ch'ing Period," *Ch'ing-shih wen-t'i* 8.2:31–54 (1972).

Nepomnin, O. E. *Genezis kapitalizma y sel'skom khozvaistve Kitaya.* Moscow, Nauka, 1966.

Nishijima Sadao 西嶋定生. *Chūgoku keizaishi kenkyū* 中國經濟史研究 (Studies in Chinese economic history). Tokyo, Tokyo University Press, 1966.

Perkins, Dwight H. *Agricultural Development in China, 1368–1968.* Chicago, Aldine, 1969.

Qingping xianzhi 清平县志 (District gazetteer of Qingping), 1798.

Rawski, Evelyn Sakakida. *Agricultural Change and the Peasant Economy of South China.* Cambridge, Harvard University Press, 1972.

Santōshō, Zainei kenjō . . . See Kokuritsu Pekin Daigaku.
Schwartz, Benjamin. "A Marxist Controversy on China," *Far Eastern Quarterly* 13.2:143–153 (1954).
Shandong fensheng dizhi. See Zhongguo fensheng dizhi, Shandong.
Shih Min-hsiung. *The Silk Industry in Ch'ing China.* E-tu Zen Sun, trans. Ann Arbor, University of Michigan, Center for Chinese Studies, 1976.
Shina shōbetsu zenshi, Santōshō 支那省別全誌, 山東省 (Comprehensive gazetteer of China by provinces, Shandong province), Tōa dōbunkai 東亞同文會 comp. Tokyo, Tōa dōbunkai, 1917.
Stenz, P. G. M. *Der Bauer in Schantung.* Tsingtau, Adolf Haupt, 1910.
Sun, E-tu Zen and Sun Shiou-chuan, trans. *T'ien-kung k'ai-wu.* University Park and London, University of Pennsylvania Press, 1966.
Sun, E-tu Zen. "Mining Labor in the Qing Period," in Albert Feuerwerker, Rhoads Murphy, and Mary C. Wright, eds., *Approaches to Modern Chinese History.* Berkeley and Los Angeles, University of California Press, 1967.
——— "Sericulture and Silk Textile Production in Ch'ing China," in W. E. Willmott, ed. *Economic Organization in Chinese Society.* Stanford, Stanford University Press, 1972.

Tanaka Masatoshi 田中正俊 . *Chūgoku kindai keizaishi kenkyū josetsu* 中国近代经济史研究予説 (Introduction

to the study of the modern economic history of China).
Tokyo, University of Tokyo Press, 1973.

Williamson, Alexander. *Journeys in North China.* 2 vols. London,
1870.

Yamane Yukio 山根幸夫 . "Min Shin jidai kahoku ni okeru
tekishi" 明清時代華北における定期市 (Peri-
odic markets in north China during the Ming and Qing),
Shiron 8:493–504 (1960).

Yang, Martin C. *A Chinese Village, Taitou, Shantung Province.*
New York, Columbia University Press, 1945.

Yang Xiu-yan 楊秀元. *Nongyan zhuoshi* 農言著實 (Practi-
cal advice on farming), in *Qin Jin nongyan* 秦晉農言
(Agricultural treatises of Shanxi and Shanxi). Peking, Ministry
of Agriculture Press, 1957.

Yongzheng Donghualu 雍正東華錄 (Records from the
Eastern Gate Yongzheng reign), in Wang Xian-qian 王先謙
ed. *Shiyi chao Donghualu* 十一朝東華錄 , 1884.

Zhangqiu xianzhi 章丘县志 (District gazetteer of Zhangqiu),
editions of 1596, 1691, 1833, and 1907.

Zhongguo fenshen dizhi, Shandong 中國分省地誌 (Gazetteers of the provinces of China, Shandong). Shanghai, 1935.

Zhongguo shiyezhi, Shandong sheng 中國實業誌,山東省
(Chinese industrial gazetteer, Shandong). Shanghai, Ministry
of Industry, 1934.

GLOSSARY

[Only the characters for special terms and names of people and places most frequently mentioned are given. Characters for district towns and well-known places are not included. Characters for authors and book titles may be found in the Bibliography.]

baigar 白干儿
baitong 白铜
baixing tian 百姓田
ban-gong 伴工
baomai shang 包买商
baoshui shang 包税商
Bi Feng-lian 毕丰䢫
Bi Ning-jie 毕宁玠
Bi Yuan-rong 毕元蓉
bing bei fushi 兵备副使

caizhu 财主
chang-gong 长工
chi 尺
Cibei qu 慈悲曲
cun 寸

da huoji 大伙计
damu 大亩
dan 担(石)
danbagu 淡巴姑
ding 丁
dingqian 定钱
dong 筒
Dongfanliu 东汎流
dongtou 筒头
dou 斗
duangong 短工
duanzai 短载

Dushanhu 独山湖

er huoji 二伙计

fucao 伏草
fujia 富家

gong 碔
gongliang 工粮
gongtian 公田
gongzhu 攻主
guandu minban 官督民办
guanliao 官僚
guantian 官田
guanzhuang 官庄

hada 哈达
han matou 旱码头
heifan 黑矾
Hengsheng 恒盛
hetao 核桃
hongtong 红铜
hu 斛
hu 槲
hutao 胡桃

jianchou 茧绸
jiangfang 浆房

297

jiangyuan 醬园
jiao 礁
jiao 椒
jifang 机房
jin 斤
Jing Su 景甦
jingtou 井头
jinshen 缙绅
jinshi 进士
Jinshu tang 矜恕堂
Jinxiu tang 进修堂
jitian 祭田
Jiujun 旧军

kecheng 课程

Li Fang-cai 李方彩
Li Hua-xi 李化熙
Li Tian-pei 李田培
Li Zi-cheng 李自成
Liaozuo 遼左
Lijiacun 栗家村
lingzi 凌子
linhuo pu 赁货铺
liuli 琉璃
Luo Lun 罗崙
luodi shui 落地税
luoleng 络梭

mang-gong 忙工
mei 煤
Meng Ji-sheng 孟继笙
mianchou 绵䌷
mihan 觅汉
Mingshui 明水
mintian 民田
mu 亩

nian 蔫
Nie Xing-de 聶兴德

Puji 普集

qianshua 牵刷
qing 顷
qinghui 请会
Qiuling 丘陵
qu 区
qutian 区田

raosui 绕缲

shanchang yezhu 山場业主
shanjian 山茧
sheng 升
Sheng Bai-er 盛百二
shengyuan 生员
shetian 社田
shimu 市亩
shizhi 市制
shu 樗
Shujing tang 树荆堂
sidian 丝店
sitian 私田
Song Jing-shi 宋景史
sui 岁
suihui 随会
Sun Kuo-tu 孙扩图
Sun Yu-ting 孙玉庭
Sun Yu-wen 孙毓汶

Taihe tang 太和堂
taiju 抬锯
tan 炭
tangming 堂名
titouqian 剃头钱

tongqi 铜碛
tuntian 屯田

Wang Lun 王伦
Wang Yu 王璵
Wang Zhi-zeng 王志曾
Wangcun 王村
wenqi cungen 文契存根
Wu Da-zhou 吴大洲
Wu Sheng 吴樫

xian 县
xiang 乡
xiangchun ya 乡椿芽
xiao mihan 小览汉
xiji 西机
Xing Dong 邢侗
xinyong 信用
Xu Hong-ru 徐鸿儒
xuansi 选丝
xuetian 学田

yaza shui 牙杂税
yezhu 业主
yiji 义集
yitian 义田
Yu tang 玉堂
Yulin 榆林

Zang Xian 藏咸
zha 砟
zhang 丈
Zhang Si-mian 张思勉
zhangfang 账房
Zhao Shi-qing 赵世卿
zhe 柘
zhen 镇
zhijia 纸价
zhongren 中人
Zhou Yi-xun 周以勋
Zhoucun 周村
zuo 柞

HARVARD EAST ASIAN MONOGRAPHS

67. Ralph C. Croizier, *Koxinga and Chinese Nationalism: History, Myth, and the Hero*

68. William J. Tyler, tr., *The Psychological World of Natsumi Sōseki*, by Doi Takeo

69. Eric Widmer, *The Russian Ecclesiastical Mission in Peking during the Eighteenth Century*

70. Charlton M. Lewis, *Prologue to the Chinese Revolution: The Transformation of Ideas and Institutions in Hunan Province, 1891–1907*

71. Preston Torbert, *The Ch'ing Imperial Household Department: A Study of its Organization and Principal Functions. 1662–1796*

72. Paul A. Cohen and John E. Schrecker, eds., *Reform in Nineteenth-Century China*

73. Jon Sigurdson, *Rural Industrialization in China*

74. Kang Chao, *The Development of Cotton Textile Production in China*

75. Valentin Rabe, *The Home Base of American China Missions, 1880–1920*

76. Sarasin Viraphol, *Tribute and Profit: Sino-Siamese Trade, 1652–1853*

77. Ch'i-ch'ing Hsiao, *The Military Establishment of the Yuan Dynasty*

78. Meishi Tsai, *Contemporary Chinese Novels and Short Stories, 1949–1974: An Annotated Bibliography*

79. Wellington K. K. Chan, *Merchants, Mandarins, and Modern Enterprise in Late Ch'ing China*

80. Endymion Wilkinson, *Landlord and Labor in Late Imperial China: Case Studies from Shandong by Jing Su and Luo Lun*

81. Barry Keenan, *The Dewey Experiment in China: Educational Reform and Political Power in the Early Republic*

82. George A. Hayden, *Crime and Punishment in Medieval Chinese Drama: Three Judge Pao Plays*